Meditations through the Ṛg Veda

Meditations through the Ṛg Veda

FOUR-DIMENSIONAL MAN

Antonio T. de Nicolás

Shambhala
BOULDER & LONDON
1978

Shambhala Publications, Inc.
1123 Spruce Street
Boulder, Colorado 80302

ISBN 0-87773-122-5
LCC 77-90878

Distributed in the United States by Random House
and in Canada by Random House of Canada Ltd.

Distributed in the Commonwealth by Routledge
and Kegan Paul Ltd., London and Henley-on-Thames.

Printed in the United States of America.

The statue on the front cover is Sūrya, Chlorite, Pāla Dynasty (7th-8th century A.D.), Bihar. The photograph is reproduced courtesy of The Asian Art Museum of San Francisco, The Avery Brundage Collection.

Contents

Acknowledgements

All those I acknowledged and thanked in *Four-Dimensional Man: The Philosophical Methodology of the Ṛg Veda* are hereby remembered and thanked again. Though the book in which they appeared is and will remain out of print, their names and their influences are not forgotten.

This version of *Four-Dimensional Man: Meditations Through the Ṛg Veda* has been completely rewritten from cover to cover, and these are the people more directly responsible for it.

My own students of the State University of New York at Stony Brook, who with innocence and generosity, uncovered for me the raw flesh of these meditations. The only way I know to thank them is to continue journeying with them.

Ernest McClain, who more than anyone else, forced me to travel the winding tunnels of my own thoughts into the music garden. He can sing this manuscript by heart, and had he not written a book inspired by my early version of *Four-Dimensional Man*, I would have never sung this new song.

Patrick A. Heelan, who considered my effort important enough to help it grow from childhood to maturity, and introduced it to the reader.

Linda Wallace, who for four years typed every word I wrote, including this manuscript, and is rushing to finish typing this page to move forever under the sun of California. For her patience, understanding and dedication, I am deeply grateful.

My deep gratitude goes to the staff of Nicolas Hays Ltd., especially to those fearless body/souls who directly contributed to this manuscript: Susan Greenleaf for easing the pain of proofreading and manuscript coordination; Rosemary B. Zeman, on whose weight and imagination the whole book's production rested; and Neil Litt for his brilliant help in editing the manuscript.

The journey and the blunders of these meditations are all mine, I have no one to blame.

Abbreviations

ABORI	Annals of the Bhandarkar Research Institute
Ait. Ar.	Aitareya *Āraṇyaka*
Ait. Br.	Aitareya *Brāhmaṇa*
AO	Acta Orientalia
A. V. (or AV)	Atharvaveda
BEFEO	Bulletin de l'Ecole Francaise d'Extreme Oriente
BG	Bhagavad Gītā
Br. Up.	*Bṛhadāraṇyaka Upaniṣad*
Comy.	Commentary
ERE	Encyclopaedia of Religion and Ethics
EVP	*Études Védiques et Pāṇinéennes*
HIP	History of Indian Philosophy
HOS	Harvard Oriental Series
IHQ	Indian Historical Quarterly
IP	Indian Philosophy
JAOS	Journal of the American Oriental Society
JRAS	Journal of the Royal Asiatic Society
Kaus.	*Kauṣītakī Upaniṣad*
OUP	Oxford University Press
PU	*The Principle Upaniṣads*, ed. S. Radhakrishnan
R. V. (or RV)	*Ṛg Veda* (When no abbreviation precedes numbers in the text, these should be understood as being from the Ṛg Veda)
SB	*Śatapatha Brāhmaṇa*
SBE	Sacred Books of the East
Tait. Br.	*Taittirīya Brāhmaṇa*

Pronunciation of Sanskrit Words

The ancient Indian grammarians of the Sanskrit language have identified forty-eight sounds as worthy of notation, and in the script that was developed over the centuries each character represents that one sound unalterably. Hence there can be no confusion about how a particular word was pronounced, though different schools of Veda transmission show slight variations in the articulation; yet compared with the haphazard correspondence of Roman notation and English pronunciation, Sanskrit notation is extremely precise.

The sequence of the alphabet again was completely scientific. The order of letters is not the historical jumble of the Roman alphabet, which imitated the sequence of Semitic scripts, but simply the path of the breath through the hollow of, the mouth from the throat to the lips, producing the vowels; through the nose, producing these vowels with nasalization; and the same breath with occlusion of the tongue to points in the hollow of the mouth from the throat to the lips, producing the consonants. Ṛg Vedic Sanskrit is earlier than the Sanskrit grammarians, more complex than Classical Sanskrit and has special rules for the accents of words which change the meaning of words.

The Alphabet

a ā, i ī, u ū, ṛ ṝ, ḷ, e ai, o au
k kh g gh ṅ
c ch j jh ñ
ṭ ṭh ḍ ḍh ṇ
t th d dh n
p ph b bh m
y r l v
ś ṣ s
h
ṃ
ḥ

Pronunciation of Sanskrit Words

Vowels

a — ā in America or *o* in come
ā — a in far or in father
i — i in pit or in pin
ī — ee in feel or *i* in machine
u — u in put or pull
ū — u in rule
ri (ṛ) — properly *ur*, but by modern Hindus as *ri* in river or in writ. *Ṛta* (*Rita*), Ṛgveda (Rigveda), *Prakṛti* (*Prakriti*), Kṛṣna (Krishna).
e — ay in say or *a* in made
ai — i in rite or *ai* in aisle
o — o in go
au — ou in loud

Consonants

Consonants are pronounced approximately as in English, except:
g — g in gun or in get (always "hard")
c — ch in church
sh (ś, ṣ — sh in sheet or in shun)
When *h* is combined with another consonant (e.g., th, bh), it is aspirated: *th* as in boathouse; *ph* as in uphill, etc. The palatal ñ is like the Spanish señor (jña, however, is pronounced most often by modern Hindus as "gyah," with a hard g).

Accent

The rule of thumb is that Sanskrit words are accented in English like Greek and Latin words: stress the penultimate vowel, if that is long. Length is indicated either by a long vowel or a short (or long) vowel followed by more than one consonant, e.g., *rāma*, *raṅga*. If the penultimate syllable is short, stress the antepenultimate, whether it is long or short: *Mahābhārata*, *Arjuna* (the antepenultimates are long), and also *Aruṇa* (antepenultimate is short, as in *Herodotus*, *Thucydides*).

The real stumbling blocks in the transcription, which follows international convention, is that of the *c* and the *v*. The *c* is always *ch*, never *k*; the *v* is always *w*, never *v*.

Foreword

This extraordinary work about the origins and originality of human language, reason and conceptual articulation leaves one, as it were, intoxicated with the divine "soma." Its shifting viewpoint is both disturbing and exciting, since it challenges all frameworks in which unexamined certainties are expressed, and attempts to lay bare the ground of all frameworks and the logic (or ordering) of their mutual relations.

The exploration of the origins of language and reason is fraught with the danger of presuming that language and reason are uniquely what Western culture presumes them to be, and of assuming with Piaget for instance, that one recovers the origins of reason when one recovers the origins of Western reason. The Ṛg Veda, however, is older than Plato and an antique though forgotten source of much that Plato found constituent of reason: its multi-dimensionality, as de Nicolás uses this term, is opposed to the linearity that Western thought inherited from Plato.

The significance of this exciting book for Western philosophers is the way it probes the most difficult of contemporary philosophical problems: the variety, interrelation and mutual exclusivity of rational thought systems. Such a problem stirs, for example, historians of science today, anthropologists of language as well as students of religion and myth; but the study of these is inhibited by the essentially linear or non-contextual historical tradition that provides the presuppositions of scientific inquiry in the West. When one leaps to a radically different culture, to that for instance of the Ṛg Veda, the separation of its rational thought patterns from our own is so great that the instruments of Western rationality alone are insufficient to make sense of it. One tries by meditation to discover the rational principles internal to it that are peculiar to it "as a text within its own context." These turn out to be, as de Nicolás shows, non-linear or contextual. He understands this to be the way complementary frameworks in quantum mechanics are created by different contexts of measurement—frameworks that are mutually exclusive (and therefore, non-linear) but ordered to one another in a lattice structure (and therefore, complementary). Complementary frameworks involve changes in the embodied subjectivity of the knower, changes that make possible mutually exclusive objectivities or horizons. Subjectivity embodied in chant and ritual displays the mutually exclusive facets of the world, not additively in a linear sense, but by "sacrifice" in which one and all are relativized both to their common ground in embodied subjectivity and to the "vision" to which they all contribute through other than by simple addition.

I warmly commend this work of hermeneutical philosophy, particularly to all who believe with Whitehead that all philosophy is but a footnote to Plato. Though true, perhaps, of the philosophy of the West, it is not true of all philosophy. Behind Plato, and constituting Plato's background, is the Ṛg Veda, proposing a philosophy of many—perhaps, four—dimensions, to which, if de Nicolás is correct, Plato and the West are themselves extended footnotes.

Patrick A. Heelan
Professor of Philosophy
SUNY at Stony Brook, N.Y.

Prologue

I was still in my teens when I arrived, for the first time, in India. I approached it hurriedly: a few months of learning English in Mallorca; some general historical readings about the glories of England in India; some romantic novels and movies; a long string of thoughts about India. After all, my journey to India was going to be a great intellectual adventure: to finish my undergraduate studies in a tropical setting. Living in the "fifties" in Spain, I did not have the benefit or handicap of "things Indian" being in vogue, least of all in book stores. So, despite my intellectual equipment I still had plenty of room for innocence.

They advised me to go by boat and enter India in the great style of the British Viceroys, through the Gate of India: Bombay. The slow boat journey, they said, would better prepare me for the new experience. By 'preparation' they meant that the fierce beating of the tropical sun if administered in gradual, daily, comfortable doses, would not soften my brains to the degree of not being able to concentrate on the intellectual task ahead of me. The preparations were geared to insure that my journey to India remained an intellectual adventure.

They were all wrong. Bombay hit me like a lightning bolt. Walking out of the docks, in that first morning haze, my lungs were furiously gasping for the familiar air they had been used to. Instead, they were mercilessly bathed in a hot and humid soup, defiantly sitting on them, challenging them to rise. A shocked gush of blood rushed to my eyes. The world, as I knew it, disappeared. The world became a bubble of air. There was only breath. Every gasp was a struggle to surface above the mass of hot air, reaching up and never making it. To surface and breathe became a lifetime. The world was just air to be reached, the body was just breath: There were no limbs, no head: just air, flowing and ebbing, alive, in breath waves.

The thing that fell away was myself: the expectations of a linear world. Without limbs, without head, the body just a gasp for breath, India, in that first morning haze, was a world in slow motion. There was not even a world; just motion. There were no forms, no figures; just masses of colors dangling without directions of up and down, forward, backward and all around. No lines separated bodies from bodies. No lines separated my gasp from the sea of color. No lines separated the colors.

The mass was amorphous, breaking into new motions without resistance, at the impulse of my breath; forming waves in a pond around a drowning stone. It was just like a live performance on an empty stage. But there was "more" performance than there was stage, and this "more" flowed and ebbed with the suggestiveness of eternal life.

There was the gasp for breath, but it came from everywhere. Where had the sounds gone? There was no sound of any–thing. Just sound; waves of indistinguishable sound; cacophonous, pulsating like a throbbing heart; louder and louder, losing the directions of up and down, outside and inside; there was only sound. Then, suddenly, absolute silence: my breath had at last stopped. But then it would rise again, with the sound of no–thing, until it would reach the silence again. Then, sound and silence would sound simultaneously: presence from absence and again its dissolution. It was a sound without melody, a live, single note was all the sound to be heard.

In that first morning haze India was a world without things; no–thing was separated from another. There were no backgrounds, no spaces, no divisions, no fields against which things were reclining and appearing. There was nothing *in* space and nothing *in* time. Nothing happened and it was all nowhere. All there was, was a pulsating presence: movement, an audial surge without fixity or direction; it was intensification and ebbing. It was exciting, it was painful. It was the seduction of the possible: perhaps a hidden invitation to disintegrate the presence into its components of past and future; perhaps an invitation to make out of the presence that space and time out of which it was made; perhaps an invitation to draw out of this a–perspectival world the multitude of simultaneous perspectives that made it simultaneously present and absent. Perhaps it was an invitation to a birth.

Where did my memory go? My anticipation? There were no sides, no lines, no dots, no things I had to perceive one after another in that first morning haze in India. There was only emptiness, that throbbing presence had begun to darken. Its shape appeared for the first time as the tail of a mythical dragon riding the sky. It was only an instant—of and out of time—but I thought the mouth of the dragon was about to appear in the dark sky and either swallow or vomit the whole of creation. A trembling fear did not allow the presence to continue. My stomach was churning in anguish; my body shivered, hot and humid. Breath again had found a body; but there had been no birth. The old Cartesian mind with neo–Kantian justifications had used the weak stomach to return to sanity, but there had been no birth. The whole body clung to the weak stomach and the mind started drawing the lines: I would stay on this side; the rest of the world on the other. There were no dragons. My body and the world were in Euclidean space and in Newtonian time; the sounds were of voices and languages I did not know yet; of carts, of cows, of things that sound . . . There was melody and noise . . . The faces were of people; the colors were of clothes and buildings . . . The . . .

My first steps on Indian soil were taken to abort a human birth. It was a clean and legal abortion. It was done with the head. Not to stand on Indian soil I would have—from now on—to continuously sprinkle my journey through India with the conceptual soil of Europe *of* which I was once born. For after all, how many times does a man need to be born?

* * *

For seven consecutive years I lived in India. For almost twenty I have been busy sprinkling my path with conceptual Indian soil. After many births and an equal number of lives I am shedding again an old skin awaiting the new sun. Myths and ideas have a quick way of becoming human flesh, but between births, where is there to go besides thought–making? Obviously, to the thought's own limit; for the flower that once has bloomed has chosen to die.

This book is a systematic exercise in the birth and death, and therefore, on the rebirth, of many thoughts; a bracket in the life of man. Yet, this is the only body–form through which one breath has found its life.

For Susie

Introduction Cautionary Notes

The tree of the Universe remains erect
its stem in the baseless region.
The sunny top craves for the hidden roots
while the roots hanker for the sun.

(R.V. 1,24,7)

Two birds with fair wings, inseparable companions,
have found a refuge in the same sheltering tree.
One incessantly eats from the peepal tree;
the other, not eating, just looks on.

(R.V. 1,164,20)

With root above and branches below, this
world-tree is eternal.

(Katha Up. II. 3,11)

They speak of the imperishable peepal tree
with its root above and its branches below . . .

(B.G. XV. 1)

As regards the most lordly part of the soul, we must conceive of it in this wise; we declare that God has given to each of us, as his demon, that kind of soul which is housed in the top of our body and which raises us—seeing that we are not an earthly but a heavenly plant—up from earth towards our kindred in heaven.

(Timaeus, 90–A)

1
Interpretation and The Ṛg Veda

When the scholar (the philologist) has done his work, the poet and philosopher must take it up and finish it.

Max Müller

I

The people of *est* (Erhard Seminars Training) describe the difference between a man and a rat in the following way: If you put a rat in front of four tunnels and put a piece of cheese in tunnel number three, the rat will travel the tunnels until it finds the cheese. If you change the cheese from tunnel number three to tunnel number four, the rat will make several passes at tunnel number three, but eventually it will move to tunnel number four and discover the cheese. Man, on the other hand, is the kind of creature that even if you remove the cheese from tunnel number three and put it in any of the other tunnels, he will continue indefinitely going up and down tunnel number three, and never venture into any of the others. The reason is because man, contrary to the rat, has beliefs.

These meditations through the Ṛg Veda are primarily concerned with developing the kind of activity that is necessary in order to get hold of other peoples' beliefs, while simultaneously getting hold of our own. In this particular case we need to travel the tunnels of the Ṛg Veda and not presuppose in any way that the Ṛg Veda must be in our own tunnel number three.

The fact that the movement of our path is determined by certain tunnels, certain controlled situations, does not in any way impinge on our freedom of movement. The philosopher's path follows the collision course of a necessary control, much as the paths of meditation do. The movement of these paths is always a movement through the paths of others. The paths of meditation begin and end at the core of the human condition–the radical beliefs of man. Meditation acknowledges the controlled situation and is capable of transcending the controls by radically falsifying them.

Human controls are neither good nor bad, they may be both but they are not necessarily either. Controls are part and parcel of being human, as is freedom. Controls are the necessary ingredient of every human action: the latent theoretical presuppositions on which all human acting ultimately rests. Meditation, on the other hand, belies the demand that the ultimate ground of man be theoretical or of any such theories. However, no falsification of theory is possible unless theory is first known as what is really falsified. Meditation is therefore, never, an excuse to hide from knowledge, but on the contrary, it is the root knowledge, the root freedom of what grounds human life. Nor is meditation the activity that grounds man in one theoretical form of life as a defense against others. Ultimately, meditation can only be meditation when it is able to be at home, no questions asked, in any form of life, everywhere.

These general promissory notes are a little premature at this stage, but they might help us understand the sort of ground level activity in which we are aiming to engage ourselves.

How can this kind of activity (meditation) find its own execution in a book? How can we meditate while reading? What is distinguishable is not necessarily separable; control and freedom are not separable, they are only distinguishable. The same may be said of knowledge and ignorance, time and eternity, individual and society, affirmation and negation. The imaginary line separating objectivity and subjectivity, reality and illusion, facts and theory, is literally imaginary: It is not empirically observable, measurable, or part of any of the dichotomies. Meditation is the activity by which we transcend whatever theories have been applied to interpret the Ṛg Veda and falsify them. Meditation is the activity by which we are able to realize that this falsification is possible because those theories are themselves their only ground or justification. Meditation is the activity by which we are able to realize that the ground Ṛg Vedic man built for himself was the necessary activity of having to live his own life. Meditation is the activity by which our expectations of what we ought to find in the Ṛg Veda stop being *our* expectations and become the expectations of Ṛg Vedic man. This means that we must simultaneously hold the ground of Ṛg Vedic man and get hold of our own in its totality. Meditation is the activity by which meaning (or at least the possibility of giving meaning) comes not only to the Ṛg Vedic text, but also to our text (our own discipline, our own life) through the Ṛg Vedic text. Meditation is the activity by which we are able to make Ṛg Vedic life the possibility of our own.

The way we have chosen is that of philosophy. However, our way of philosophy should be radically distinguished from any *apriori* method, like those of the social sciences, which proceed from a set of criteria through which the task of interpretation must proceed and to which the results of such interpretations must conform. Our way of philosophy is a disciplined effort to traverse the path of others: in this concrete case, those who have interpreted the Ṛg Veda. At a radical level, interpreters from any discipline are unable to travel the trail of the theoretical and other presuppositions they left in the wake of their own path. In this sense, we want to avoid identification of philosophy with any definition of philosophy. Rather, we would like to discover what philosophy is as we are forced to do it while traveling the paths of multiple rationalities at the root level at which they constitute themselves.

Through this philosophical mediation we hope to gain for philosophy and the sciences the *distance* required for them to acknowledge themselves in what they do to themselves and others. We also hope to discover the very determined forms of "history" and "culture" beyond the Western determination of "history" and "culture," and above all, we hope to suggest the root level at which all men are equal as 'man', the level at which they act as interpreters of themselves and their worlds, and thereby constitute a multiplicity of histories and cultures. It is at this root level of self–constitution and self–liberation that the activities of meditation and philosophy coincide, and an undefiled anonymity and plurality of names, forms, history, culture and man manifests itself.

The task of the philosopher has taken many forms and styles, but never a final form. The philosopher's task, contrary to what Max Müller suggests, is never to finish anything. On the contrary, the philosopher's task is always a new beginning. In trying to journey through the Ṛg Vedic text with a philosopher's eye, the reader should be cautioned not to project any false expectations about what philosophers do when interpreting any text, especially when this text belongs to a cultural body different from the philosopher's. The reader should be aware that prior to the task of interpreting any text, from our culture or from any other, the philosopher must beware of the problem he is facing. Before interpreting the text, the philosopher must uncover the necessary and sufficient conditions for the text to be read within its own cultural context. On the other hand, since a culture is as problematic as philosophy itself, the philosopher has to face the problem of uncovering the necessary and sufficient conditions for the cultural context within which the text appears as such a particular text. Therefore, the task of the philosopher is not so much to arbitrarily interpret, but rather to uncover the radical interpretation from which texts were written or chanted by a particular group of people or a single author. It would be a great misunderstanding if this book was taken in its totality as another interpretation of the Ṛg Veda; this book is not an interpretation but rather a radical and systematic effort to retrieve the necessary and sufficient conditions (the radical presuppositions) upon which an interpretation of the Ṛg Vedic text would make sense. An interpretation of the Ṛg Veda is only possible if these radical presuppositions—cultural and contextual—are first made evident.

As philosophers, we must presuppose that for philosophy to remain rational, it is obliged to recognize the rationality it faces when confronting others; rationality is culture–dependent, and philosophy must constantly feed itself through rationality by recognizing it in others as they radically orient themselves in the worlds they create. No one rationality is justifiably rational, for no single rationality can know itself. Rationality needs the other for its own life.

Rationality, therefore, is radically historical; the need to know others as they knew themselves is the first task of the philosopher. But since others, texts, and cultures, have already been reduced and colonialized to the one form of rationality sanctioned by Western and Eastern philosophers and scholars, our task is primarily to liberate interpretation from these colonialistic controls. Our task is to draw out the dogmatism of these interpretations and the presuppositions on which they are based, and to point out the necessary and sufficient conditions upon which a *comprehensive* interpretation of the Ṛg Veda could be possible. But our main task as philosophers is to uncover presuppositions, and our main clue as philosophers is language, i.e., language and languages as found and used in the Ṛg Veda. In this sense, we understand language as the empirical evidence of what we call a culture, not in any defined form, but as the source of meaning for any name and form. Thus language takes into account not only the *external* tokens of sound, gesture, and word, but also the *internal* tokens of intentionality, conceptualization and purposive action. In this sense, we not only examine language as used in the Ṛg Veda, but also the presuppositions which such a use entails. Therefore, this comprehensive interpretation must include the totality of frameworks or horizons within which and through which Ṛg Vedic man's intentional activity is manifested. The religious and/or philosophical discourse that can be extracted from any sampling of texts grounded in a Western cultural reference has been proven unable to rise to the task.

To gain a radical ground from which a comprehensive interpretation of the Ṛg Veda could be possible, three original claims are proposed:

1. Though Indian philosophical tradition originates in the Ṛg Veda, the Ṛg Veda still remains a text out of context; i.e., Vedic exegesis has considered the Ṛg Veda not as its own source of explanation, but has relied heavily on later Indian and Western sources and methods extrinsic to the Ṛg Veda. I am opposing, therefore, those interpretations of the Ṛg Veda which claim it to be:

a) a book of rituals (*Ādhiyājñikā*);
b) a religio–cultural mythology, dealing exclusively with gods, (*ādhidaivika*);
c) or even an esoteric spiritual document, (*ādhyātmika*).

None of these interpretations, when taken in all of their dogmatic claims, accounts for the Ṛg Vedic text itself, but rather are such interpretations because of other interpretations and methods exterior and posterior to the Ṛg Veda.

2. From the viewpoint of philosophy, the Ṛg Veda must be considered as a 'complete linguistic whole.' The linguistic–contexts within which and through which Vedic man expresses his intentional activity form a linguistic universe which has meaning only if taken as a whole: our universe of discourse is the discourse of this particular universe called the Ṛg Veda. The opposite of this approach is to 'talk' of the philosophy of the Ṛg Veda simply by translating certain obvious philosophical texts; philosophy thus turns into discourse about 'philosophic discourse' and obviates the more difficult task of cultivating a philosophical activity. But philosophical activity, to be such, must share that way of 'viewing the world' which produces 'philosophic discourse' in the first place, and only this philosophical activity is the ground on which the resulting 'vision' of the world of Ṛg Vedic man's goal and intentional acting can be radicalized.

3. The languages found and used in the Ṛg Veda are four; i.e.,

i. Non-existence (*Asat*)
ii. Existence (*Sat*)
iii. Images and Sacrifice (*yajña*)
iv. Embodied (*Ṛta*) vision (*dhīḥ*)

These four languages function as four spaces of discourse, four ways of viewing the world within which human action takes place and from which any statement in the text gains meaning. The languages of Non–existence, Existence, Images and Sacrifice show the human situation within certain disparate linguistic contexts embodying different ways of viewing the world. These may be integrated within a transcendent context, not by rejecting the reality of any of the previous frameworks, but only by changing to a transcendent 'viewing' of the world implicit in the internal dynamism of the languages themselves. This integrating and transcendent context is a Language, as well, and the totality of its manifestation is the result of viewing the world from the heights of a cultural embodied vision. In this manner, a *complementarity* of languages is suggested under a transcendent and unifying language: and each language is torn from its opposing demands of exclusivity in exchange for a way of viewing and acting in the world which is eternally (*nitya*) efficient.[1]

It will become evident that the structure of the Ṛg Veda takes sound and its criteria rather than sight and its criteria as the radical presupposition through which the sensorium and the cultural body orient themselves in the Ṛg Vedic world, and this discovery will force us to re–examine the whole problem of embodiment.

The context–dependence of one language on another can be formalized in a logic. This I do on the lines suggested by P. A. Heelan for N. Bohr's complementarity with the added corrections which the internal logic of the Ṛg Veda demands. It appears that such complementarity or contextual logic offers a very suggestive 'model' for positive dialogue between rival philosophies, and even more important, within human experience itself.

It is, however, important to bear in mind that a book of this type is undertaken in the hope of clarifying not only a particular aspect of Eastern philosophy but also of increasing philosophical understanding in general. This book will bring out a theory of language and a theory of context–language dependence the epistemological foundations of which vary greatly from those in the West, and the comparison should be fruitful. For reality is neither contained nor expressed in any one context–language, but it is lived in a transcendence of human dependence on a context–language, and it is as a *result* of this human, toilsome, complementary activity of dependence and transcendence (sacrifice) that Vedic man achieves in one auspicious intuitive moment that vision–identity of the *Real* which could make 'his' action cosmically efficient. It is also in this dialectical activity that the philosopher comes to grips with different concepts—different from those with which he is familiar—of space, time, in–action, and immortality.

For example, immortality is not a condition of a biological body and its death for Ṛg Vedic man, but rather, a condition toward a different way of viewing the world neither in space nor in time and which biological death does not alter. Within a radical and comprehensive interpretation of the Ṛg Veda such opposing categories as death and immortality, space and time, action and efficacy, etc., seem to fall into place.

II

No one acquainted with Indian Philosophy is unaware of the philosophical gap which exists in Vedic Philosophy accounting for certain unsolved anomalies in Oriental studies. For example, we have a vast philosophic literature in Buddhism, Jainism, and the Six orthodox systems of Indian philosophy: *Sāṃkhya*, *Yoga*, *Mīmāṃsa*, *Vedānta*, *Vaiśeṣika*, and *Nyāya*; yet the Vedas, and in particular the Ṛg Veda, which is allegedly the direct or indirect source of all these systems, remain ineffective as philosophical tools.[2] (See also the second part to Textual Appendix III.)

The Ṛg Veda at a first glance is an anthology of songs and poems. It contains diversified elements of poetry, mythology, religious beliefs, magic and, primarily invocations of songs of praise to various gods. They represent only fragments of an immense cultural lore which combined popular religion with priestly cults, codified and used later on for sacrificial purposes.

The novelty of our approach, and obviously its justifiable need, is a systematic effort to create the necessary and sufficient conditions for the Ṛg Vedic text to give us its own *meaning*. But since *meaning*, any meaning, is dependent on certain definite *criteria* that make it possible, the novelty of our approach will demand that the only criteria we use for meaning in the Ṛg Veda are the criteria which the Ṛg Veda itself provides.

Whether we like it or not, whether we consider it a gain or a loss, all we stand on, or can stand on when trying to discover the origins of Indian tradition or the Rg Veda, is the hymns themselves. There are no other sources except the chanted hymns. It is, therefore, essential, given this fact, that we get ourselves ready to move, in one swift jump, from the prosaic, discursive, lengthy and conceptual ground on which we are accustomed to stand, into the moving, shifting, resounding, evanescent, vibrating and always sounding silence of the *musical* world on which the Ṛg Veda stands. But this means that the criteria for the meaning which we are seeking cannot be reduced to explicit statements chanted in the hymns. The main criteria for meaning are implied in the context and the structure of the hymns themselves: the intentionality–structures of the Ṛg Vedic poets, the implied theory of harmonics derived from the use of the hymns, and the mathematical number and measure through which the harmonics of the hymns can be identified.

The full theory of harmonics and mathematics we shall leave for others to develop, while our primary purpose in the pages that follow will be to bring out the intentionality–structures—the context—of the Ṛg Vedic poets and on which or with which harmonics and mathematics stand. One must also learn to say the least, so that the maximum involvement of others is accomplished.

Therefore, the first 'linguistic fact' to attend to in the Ṛg Veda is that its hymns are composed in a very elaborate meter, with great literary skill, and that they are meant to be chanted.[3] We must take this linguistic fact literally and remember at every step of our interpretation that Ṛg Vedic man *literally* stands on music. This applies not only to the chanters of the hymns (*ṛṣis*) but to the whole population of the people. The criteria by which to give meaning to the hymns cannot be the criteria by which meaning is given to poetry or prose. The hymn is, in fact, the sonorous embodiment of certain definite criteria by which a musical theory becomes a particular chant. Since the tonal systems, however, are infinite, the selection by the musician (*kavi*, *ṛṣi*) of a finite number of them, not only closes him within a certain limitation or determination—just tuning, meantone temperament, equal temperament, etc.—but, more radically, it forces him to constantly face the internal incompatibility of any such selection. In order to be able to accept "a democracy" or "a plurality," of such systems, the tones of every conceivable system must constantly face and submit to a radical sacrifice. This is the sacrifice that is the result of a radical disorder, which for the sake of functioning within a particular order, is usually ignored or repressed. It is to the credit of the Ṛg Vedic seers that the hymns and the sacrifice are the original sources to which they return again and again when they have to reorient (recreate) themselves. These are all important points in the interpretation of the Ṛg Veda. What the Vedic listener experienced as a *whole* in the sacrificial recitation can be lost in fragments and in countless atomic centers of meanings when a 'prosaic' (analytic) reading or listening is applied systematically to the same verses. What Vedic man *knew*, we do not know, and yet it will depend entirely on recovering that way of 'knowing' for the Vedic hymns to make sense to us. Although Vedic exegesis had to approach the Ṛg Veda with analytic crutches, to depend on them exclusively now might work against the understanding of the Ṛg Veda which Vedic exegesis is seeking.

In sum, we may say that we are not trying in any way to reconstruct the *text* of the Ṛg Veda, or that we consider that such a task is possible, feasible, or even desirable. We may even dare to suggest that such a feat, even if it were possible to accomplish, would be, within the context of this book, a trivial feat. Our present task is more radical in the sense that through the collection of texts known as the Ṛg Veda we are trying to understand a human ground which is different from ours. Through its discovery we will be able to free ourselves from our own determination, even though this same ground we are about to discover was in many ways the determination and at times the emancipation of Ṛg Vedic man and the tradition that followed. We consider that if man's appearance on this earth, like our own appearance on this earth, is not to be considered a historical triviality, then these meditations in which we are engaged are not only necessary but are also the sufficient condition for the given fact that man has to live with man in a plurality of societies, democracies, dependencies and rationalities. There are, of course, other alternatives; but all these other alternatives, coincide in the crypto-agreement that man's appearance on this earth is a triviality, at best to be given full meaning in a heaven away from this earth, or at worst a nuisance of this earth which must, at all costs, be radically controlled. But about these things, more later. Let us now proceed with our preparations for meditation.

III

It is not now my intention to proceed to criticize Western or Eastern exegesis of the Ṛg Veda. Frankly, I would not know what it would mean to pronounce anyone right or wrong. Exegesis is made in relation to a concrete horizon or framework. The owner of such a horizon or framework succeeds if his claims are bound by that horizon by that horizon, or state what, within that horizon, is or is not the case. Horizons or frameworks are neither right nor wrong, they are more or less constraining, more or less liberating, wider or narrower: they may contain the totality—actual or possible—of human experience, or they may reduce human experience to only a part of its actuality or potentiality. What I, therefore, am about to point out has only to do with frameworks—some at least—of Ṛg Vedic exegesis. The underlying critical claim is that no one framework can do justice to the Ṛg Veda except the Ṛg Vedic framework itself.

Indian exegesis of the Ṛg Veda is, like its Western counterpart, based for the most part on later and exterior frameworks: Yaska's and Mādhava's[4] etymological-cum-naturalistic-mythology; Sāyana[5] with his ritualistic interpretation, and, in modern times, the 'esoteric' and 'mystical' interpretations of Sri Aurobindo[6] and V. S. Agrawala.[7] Some of the interpretations given to the Ṛg Veda texts are not only foreign to them but even to Indian Tradition itself. However, all these authors bring to Vedic exegesis a tremendous richness of information and insights which are in any event useful and textually necessary.

Western scholars, since the discovery of Sanskrit in the 18th century by Coeurtdeau, a French missionary, and Sir William Jones, a British judge,[8] have approached Vedic exegesis from the viewpoint that their own Western disciplines allowed. The greatest effort at textual fidelity, and in many ways an exceptional work, has been provided by Louis Renou.[9]

There is no doubt that Western comparative philology has provided the most serious approach at interpreting the Ṛg Veda. No matter how adequate or inadequate one may find the framework through which each philologist or school of philology approached the Ṛg Veda, one cannot ignore or discard any of them. The work of these pioneers is what makes possible any further advance in understanding.[10]

The purpose of mentioning a few here is to add concrete examples of the relation that holds between interpretation and frameworks and how these interpreters progressively advance towards a more and more exclusive understanding of the text in and for itself.

The Ṛg Veda has been understood by these scholars as:

1. A sort of *referential literary document*, useful for comparative rituals and mythologies;
2. A text with a certain independence from other texts;
3. Some combination of numbers 1 and 2;
4. A possibly complete independent linguistic text where one should attend only to the use of words and groups of words within the constantly self-referential text itself, rejecting outside criteria and influences.

Under the first group we may include two groups of scholars, those bent on seeing in the Ṛg Veda a parallel of the Iranian culture: Thieme[11] or Gershevitch,[12] for example; and those who see the Ṛg Veda as a source of material for mythological and religio–cultural ideas: Zimmer,[13] Hilldebrandt,[14] to a great extend Oldenberg,[15] and his modern exponent Gonda.[16]

In the second group we may include Oldenberg and to a greater extent Bergaigne.[17] They tried to see in the Ṛg Veda a text with a greater independence than had previously been acknowledged. Bergaigne is, in this sense, the most radical of the two interpreting the Ṛg Veda as mythology: his 'ideological' approach, though insisting on an interpretation of the Ṛg Veda based exclusively on the text itself, also introduces an ideology too final not to be premature. (As we shall see later in this book, the 'language of Sacrifice' of the Ṛg Veda demands that the 'idol' of conceptual 'personification'—on which myth is based—die, so that man may live.)

The third group of philologists, who share in certain characteristics common to the above two groups, are: von Roth,[18] Geldner,[19] Grassman,[20] and Ludwig.[21] And finally, there is the fourth group: Louis Renou.[22]

Renou's Ṛg Veda is a text in itself, a text in use, in the process of composition, compiled in response to 'literary' (or if preferred) archeological, rather than liturgical needs, it is an anthology. "It could almost be said without paradox that the work stands outside the Vedic religion. Unlike the others it does not claim to be a practical manual."[23] Renou is very well aware that between the Vedic text and the following Indian texts there are great cultural gaps. It is only in these later contexts that the word of the Ṛg Veda becomes 'holy word,' i.e., it is no longer dynamic, but becomes stagnant in order to achieve external ends. The *ṛc*, alive and dripping inspiration, changes into a mantra, but by then the integrity of the Ṛg Veda is lost and we have instead and in succession: liturgy (*Brāhmaṇas*), speculative philosophy (*Upaniṣads*), and even historical poetry (Epics). It is Renou's Ṛg Veda that points most directly to the 'spirit and the letter' of the Vedic *kavis*. Unfortunately, Renou's untimely death prevented his ideal from being completed.

IV

Next to this gigantic effort of philologists to provide an understandable translation of the Ṛg Veda, the effort of others to isolate *a* religion or *a* philosophy of the Ṛg Veda cannot but appear somewhat naïve and uncritical. In order to obtain a religious or philosophical framework, texts have been isolated uncritically often for the purpose of fitting other religious or philosophical frameworks.[24] "The historico–religious or the historico–philosophical frameworks have tried to gain a non–situated objectivity of all life and of all manifestations of life and have avoided, in the name of objectivity, any kind of personal involvement. Though the aim may be very high, i.e., to 'know everything,' one may well end up understanding nothing.[25] Furthermore, the use of such an uncritical approach has proliferated religious and metaphysical statements which, to say the least, are confusing, untrue, and sometimes meaningless.

To sum up:

1. A recovery of the Ṛg Vedic text, in itself and for itself, can only be completed when: a) what Ṛg Vedic man had in mind or knew becomes

evident and b) this knowledge is reflected in the translation of the Ṛg Vedic text. The reason for this is that the Vedic text is a creation of men and for men with the same things in mind.

2. What philologists, and other scholars, have offered so far in the understanding of the Vedic text are only partial insights as to the reality of the total text. The totality of the text can be secured only if all the partial insights are taken into account and if the secondary elements, which in the partial interpretation were added by the structures of explanation, are dropped.

3. This sampling of partial insights and interpretations is what is understood in this book as the complementarity of explanations. Comparative interpretations are juxtaposed not just as bricks in a building, but in the following manner: partial views are not only contrasted but also synthesized into a comprehensive viewpoint in which each lower viewpoint is complemented with insights from other viewpoints. This results in a real increase in interpretative insight, a widening of perspective and in fact a *change of viewpoint* brought about by the activity of synthesis itself.

4. This change of viewpoint is necessary in order to gain the Ṛg Vedic viewpoint. However, since the structural characteristics of the disciplines approaching the Ṛg Veda make it almost impossible to attain a complete freedom in viewpoint–changing, I suggest that a comprehensive and radical philosophical approach to the Ṛg Veda is necessary in order to discover the functional characteristics through which the text is still a living body.

5. Since every form of human life is ultimately grounded on a dark soil of hidden beliefs and presuppositions, philosophical activity cannot be content with just describing the surface of the world, *the consciousness of* which it is aware. It must also be able to uncover the consciousness men *count on* in order to act, reflect, and communicate; for it is this consciousness man counts on that is the most problematic in man and in philosophy, and unless man is able to get hold of it in himself and in others, despite the affirmations and negations to the contrary, there can be no cultural movement of the body of man: The human body will forever remain a fixed point in the fixed space and time of its uncovered beliefs. These meditations are just the systematic effort at setting the cultural body of man in movement.

2
The Way of Critical Philosophy

A picture held us captive, and we could not get outside it for it lay in our language and the language seemed to repeat it to us inexorably.

Ludwig Wittgenstein

We cannot know our world until we find a compass that can chart what world we know.

Theodore Spencer

I

We stated earlier that the philosopher's task is never to finish anything, but rather a constant new beginning. We further had the audacity to suggest that philosophy and meditation coincide at the root level of their own anonymity. Obviously the above two statements are the result of a laborious and prolonged reading of the history of philosophy. In their concise form they might appear not only puzzling but even confusing. Let us, therefore, retrace our steps and try, in plain English, for some kind of translation.

The task we set for ourselves in this book was to reach the ground on which Ṛg Vedic man stands. We soon realized, however, that this task was an impossible one unless we were capable of running up and down, backwards and forwards, the ground upon which we ourselves as interpreters stand. But as soon as we decided on this project, a sense of desperation overcame us. If philosophy was to be our way to reach the Ṛg Veda, then the very idea of our project seemed impossible. For philosophy, as traditionally understood, had systematically focused on theory and communication, and by doing so had systematically closed itself within its own theories and its own discourse about them. There was no room in it for a foreign rationality. Even critical philosophy, in the wake of the Kantian critique, was no more than a deliberate justification of a particular theory of knowledge (scientific method) which took its own theoretical ground for granted. In a word, if we were to follow the path traditionally assigned to philosophers by their own tradition, we could never make it to the shores of the Ṛg Veda. What we needed was a way which could not only produce theories which could be verified, but a way which could radically falsify all theory, if our project as philosophers was primarily to stand under (understand) the determinations and controls of any and all theories by which men live. It is for this reason and, in a sense, for this radical freedom, that we had to turn and develop philosophy as a critical activity. In doing this our focus is not so much on theory and communication, but rather on the activity itself of doing philosophy. What philosophers do is as constitutive of philosophy as theory and communication. And what philosophers *do*, radically contradicts and denies what philosophers *think* they do and what they *say* about their thinking. But having said all this, we are forced to retrace our steps a bit further.

The problem of philosophy was dramatically and unknowingly prophesized by a man of Elea called Zeno. Zeno of Elea (489 B.C.) did not think of himself as a philosophical prophet, nor did Western tradition consider him as such. In fact, he is very lucky to receive a couple of pages of acknowledgement either in the Western histories of philosophy or mathematics. Why we have chosen to elevate him today to the rank of prophet might become clear from what follows, provided we take what follows by way of illustration and avoid making of it a formal thesis in the form here presented.

Zeno of Elea was a deciple of Parmenedes. According to the master, only the One is real, and the One is Thought: this is the Way of Truth. The rest, the multiplicity, is illusion: the Way of Seeming. The Pythagoreans, on the other hand, claimed the multiplicity to be real and denied the supremacy of the One. Zeno understood or misunderstood the pluralism of the Pythagoreans to mean the pluralism grounded on a pluralism of many discreet thoughts. In order to defend his master he thought that all he had to do was to prove the contradictions inherent in the Pythagorean position as he understood it. This he did with four arguments which we know mostly through Plato and Aristotle and are generally known as Zeno's paradoxes. For the sake of brevity we shall consider only the paradoxes of the "crossing of the stadium" and of "the race between Achilles and the tortoise."

Let us suppose that you want to cross a stadium or race–course. In order to do so, you would have to traverse an infinite number of points. Moreover, you would have to travel the distance in finite time if you wanted to get to the other side at all. But how can you traverse an infinite number of points, and so, an infinite distance, in a finite time? We must conclude, said Zeno, that you cannot cross the stadium.

The same argument is even more dramatically stated with the race between Achilles and the tortoise. Achilles and the tortoise are going to race. Since Achilles is a sportsman, he gives the tortoise a start. Even though Achilles runs ten times as fast as the tortoise, and though the tortoise has only 100 yards' start, by the time Achilles reaches the place where the tortoise starts the race the tortoise has already gone a tenth as far as Achilles, and is therefore ten yards ahead of Achilles. Achilles runs this 10 yards. Meanwhile the tortoise has run a tenth as far as Achilles, and is therefore 1 yard in front of him. Achilles runs this 1 yard. Meanwhile the tortoise has run a tenth of a yard and is therefore a tenth of a yard in front of Achilles. Achilles runs this tenth of a yard. Meanwhile the tortoise goes a tenth of a tenth of a yard. He is now a hundredth of a yard in front of Achilles. When Achilles has caught up this hundredth of a yard, the tortoise is a thousandth of a yard in front. So, argued Zeno, Achilles is always getting nearer the tortoise, but can never quite catch up with the tortoise.

These are the paradoxes. Mathematicians and philosophers might ask, "So what, why to make a point of problems already solved?" But this is precisely the point of bringing these paradoxes up for new consideration. The problem of Achilles and the tortoise has been solved in mathematics as a problem of quantification and mathematical language. But this solution has led mathematicians into new problems and new mathematical languages. To illustrate this point let us put down in numbers the distance which the tortoise traverses at different stages of the race after Achilles starts. As we have described it above, the tortoise moves 10 yards in stage 1, 1 yard in stage 2, one–tenth of a yard in stage 3, one–hundredth of a yard in stage 4, etc. Suppose we had a number language like the Greeks and Romans, or the Hebrews, who used letters of the alphabet. Using the one that is familiar to us because it is still used for clocks, graveyards, and law–courts, we might write the total of all the distances the tortoise ran before Achilles caught him like this:

$$X + I + \frac{I}{X} + \frac{I}{C} + \frac{I}{M} \textit{ and so on}$$

The awkwardness of this script is that there is nothing to suggest how the distances at each stage of the race are connected with one another. Today we have a number vocabulary which makes this relation perfectly evident when we write it down as:

$$10 + 1 + \frac{1}{10} + \frac{1}{100} + \frac{1}{1000} + \frac{1}{10000} + \frac{1}{100000} + \frac{1}{1000000} \text{ and so on}$$

It took the French Revolution to simplify the above notation into a decimal spelling:

10 + 1 + 0.1 + 0.01 + 0.001 + 0.0001 + 0.00001 + 0.000001 and so on

Which in turn can be translated into:

11.111111 and so on

Which in its most elegant form can be read as:

11.i.

We recognize the fraction 0.i as a quantity that is less than $\frac{2}{10}$ and more than $\frac{1}{10}$. If we have not forgotten the arithmetic we learned at school, we may even remember that 0.i corresponds with the fraction $\frac{1}{9}$. This means that the longer we make the sum, 0.1 + 0.01 + 0.001, etc, the nearer it gets to $\frac{1}{9}$, and it never grows bigger than $\frac{1}{9}$. The total of all the yards the tortoise moves till there is no distance between himself and Achilles makes up just $11\frac{1}{9}$ yards, and no more.

In mathematical language it is a problem that has needed only the discovery of a number–language constructed in order to solve it: what mathematicians describe as the convergence of an infinite series to a limiting value, which translated means that if we go on piling up smaller and smaller quantities as long as we can, we *may* get a pile whose size is not made *measurably* larger by adding any more. The whole history of mathematics, from the process of division carried on indefinitely, through infinite series, limits, transcendental numbers, irrational quantities, complementarity, the indeterminacy principle, etc., is a history determined by the problems it encountered and its ability to resolve them. Ironically, however, the origins of mathematics are lost in the origins of music, and with this ignorance mathematics has lost its freedom. At the other end of the story in contemporary mathematics, as used in quantum mechanics for example, the language of mathematics is no longer translatable into ordinary English. For what mathematicians talk about: atoms, electrons, particles, etc., is not what they observe, measure, and control. Ordinary language has not yet caught up with contemporary mathematical language where in its most strict sense mathematicians could only speak properly of no–thing. They could speak a lot about what they *do*, but about this we shall be able to say more later.

As for philosophers, they have still to solve the problem of the One and the Many. Since philosophers like Zeno took it for granted that the problem was grounded in Thought, neither rhetoric nor dialectics have been able in 2500 years to move in any other way but in philosophical circles. The circular movement, however, has created a proliferation of many other epistemological, ontological and metaphysical problems grounded on thought, or as contemporary philosophers would say, "on the consciousness of." As a result we have that up to this day neither Achilles nor the tortoise did ever finish the race, nor has anyone been able to run the full length of the stadium, nor historically moved *behind* these beginnings. In other words, Parmenedes' proclamation of Thought as the ground of reality has determined for us, as prophesized by Zeno, a host of new thoughts, of new theories, which multiplied of their own inertia other thoughts and theories; but it never allowed us to finish the trajectory of any Thought except to see it continued in another thought; for we were never able to question—stand under—the original Thought which controlled and determined our circular trajectory; nor could we read the previous history of man in any other form.

Thought in man is never neutral. It acts, it multiplies, it divides, it becomes flesh, it becomes joy and it becomes suffering. It is determination and it is crisis. It is, in fact, a cultural reduction and determination of a human path. But man does not live by Thought alone, nor is Thought a cultural determination for all men. There is room for freedom. Man must somehow mediate himself through other men; which means that he must be able not only to discover other men's controls, but above all, he must avoid the philosophical exaggeration of believing that the life of all men, and even reality, are all controlled by the same Thought. For after all, life is continuous, it runs the length of the stadium and Achilles beats the tortoise every time they race.

It is hoped that by now the reader has been able to discover the ironical note we struck when we proclaimed Zeno a philosophical prophet. If we consider the history of Western philosophy, or for that matter what is traditionally understood as Western culture, as a large stadium to be crossed—a whole sentence to be finished—a race to be run between Achilles and the tortoise—or one great discourse to be ended—then we find that the very idea of this enterprise was determined by its very origin to be an impossible task. Parmenides fixed the railroad tracks of the journey for us. Zeno, unbeknown to himself, prophesized for us the impossibility of reaching this journey's end. Man instead will be condemned to Sisyphean labor. But as it is customary with us, we have for the sake of clarity to retrace our steps again.

The first determination of the journey, the Way of Truth, was the identification of the One with Thought. The second determination, the second rail of the railroad track, was the identification of Thought with Being. As Parmenides sums up the position at the end of Plato's *Parmenides*: "If One is not, then nothing is." Which would be fine if this identification had not in turn given birth to new thoughts and new identifications, new problems and new languages, with dramatic results, not for Thought and Being, which are still alive and procreating, but for Western man condemned not only to endless wandering, but even more dramatically, condemned to death at the hand of the original determination of Thought and Being.

If we focus again on what philosophers do rather than on their theories and communication, we find, with astonishment, that they are more willing to sacrifice even unto death what they do for the sake of the lives of their theories and communications. Or in other words, when we take Thought and Being from their origin to what philosophers and natural scientists are doing today, we find that Thought and Being have not only become flesh, but they have done so at the *expense* of the life of every individual from the West or the East.

Let us again avoid multiplying the thoughts of man by developing the above in a formal thesis. Philosophers, myself included, have been continuously doing that, but let me point out only in a schematic and suggestive way how thinking has been systematically reduced to having thoughts, and this in turn to the brain, and lastly to human behavior, while the language of Being has been equally reduced to the language of a logic, of a grammar, identified with word, and proclaimed in this fashion as able to control universal human behavior. It is not the case, as Heidegger contends, that we have forgotten Being; but it is rather the case that because we have not forgotten Being and Thought, man has condemned himself, as Heidegger also contends, to being Being–towards–abstraction and Being–towards–the–end: Death.

Nietzsche, that young, philosophical prophet of modern man, has hinted to us the need to retrace our steps to the origin of our steps in order to avoid all this determinism. In *The Will to Power* he says:

> *Our oldest metaphysical ground is the one we will rid ourselves of at last—supposing we could succeed in getting rid of it—this ground that*

has incorporated itself in language and in the grammatical categories, and has made itself so indispensable at this point, that it seems we would have to cease thinking if we renounced this metaphysics. Philosophers are properly those who have the most difficulty in freeing themselves from the belief that the fundamental concepts and categories of reason belong by nature to the realm of metaphysical certainties. They always believe in reason as a fragment of the metaphysical world itself; this backward belief always reappears for them like an all-powerful regression.[1]

Nietzsche, of course, is not offering a logical solution within the scheme of things grounded on Thought and Being. What he proposes is a strategy to be followed, a new activity to be developed, a new analysis that if *practiced* would liberate the reader from the determinations of Thought and Being. This approach would be diametrically opposed to Heidegger's way of dealing with the same problems. In the "Letter on Humanism" he speaks of

. . . *the metaphysics which, in the form of Western "logic" and "grammar," early took possession of the interpretation of language. Today we can but begin to surmise what lies hidden in this process. The freeing of language from "grammar," and placing it in a more original and essential framework, is reserved for thought and poetry.*[2]

And elsewhere, recalling that *Sein und Seit* (Being and Time) remained unfinished he writes:

Here the whole thing is reversed. The section in question was suppressed because the thinking failed to find language adequate to this reversal and did not succeed through the aid of the language of metaphysics.[3]

And so the wheel goes on, from philosophy to linguistics, to the natural sciences, and back to philosophy. And it is also obvious that to follow this path systematically will again keep us within the tracks of Thought and Being, but would never allow us to reach the shores of the Ṛg Veda. What we shall do instead is presuppose that the whole history of philosophy and of the social sciences is the stratification of one great discourse, and try a textual strategy whose *practice* might catapult us outside of it.

Our first critical move is to point out that neither Thought nor Being are a *universal* radical ground. They are not universal radical ground in at least two senses. First, in the sense that not all men or communities of men or cultures have historically taken Thought and Being as their radical ground. Second, in the sense that even for the Eleatic philosophers, Thought and Being are not ultimately grounded on themselves but rather on the preconception and preaffirmable *belief* that Thought and Being will work as a way, or a method, in opposition to other ways and methods. The Way of Truth is the incestuous child of Greek life and Greek interpretation; but the child, even in its cradle, destroys its fathers and forefathers and proclaims itself the absolute and universal procreator of all life. What is only in its origin a temporary, public, and particular form of injecting meaning into the world becomes, through the magic of power, a demand and a resolution to absorb all life into its particular form of giving meaning to all of life. The Way of Truth, which is particular, public, and derived, becomes a *universal* scheme to subjugate all men not only to the fixity of Thought as their ground, but also to limit Being only to the moves possible within that particular ground of Thought. The subsequent moves in the history of philosophy, through dialectics and logic on the one hand, and rhetoric and grammar on the other, have only been moves of power in the same direction but never moves to liberate man from these original controls.

With these preliminary notes in mind, the reader might be able to understand the almost impossible task we face in our effort to reach the text of the Ṛg Veda. The Ṛg Veda has been approached by investigators within a logical space of explanation given them either by a Western philosophy or a Western science or a later Indian philosophy. The claims so made do not reveal Ṛg Vedic man in his authentic given order, but rather within the conceptual order of the particular structure of explanation. Were we to change the language—and with it the conceptual system it expresses—we would undoubtedly create as many different understandings of Vedic man as the different languages we use. Yet, one may easily be trapped within "conceptual spaces;" the aim would be to *free* oneself by *becoming*, in one auspicious instant, as the *Ṛṣis* understood it, the intelligible *Vāc* (Word) operating to transcend conceptual spaces. This latter way of acting corresponds both to Vedic man's intentional mode of action and to the incorporation and subsequent falsification of the complementarity of frameworks as described in the previous chapter. In both cases, spaces of discourse are to be transcended through action—the action of using them without resting permanently in any of them—in order to work out the wider perspective of the world and the reality which is most comprehensively human.

These are claims which only philosophy as we *do* it here can handle. Philosophy deals with many conceptual systems and intentional frameworks—actual or possible—and is concerned with their relationships as well as with the possibility of transcending them by their relations to human action. The most important new element generated by the *human* action of critical philosophy is the change of perspective on the world which such an activity produces as it actively avoids resting permanently in any one theoretical framework. Its path is to focus on the activity that enables us to bring out the dynamic and anonymous reality that holds between that which is structured and the structuring activity; between language and its source; between symbol and reality, and the spaces of discourse in which they appear. We will then have a way of doing philosophy capable of reaching the Ṛg Veda.

It is obvious, therefore, that the Ṛg Veda is the only source we can count on for understanding the Ṛg Veda. The main clue, and in fact the only one we can lay our hands on, is Ṛg Vedic language or the understanding of language as found implicity and explicitly in the Ṛg Veda. But this poses a problem. The philosopher who approaches the Ṛg Veda is already doing this with the crutches of his own linguistic framework. Such a framework comes equipped with theoretical constructs: categories, ontology, metaphysics and ethics, and also supposes a theory of knowledge. Philosophical inquiry may reduce itself to explaining that slice of human experience that fits the investigative framework, rather than enlarging itself, and examining human experience in its wider intentionality, and so, allowing philosophy to live. Therefore, it is not to be supposed that one might fruitfully use any one of the Western philosophical frameworks in the case of the Ṛg Veda—not even the most general of them all: the metaphysical frame of Being and its subservience to Thought as universal human ground.

The fact is that philosophy and method are so linked together that the philosophy which possesses the market place often drives other philosophies out of the city. Some have described metaphysical speculation as "nonsense," rational principles as "elective analytical postulates," and ethical statements as "emotive;" but the fact is, philosophy cannot be purely deductive, nor purely inductive, nor purely transcendental. Its method must coordinate and perhaps subordinate all these methods in a complementary fashion. Man is not neutral in respect to the construction and use of his intentional structures, neither in respect to the forms of knowing assumed by transcendental philosophers, nor in respect to the content assumed by empiricists, nor in respect to the forms of the objects known assumed by rationalists. This assumption of neutrality lies at the root of the Western dispute on philosophical methodology. Defenders of the purely deductive method have assumed a human power attributable only to the creative intellect. Defenders of the purely inductive method have assumed human impotence attributable only to man's complete dependence on the givenness of objective events. Defenders of the *transcendental* method have assumed that the receptive categorizing mind and its *data* are the measure of the *real*. (Although Kant himself went far beyond this assumption in his ethical doctrine; here, at least, he understood that the *real* is the *active*.)[4]

What is common to all these groups is that:

a) the 'structural' rather than the active and *functional* characteristics of human experience determine 'Reality'; and

b) *final knowledge* and the Real are both a result and a reduction of the sources of knowledge emphasized by each group.

These two common characteristics of philosophies can be made even more explicit by considering the active or *functional* characteristics of a conceptual system.

A conceptual system takes on existential import when the system as a *whole* is used to refer to that which is not *in the mind or in the senses*.[5] To use a system to refer is not itself to mean or to assert something; it is only the precondition of meaning or of asserting *anything* about reality. On the other hand, having a system to refer presupposes having a meaningful notion of knowledge and of reality. This may be exemplified by seeing that to have Being as the primal concept of the mind means no more than to be disposed to use one's conceptual system to refer to the objects of experience. Now, this referring to the objects of experience takes several forms but its model may be gathered from the *realist* way of using it. 'Being' is there used in the following way:

a) 'Being' is not an element *in* the conceptual system;

b) but a dispositional tendency to *espouse* the formal intelligibility of the conceptual system and the contents of sense experience so as to

c) create a reference to a domain of things, processes and events conceived, not as the product of subjective constitution, but as already out there in the public domain independently of any human involvement (noetic or otherwise).

Therefore, any judgment of the form 'is' or 'exists' in this system expresses an isomorphic relation between propositions as mental forms and the "real world." The judgment itself, however, is not a factor *in* our conscious experience, but rather a presupposition *of* our conscious experience; that is, it is not something we are *naturally* disposed so to do.

Yet, no matter how *natural* this disposition may be, neither the *contents* of a conceptual system nor their *counterparts*—the organic states of the sensory system—are in their own right *significant* or *intentional*. They only signify or represent a state of affairs (themselves experienced) because *we* take them to do so. The natural intentionality and disposition of the mind can be committed to a knowledge and a 'reality' which are constructed so by us in response to an already committed way of 'viewing the world,' 'knowledge' and 'reality.'[6]

Whatever else philosophy may do, it certainly is a human activity involving and involved in discourse. Any commitment of the natural disposition of the mind to inform experience with knowledge and reality is reflected in discourse. The linguistic framework, once admitted, makes the syntactical moves which, with the syntax of our language, determine the *relations* of 'is,' 'exists,' 'know' and 'real.' What in the original natural inclination of the mind was only one of many logically possible moves, becomes for the committed mind a representation of and a claim to limit the possibilities to one linguistic framework. The mind committed to the framework could then open itself only to one possibility of relating to the world (for example, that 'what exists in reality' is a set of objects with properties) and not open itself to the possibilities that what is experienced in one way may be experienced in many other legitimate frameworks endorsed by the natural inclination of the mind. The possibility that there are other possible logical moves about the 'real' is obvious. Let us mention, for example, Buddhist tradition, where the 'real' is 'non–indirectly' signified but not as a set of objects with properties, ("What is evident–*pratyakṣam*—to men is concealed–*parokṣam*–to the gods and what is concealed to men is evident to the gods.")[7]

Therefore, to raise significant questions in philosophy about the world, reality, knowledge, or existence, is not to raise questions about those *things*,[8] but rather to question the very relationship of our conceptual system—as admitted in use—to "that which is." This questioning is, in a sense, transcendental, because it does not focus on the objects of knowledge, but rather on knowing itself. This is a knowing which transcends itself, becoming aware of its own controls, the moment we reflect on the fact that we naturally *use* intelligible forms to *refer* to "that which is" without being able to know the *cause–originator* of "that which is." What for us, within any given framework, is *immediately* given is only our commitment to our own construction. The mediate experience, originator and cause of the immediately given, remains forever directly unknowable, uncontainable in any one framework and therefore, unspeakable. Yet, what cannot be directly *conceived* as that which makes our experience transcendentally *real* can be reached in other ways by complementarily transcending the different spaces of discourse, and it can even be directly experienced, so that the way of human knowing and the direct *source* of human experiencing coincide to become that way of human seeing which would make human action most efficacious. Liberating knowledge is, again, a philosophical task; for to question knowing in the above sense is to question *human action* in every sense: social, religious, linguistic, ethical. One may take the *indirect* creation of man, as reflected in his language, as the 'real' and defend it with one's own teeth to the death,[9] or one may transcend it in 'living sacrifice' and *become* that *direct* way of efficacious acting which keeps these worlds going. This latter alternative is the Ṛg Vedic enterprise.

II

Philosophy, in its constraints of Thought as ground of Being, universally accepts the above mentioned dichotomy of our two sources of knowledge: the indirect one (called understanding, imagination, etc.) and the direct one (called sensibility, perception, etc.); the two sources of knowledge are understood as a 'nonsensuous' and a 'sensuous' source: a *mundus sensibilis* (*kósmos aisthetós*) and a *mundus intelligibilis* (*kósmos noetós*). Philosophies will vary, both in the East and the West, according to the interpretation (language–value) given to the relation between these two worlds and their corresponding space of discourse. The same possibility of accepting and depending on new and different ontologies remains open when confronting the objects of the senses; the language of sensible objects is as interpretative as the language of ontology in the sense that a physical object is an intermediary construct for the sake of meaning within a given framework. As Quine remarks:

> . . . . *in point of epistemological footing the physical objects and the gods (of Homer) differ only in degree and not in kind.*[10]

What is said of physical objects applies also to 'forces,' 'abstract entities,' and 'powers.'

> *Epistemologically these are myths on the same footing with physical objects and gods, neither better nor worse except for differences in the degree to which they expedite our dealings with sense experience.*[11]

This, however, is only part of the problem; for ultimately all philosophies function on the implicit understanding that the language they are using has a certain value: some claim an isomorphic relation between the language of the senses and that of the understanding and the reality determining both, while others hold that the language of the senses and of the understanding are both heterogeneous of the real, in the sense that one contradicts and negates the other.[12] Language, in this view, leads to knowledge only non–indirectly. Direct knowledge is not in language (and its static conceptualization), but in that continuous efficacy out of which language arises; for language constantly points back to itself and also to its source.

It is worthwhile at this point to explicitly state that this view of language does not permit any philosophical system to contradict any other, since none of them contains—or is directly—the real; but all philosophical systems are necessary—at least insofar as I encounter them—to gain not only new knowledge but also freedom by transcending them all at the active level which later on translates as intercommunication.[13] Therefore, philosophy must turn to the complementarity of frameworks and their falsification.

Philosophy has to contend with the admitted fact that human existence is problematic, i.e., there is a nonintelligible surd at the root of our experience. This nonintelligibility can be taken seriously, for after all, it is the source of all intelligibility; or it may be discarded as unspeakable, and therefore unknowable and logically meaningless (Positivists). While the latter will claim that the former does not 'know what he is talking about,' the former will reply that 'what he knows, in the transcendent sense, cannot be put into words because of the limits of language and of empiricism itself;' one can make claims in the name of empiricism without enrolling in any of the current empirical schools. In fact, one may claim, in the name of empiricism, a more radical empiricism than any of the ones in vogue, but here again, the difference is not so much of language as of philosophical methodology.

To *perceive* consciously is already to interpret reality in terms of *what we take to be the case*, but taking is already a way of informing. We notice and become aware of our experience in terms of *those aspects* to which we have already given form (interpreted in intelligible terms). Language repeats, in a functional way, the role played in the conceptual system by the concepts it expresses. However, since language itself has been taken by most philosophies as saying something positive about what is, and since saying is linguistically a process involving both the body and the mind, we find ourselves with two apparently irreducible languages: a language which describes physical states, and a language which refers to mental states. Any efforts by conceptual empiricists, behaviorists, and idealists[14] to reduce the one to the other have not succeeded; nor have the efforts of some phenomenologists[15] to enclose both worlds in one linguistic performance, by which reality is physico–mental, avoided the difficulty, because they must presuppose both languages. In fact, the problem seems unsolvable as long as the men of these philosophies do not transcend their own frameworks. Instead they create pseudo–problems—only reflected in language—by dogmatically taking the atomization of language and its separateness of the things of the world as real. These limits of separateness which commonsense language inflicts on reality: subjects and objects, man and the world, agent and re–agent, observer and observed, life and physiology, mind and bodies, I and other—are the result of what Wittgenstein called the 'bewitchment of language' on the one hand, and on the other, of a way of 'viewing the world' which is bound by that same commonsense language and its perspective. Ṛg Vedic man, in contrast, refused to create new problems by separating the inseparable, and searched instead for that other way of *viewing* the world which happens as a result of transcending common sense language and its viewpoint: the executive subject of that efficient *action* of which these worlds are the symbol: *janmad yasya yataḥ*.

Let us try and sum up the main insights which preceded:

a) There are many possibilities of describing the world and, by consequence, of interacting with it.

b) None of these logical possibilities has, in principle, preeminence above any others.

c) The choice, by philosophers, society, man, etc., of one over the other answers to other needs rather than the logical ones on which disagreements amongst philosophers seem to be based.

d) The main reason for choosing one logical description of the world rather than another and/or with the exclusion of the others, is the result of a preconceptual vision of the world received through language, accepted, and uncritically adhered to almost like a dogma.

e) A corrective of this impasse is suggested in a way of focusing on the activity itself of *doing* philosophy, which not only accounts for the complementarity of actual context–languages (frameworks, horizons), but which may transcend the limitations of a single set of possibilities, and liberate man from their controls.

f) The result of this journey into the complementarity of languages would be a new way of *viewing the world*, and therefore of interacting with it; making freedom possible by falsifying all controls through the knowledge of the controls themselves.

With this summary in mind and in order to make the case for the philosophical way a valid one in the Ṛg Vedic case, I will try to show in more detail what is here understood by *a*) 'vision' or 'way of viewing the world,' and *b*) complementarity of context–languages and falsification.

III

The interaction of man with his world depends entirely on how he understands the *nature* of his *relationship* to himself and to other things or events. I propose therefore that:

1. The nature of this *relationship* is entirely dependent upon the type of framework, or world–view, from which man decides, or is habitually compelled, to relate to other things and events;

2. that within Western man's experience, there are at least two distinctive ways of viewing the world, which, for convenience sake, I shall call 'the commonsense–Classical–Physics viewing' and the 'Modern–Physics–Eastern viewing' of the world;

3. that man's condition is such that he is *bound* to use both view points if he is to solve the problem of "what–is–really–the–nature–of–things," and that by doing so, man becomes capable of finding his own liberation. This activity is one of complementarity, and liberation would correspond not only to a 'new way of viewing the world' and acting effectively within it, but also to being able to actually falsify and cancel out all thought, even if this activity in turn gives birth to new visions and thoughts.

There is obviously no solution to the situation of paragraph 1; since the problem there seems to be the premise behind the situation: Philosophers have been questioning the relation of man to the world with a preconceived notion of what this relation ought to be; we have seen the results earlier. They have placed side by side a multiplicity of actual particular languages and they have been more concerned with negating each other's claims than with transcending each other's limitations. This impasse of philosophers is the result of a preconceptual way of viewing the world which makes man a prisoner of his own language; internal intentionality and external tokens are used by man as in a formula, so that he sees what is as if the entities and atomic events, together with their boundaries, were the *real* constituents of reality. What is needed, rather than an answer or a negation of such a position, is a new reformulation of the problem: "If we want to have new knowledge, we need a whole host of new questions."[16] This is, after all, part of the faith of science; that if serious people work diligently on a problem for a long period of time and cannot arrive at a satisfactory answer, then they are asking the wrong questions and new ones are needed. What would then be, in man's relation to all that is, the nature of this relationship, if we were to formulate it in a "modern–physics–Eastern–way–of–viewing–the–world?" Let us try this new formulation:

> *If the boundaries of atomic entities and events, and those things and events, as expressed by our commonsense language, such as I, you, space, time, birth, death, subject, object, etc., did not really invariently exist, what would then be the relation of what exists, and how would it then be apprehended?*

Western man has a certain experience of certain implications of such a formulation within, what I have called, the Modern physics (particle theories and field theories) viewpoint. For clarity's sake, I will contrast here the two approaches so that the new formulation gains wider perspective.

The approach of *Classical Physics* corresponds very closely to the commonsense approach in the following sense: *It operates on the assumption that we should primarily search for individual, unique, atomic entities like things, and events, and only secondarily that we should see how these atomic units combine into classes of units and classes of classes of units and so forth.* The primacy of reality within this framework, is the atomic individual unit, separated from the rest of reality. This atomic individuality is considered the most real. But reality so conceived is a decision to establish *invarience* as a universal condition for knowing what is. On this view, *something*—nature, society, the individual, thought, being, space, time—must be presumed constant or invarient, so that their *regularities* may be explained, predicted, and controlled. On this view, not only invarience is established as the ground of reality, but the criteria through which invarience is so grounded are also universalized in such a way that nature, society, the individual, thought, being, space and time are radically and systematically suppressed.

The approach of *Modern Physics* corresponds to the Eastern view of reality in the following sense: *It operates on the assumption that whenever we are in search of anything, we are primarily in contact with a totality, the most 'real' aspect of any entity being the total pattern. Our perception of 'it' defies any atomicity or real identification. It is only secondarily that classification of individual entities is made possible, and for this we revert to ordinary symbolic manipulation. In other words, to perceive anything apart from the total field is to perceive it as a subsystem, an artificially created aspect of a field of stresses, i.e., a pattern. In fact, according to the law of complementarity, what can truly be said in one context–language, the same cannot be truly said in the other context–language.*

In the view of Modern Physics, we cannot simply say, "Here is an electron;" but, either we say with Sir James Jeans: "Here is an area where the field is strong,"[17] or else we revert to the viewpoint of Classical Physics and say: "Here, on this instrument, at this place, at this time, there is a signal (that manifests the presence of an electron)." In this view *what is* appears as a *quantum*, a whole, a totality; the identifiable parts of this totality are artificially created for purposes of linguistic communication and conceptualization: they are artificial subpatterns. The separation is totally false in relation to what is.

The difference between these two world views cannot be underestimated. It is in relation to these two pictures of reality that man relates to himself and to everything else. A man who *views* the world from the framework of Classical Physics cannot help but insist on the atomic and abstract demands of its viewpoint and act accordingly. The universal search for absolutes condemns man to die by those same absolutes; for in his search for abstraction man not only cancels out the concrete particular flesh facing him, but his own flesh becomes the invarient and fixed limits of the universalized criteria he so uncritically accepted.

On the other hand, to *view* the world from the Modern Physics viewpoint means to discover the form of knowledge of any reality in a systematic exercise *through* the total and particular reality as we encounter it. Reality is here understood as a 'whole' and as a 'total picture;' to know it and its language in the Classical–Physics–commonsense view has no meaning at all; for to know it on those terms would lead to a total falsification of what was previously presupposed that could be affirmed or denied. In Modern Physics, language, affirmation, and negation are restricted to and dependent on the particular context under consideration, and so are the criteria for their use; what is invarient is the particular norm, criterion, or ratio of the language in use. Invarience, as a universal requirement of language or of reality, is thereby completely falsified. The same applies to the universal invarients of nature, society, the individual, thought, being, time, space, etc. Now we are involved in a way of rediscovery!

Modern Physicists have tried to make us aware of the consequences that the new perspective would inflict on our lives:

> *we distinguish between living and dead matter, between moving bodies and bodies at rest. This is a primitive viewpoint. What seems dead, a stone or the proverbial 'door-nail,' say, is actually forever in motion. . . We shall have to learn to describe things in new and better ways.*[18]

Or, in the view of Sir James Jeans, there is need to consider as actually existing (according to the laws of complementarity) the totality of the efforts of man, successes or failures. In the continuum, they all live in the present:

> *. . . the twentieth century physicist is hammering out a new philosophy for himself. Its essence is that he no longer sees nature as something entirely distinct from himself. Sometimes it is what he creates and selects or abstracts; sometimes it is what he destroys.*[19]

It is in this light that one can read the meaning of the following texts of Indian Tradition:

Release us from the bonds of Death, not those of life.
R.V. 7.59.2

THERE, where the eagles vigilantly raise their voices
for the sake of a share of IMMORTALITY, of sacrifices,
THERE the mighty Herdsman of the whole world, the Wise
One, has entered me, the ignorant one.
R.V. 1.164.21

Two birds with fair wings, inseparable companions,
have found a refuge in the same sheltering tree.
One of the birds incessantly eats from the peepal tree;
the other, not eating, just looks on.
R.V. 1.164.20

They speak of the imperishable peepal tree
With its roots above and its branches below. . . .
B.G. 15,1

From the unreal lead me to the REAL!
From the darkness lead me to LIGHT!
From death lead me to IMMORTALITY!
Br. Up. 1.3.28

With the Classical Physics viewpoint of the world, we were primarily concerned with discovering notes, classifying them and aiming, through their different classifications, to compose a symphony that would eventually sing the world so conceived. Suddenly, with the discoveries of Modern Physics we have realized that the symphony was already there; that the songs were already being sung, and that the true sound of any note was dependent on how well one knew the symphony or the song in which the note was embedded. One could say that one single note is the whole song; that in order to play one single note, one has to know the whole song; or that while playing one single note one is playing the whole symphony. Silence underlies both as the condition of possibility. Perhaps this musical metaphor helps clarify what has preceded it.

It would, of course, be a complete misunderstanding of what we have sketched if we gave value to one way of viewing the world in preference to the other: The human condition is such that both viewings are essential to man, and he cannot be fully human without being at home with both. The interrelation and integration of both, in every man's life, is what we understand by complementarity. But this means that man must learn to read the particular and invarient in every situation and learn to surrender the demands of one form of particularity and its criteria to become universal thought, being, ground, and control. The Ṛg Vedic understanding of complementarity can be advanced considerably by attending to the laws of complementarity as provided by the new Logic of Quantum Mechanics; and by seeing how physics, an activity of Western man which started under the determination of Thought and Being, has, by the dedication to that same activity, carried to its limit, the ability to cancel out its original determination.

IV

The propositional Logic of Quantum Mechanics and Classical Logic, (or General Propositional Logic)—be it Aristotelian, or as developed by Russell and Whitehead in *Principia Mathematica*—are opposed to each other in the following sense: Classical Logic is a propositional Logic of two–valued truth–functional propositions, the logic of classes and of quantization. It functions on the level of statements about quantum events. On the other hand, quantum Logic[20] is a logic appropriate to the context: language about contexts and the language appropriate to the contexts. It is a two–valued propositional logic which varies only in dropping the distributive laws for 'and' and 'or,' and replacing them by some weaker form of connection, like a modularity principle.[21] This quantum logic is an orthocomplemented non–distributive lattice. Since this logic is formalizable, it becomes possible to clearly determine complementarity and exhibit the logical structure of the dialectic of context–language dependence. This is the core of Bohr's notion of complementarity.[22] (For the most important terms, definitions, axioms and formulae of both classical and quantum logic, see Appendix I.)

Let me illustrate these claims with some examples:

1. In classical mechanics, all 'physical contexts' were simultaneously realizable; i.e., measurable. On the other hand, in quantum mechanics, complementary quantities cannot be measured simultaneously without a reciprocal interference occurring in the measuring process; which means, that not all physical contexts can be realized simultaneously without some being in some way altered by the presence of others. So that in a language, if the physical contexts A and B are united in a combined physical context (whether unchanged or interacting mutually to constitute a single new physical context) the question arises as to what is the relation between L_A and L_B, the languages corresponding to the old physical contexts in isolation from each other, and L_{AB}, the language corresponding to the new context AB?

2. In classical mechanics, it is possible simultaneously to measure the position and momentum of a system. So that when A denotes the physical context for a position measurement, and B denotes the physical context for a position measurement, then AB exists, and at least at the kinematical (descriptive) level, L_{AB} is the set theoretic union of L_A and L_B, i.e., $L_{AB} - L_A = L_B$; and $L_{AB} = L_A$.

3. Let us proceed now with the language of microphysics. Let an atom be the given physical system. The first measurement is a momentum measurement of the atom constrained to stay in a box. Let A denote this physical context, which is a context within which the atom's momentum is quantized. The second measurement is the measurement of the atom's momentum in a universe divided down the center by a wall that is impenetrable except for one small hole, and is otherwise without boundaries. Let B denote the second physical context and L_B the language of the situation. In the second situation, the atom's momentum is not quantized, but its wave function is a superposition of symmetrical and anti-symmetrical left and right terms. The two original physical contexts can be combined by placing in a box divided (not necessarily at its center) by a wall impenetrable except for one small hole (as in diagram below). Let AB denote the combined physical context and L_{AB} the momentum language appropriate to this context. It is clear that L_{AB} is not just the set theoretic union of L_A and L_B. (To facilitate the formalization of the

notion of complementarity, it is supposed that L_{AB} contains L_A and L_B as limiting cases of the divided box context, i.e., it becomes identical with L_A when the dividing wall coincides with one or other of the end walls of the box, and with L_B when the dimensions of the box become very large.)

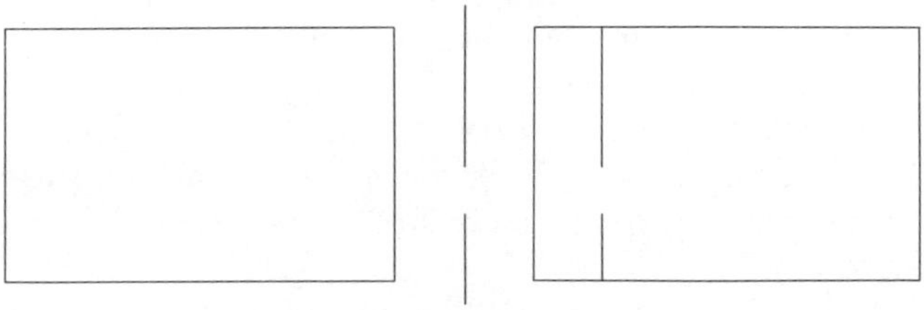

A *B* *AB*

Diagram of the complementarity contexts A and B and of the combined context AB

L_{AB} contains L_A and L_B set theoretically, that is,

$$L_A \subset L_{AB} \qquad (1)$$

and $$L_B \subset L_{AB} \qquad (2)$$

but $$(L_{AB} - L_A) \cup L_B \neq L_B \qquad (3)$$

and $$(L_{AB} - L_B) \cup L_A \neq L_A \qquad (4)$$

(3) and (4) formalize the result that, by combining the two separate physical contexts, new possibilities are generated which enlarge the manifold of possible events beyond what was included in the original manifolds. The universe of the combined physical context is larger in potentiality than the set theoretic union of the potentialities of the physical contexts in isolation. That the two measurements can be combined in one physical context is clear from the way the Indeterminancy Principle is used by Bohr, Heisenberg, and their followers. This Indeterminancy Principle is used in two different ways—as an inequality between the standard deviation between two sets of data,[23] and as a limitation imposed by the theory on an individual system in one and the same context.[24] It is this latter use which justifies the suggestions made here, i.e., that combined position and momentum contexts exist. In fact, since ideally precise contexts are impossible, they are all that exist. Man's life, as much as man's science, is grafted in them.

Therefore, the possibility exists, for philosophy and for man, to continue viewing the world on the classical model as an objective whole, and remove all subjective variations from it. A viewing of this sort gives us a public object only in its systematic aspect in an objective (scientific) domain which, on constitution is already a closed system. It is true that the linguistic token becomes an autonomous object, and because of this linguistics constitutes itself as a science; yet, the cost of this feat, in philosophical terms, is the constitution of a closed, finite system of signs lacking external reference within a semilogical system; the object is an abstract one with only *internal relations.* The arguments for such an idealized linguistic object will take the form of the old arguments between empiricism and idealism with a stop in between for realism. In this impasse, philosophy has only turned one more spoke of the wheel; understanding remains static.

On the other hand, there is also the possibility of viewing according to the Modern Physics model. Within this model, the way of procedure is through a community of inseparables (subject–object, observer–observed, mind–body, etc.) which were artificially created in the first place, and which indirectly indicate man's progress in transcending the knowledge of his own context–language dependence through the activity of the men of science, philosophy, and by man in general. The philosopher of science, the propagandist of the scientific method and the advocates of progress and civilization find, in the new formulations of Modern Physics, a new way of referring to the Real, as the result of a new way of viewing what "is." Philosophers and scientists are trying to find new ways of communicating this new vision, aware however that Complementarity and the Indeterminacy Principle are the limiting conditions of the language of such communication. Thus, it is uncritically believed that Complementarity, in its classical sense of *transcending* actual context–languages, accounts for some sort of dialectical progression within the language of mathematics and, by implication, of philosophy and human life. The Indeterminacy Principle, on the other hand, would on the same assumptions establish the rational limits within which such communication would not only be *descriptive* (establish the relation of objects to subjects) of the Real, but principally it would be an *explanatory* communication–language (establish the relationship between instrument–objects and instrument–objects) of the Real. Such a language would, of course, be rational, objective, and controllable in use as much as the reality it proposes to know. As Professor P. Heelan remarks:

> *. . . (It) was merely a historical accident that it took the existence of quantum mechanics to bring out the awareness of the structural character and the shift of structures through dialogue of both, our experience and our linguistic performance.*[25]

And so the wheel goes on. Thought has turned one more spoke of the wheel; Being affirms this movement, and Language, the faithful mirror of Thought and Being, tautologically reflects this new step of the dance that they started together so long ago. But if this is the only dance there is, we could never learn new steps or dance the Hindu dance; unless, of course, we could stop the movement of Thought–Being, and be able to discover the moving rhythm which determines the dance of Hindu feet. And so once again, we are forced to retrace our Western steps to the original determination of which every step of the dance has been a movement. Achilles might finally catch up with the tortoise.

V

The historical accident of the discoveries of quantum mechanics and their relation to linguistic communication, complementarity, indeterminacy, and vision, makes our project of landing on the text of the Ṛg Veda possible, not because of the theories and communications of these discoveries, but because of what the *activity* which led to these theories and communications has done to theory and communication. The Way of Truth, which required for its traveling, that the One, Thought and Being, remain Invariant as the Absolute ground of the journey, gives way at the end of this journey to the Way of Criteria for Truth. The Invariant One, Thought and Being, on which the Way of Truth started its predetermined journey, turns along the way into a myth: The Myth of Invariance. What started as a requirement for the Way of Truth, developed as it moved along, the characteristics of what it really was to begin with: the absolute and *invariant criteria* for obtaining any truth along its predetermined path. It is only because the men of the sciences and of philosophy were determined to focus on the absolute forms of theory and communication, through which criteria for verification are communicated, that they did not realize that, with every shift of criteria, and as a condition of their invariant character, they were simultaneously, and through their own activity, cancelling out and radically falsifying, the Absolute Invariant Ground on which they thought they were standing. But now that we have said all this, let us not fall again into the hands of Zeno and develop a formal thesis; somebody must cross the stadium from end to end. I will only offer some suggestive instances as strategic clues towards the path we ourselves have followed many a time.

Let us go back again to the beginning. Western philosophy, as much as Western science and the natural sciences, takes as its absolute and arbitrary beginning what is foggily identified as the beginnings of Greek rationality. Above all, Platonism and Aristotelianism have come down to us as two opposed ontologies fighting for absolute priority over each other. According to this view, the Platonists are presented as believing that classes, orders, genres and ideas are absolutely real, while for the Aristotelians the Platonic view is only a generalization, and the absolutely real is the individual substance, the particular concepts, and the categories derived from them: a universal set of principles of logic and a universal chain of causes and effects. For the Platonist, language is nothing more than an approximative set of symbols; for the Aristotelians, it is the only geography of the universe.

However general the above picture might appear, it is still an accurate one for the following reason: no one has really bothered to destroy it; or to put it in more Eastern and suggestive terms, no one has bothered to discover how the face of this newborn child looked *before* it was born.

Parmenides was no more an absolute beginning than those who followed after him. He was already a man *in medias res*, in the middle of things. For Parmenides to proclaim the Way of Truth, he had to cancel out the Way of Becoming of Heraclitus, the Way of the Elements, and the Way of Destiny (*Moira*). He had to empty the heavens of gods, the temples of oracles, and divert the attention of man from the entrails of the animals. As a substitution for this ground, on which Greek men had stood for centuries, Parmenides offered Thought. This new Ground became the One; it became Being; and this was finally the new way: The Way of Truth. But while Parmenides was apparently making claims about an absolute metaphysics about Being as One and True, he could only do that on the tacit assumption that Thought as ground would not be questioned, and that Being and Truth be given absolute and ontological priority over the Many and things. The truth of the matter is, however, that, in view of the subsequent development of the history of philosophy itself, this demand of the beginning was not so much to establish a metaphysics, and the priority of one ontology over another, but rather, to elevate the criteria of one particular epistemology to the heights of metaphysics. What he offered as the Way of Truth could only be the epistemological conditions which needed to be satisfied so that a proposition could be rationally affirmed as virtually or absolutely unconditioned. In this way he determined, invariantly he thought, the absolute ground of the world; while in fact, he only established the *invariant criteria* by which a valid assertion of a particular form of truth could be made every time the criteria were accepted. But since Thought itself was never questioned in this sense, and was uncritically taken for what it was not; namely, the ability to stay within its own limits; Western man had no other alternative but to follow Zeno's path, dividing his thoughts, multiplying his ontologies, and dividing again, forever unable, perhaps afraid or bewitched by his own achievement, to overcome the original determination. In this sense, human freedom, from its beginning, was already determined to be radically impossible; while human understanding of other people and other cultures was condemned to be possible only if and insofar as other people and other cultures could be radically emasculated or lobotomized, to stand, theorize and communicate from within the limits of our own determination. In this view, the understanding of others could be no more than a systematic effort at conceptual colonization, uprooting the flesh of all man, and transplanting it where we could recognize it, in our own conceptual ground. Only by then, they are no longer "them," but our own fleshless, disembodied ideas.

But of course there was no way in the world for Parmenides to know that Thought was the absolute ground of all man. It is ironical that the Way of Truth could not verify itself. What it could do instead, and in fact did, was to establish itself as the crypto–premise for affirming any truth. But since Thought in its Greek form was already a particular form of thought, the determination became even more fixed when all the moves of Thought had of necessity to follow the moves of Greek language and grammar. In philosophical terms, these moves were exemplified by the rhetoric of the sophists and the rules of rhetoric, the definitions of Socrates and the rules of definition, the dialectics of Plato and the rules of dialectics, and the logic of Aristotle and the rules of logic. With every step of the history of philosophy we find again the same determinations of the origin. Thought is taken for granted, new criteria, invariantly established, are proclaimed, new languages are developed to communicate the criteria and elevate them to the rank of metaphysical and ontological invariance. Ontological priorities take the place of the world—on the one hand, the priority of ideas; on the other hand, the priority of sensation and material substance. In either case, the teleology of Thought is imposed on the world and on man, and the Way of Truth turns out to be a long journey of hope, either for the Absolute Good or for the Absolute Truth. In either case, man is condemned to an idea of temporality, which is the result not of Time, but of a particular way of measuring the moves of a particular form of thought. In fact, Time, grounded on Thought, cannot be anything else but an idea of time.

There is, of course, a further element needed so that Western man, as we know him today, emerges in his full determination: individuality. The idea of the individual as an agent of action had to be exaggerated so that thought could move, either towards the absolute objectivity and fixity of the Unmoved Mover (Aristotle), or towards the uncontaminated One and Good (Platonist, neo–Platonists). In either case, the *efficient* subject or cause is exaggerated in such a way and to such an extent, that it completely obscures the *final* cause towards which it is already projected. What is not seen through this exaggeration of the individual, is that the final cause is nothing else than Thought (as the original cause of the whole movement;) and that the efficient cause, the individual, could be dispensed with; for after all, it is not such an efficient cause. But this idea of the individual had to stay with us as long as the whole system of Thought as ground stayed with us. Our whole system of law was born and grew stronger as the Way of Truth failed, and was fastened onto the individual who could not know all he was supposed to. Medieval philosophy and theology would turn the law into a way of salvation for the individual, while the natural sciences, and medicine, in particular, would give final structural form to these individuals with the ideas of the organism that they inherited from Greece. The idea of the organism is the most vivid example of an idea that is not neutral, but that *informs* man: the idea of the organism has become flesh, even while the organs of man are individually for sale or hire in any modernly equipped hospital.

It is again obvious that once Thought was taken for granted and remained unquestioned, the primary focus of Western man was what he could do with it rather than what he was determined to do by it, even if in the process man had to pay the high price of de–fleshing the flesh so that Thought might live. The momentous advances of Western sciences were based on the erroneous belief that everyone else namely, Pythagoreans and non–Western cultures had been doing science of a primitive kind because they had only been able to work with *descriptive* and *observational* concepts, rather than with explanatory concepts. A descriptive language or method is concerned only with how things relate to a subject; while an explanatory language–method is concerned only with how things relate to things. In its search for absolute explanation, prediction, and control (the method of the sciences), ontological priority was again given to a set of criteria to establish particular truths, and this was proclaimed to be the invariant picture of how things are. While all the time, all we had, and all we could give to our viewpoint of cultures, was an invariant set of criteria that guarantee certain truths every time the criteria were applied, and that, for this same reason, cancelled the ontological priority. If anything is to be drawn out of Modern Physics, especially quantum mechanics, it is the invariant character of the criteria of explanation, prediction, and control, and the context–language of their applicability. At, last we can see that the criteria of explanation, prediction, and control are such because they have a limit; and this limit is the context of both their applicability and their discourse.

If we were able to redo the history of philosophy, focusing exclusively on what philosophers have done as philosophers, we would see that the path of philosophy is strewn with unwilling corpses of theories and languages about theories. Where Parmenides proclaims the One, the Sophists proclaim the Many. Where Plato proclaims ideas, Aristotle proclaims sensation; but where Aristotle proclaims substance, Kant affirms the absolute categories of the mind instead; though in order to do so, he has to posit as their condition absolute time and absolute space. Berkeley affirms the existence of objects; for after all, God perceives them; but Berkeley denies absolute space—and while he affirms that an object equals sense impressions, he denies any object behind these sense impressions. Then Hume affirms that perceptions come in bundles, and that their rapid succession is their only justification; but in this way he denies the necessity of maintaining a subject to account for the perception of change. The ontological and epistemological determination of Thought continues through Descartes, but by this time, Thought has been reduced to "having thoughts." Thus from then on, thought is more generally understood to be the action of a substance called the *mind* facing another substance called the body. Having thoughts, and understanding these in turn as being extended, affirms their absolute temporal condition; but because time is so conceived as an attribute of two substances, we again find a host of problems determined by the *duration* of the ideas which gave birth to those problems. Duration and temporality are identified with the criteria of their measurement, thus Time and Space are reduced to a particular theoretical form of spatiality and temporality. In Kant, time and space become absolute, while in Hegel and Marx, they become historical or futuristic as the condition for Spirit and Matter to reach their fulfillment. But since Matter and Spirit are ideas, historicism at the hands of Dilthey will try to lump them together in a universal effort to bring together the whole world as a catalog of ideas.

Contemporary modern philosophy in the form of language analysis or of phenomenology tries to bypass these problems by focusing on language. Both movements, however, initially presuppose a strict logic to which language must already conform, previous and independent of how language is used (early Wittgenstein, Husserl, etc.); but when this demand becomes unbearable, language is again grounded on rhetoric, or dependent on peoples' use of language (later Wittgenstein, Heidegger, etc.).

In both instances, theory is overemphasized; analytic philosophers reduce all analysis of languages to the positivistic demand that the logical category of fact is a standard measure of the real; while phenomenologists ground the measure of the real on the "consciousness of."

No matter how many times we turn the wheel, its moves are already determined by our decision that it follow the moves of one particular form of thought. The efforts of phenomenologists, existentialists and analytic philosophers to solve this impasse has only accentuated the trap in which man has closed himself. The only thing that emerges clear out of these philosophies is that man is condemned to a temporality which is itself only an idea and which will last as long as man is incapable of reaching behind the idea of temporality to the Time of which man is made. For the idea is determined by its own condition as idea and it lasts only as long as the idea is able to live or die. We may either prolong our ideas and die before they do, or kill them at their root and renew our lives through their presence. The present is *all that is*; but the present includes not only theory and communication, but also what philosophers had to do in order to build theories and communicate. Critical philosophy and meditation coincide at this level, being able to cut man off from his determinations.

Critical philosophy would be impossible if there were no consciousness more radical than the *consciousness of*; if man was condemned to follow the predetermined path of one particular form of thought. But as Ortega y Gasset pointed out, there is a more radical consciousness: *the consciousness I count on* in order to decide which particular form of consciousness to follow or reject. Nietzsche expressed it as a radical *belief:*

> *Critique of 'reality': where does the 'more or less real,' the gradation of being in which we believe, lead to?—*
>
> *The degree to which we feel life and power (logic and coherence of experience) gives us our measure of 'being,' 'reality,' not–appearance.*
>
> *The subject: this is the term for our belief in a unity underlying all the different impulses of the highest feeling of reality: we understand this belief as the effect of one cause—we believe so firmly in our belief that for its sake we imagine 'truth,' 'reality,' 'substantiality' in general.—'The subject' is the fiction that many similar states in us are the effect of one substratum: but it is we who first created the 'similarity' of these states; our adjusting them and making them similar is the fact, not their similarity (—which ought rather to be denied—).*[26]

We would most probably do nothing about this situation were it not for the fact that the situation itself has become unbearable. Underlying the achievements of a method that allowed us to fix nature, society and the individual on a theoretical ground by means of which the regularities of nature, society and the individual could be explained, predicted, controlled, and eventually gotten rid of through these regularities, there is the absolute *falsification* of that method; a falsification that finds its confirmation in the continuous crisis of nature, society and the individual. But while the crisis of nature does not bother us too much, the crisis of society and the individual hit us closer to home, where it hurts. Social crisis and individual crisis are the mediating grounds and constant falsifications of any theory imposed on them from the outside. It also provides the society and the individual with the means towards a firm resolve to live in the authenticity of their own radical corporality. Unfortunately, neither societies nor individuals move for their own authenticity and corporeal life at the radical level at which they are constituted; and so, their freedom escapes them and us. They have settled, instead, for a second–hand and more epidermic so–called radicality, where both societies and individuals plant their own theoretical feet for the sake of expedient political survival or expedient therapeutic stupor. And so the wheel goes on.

In sum: The whole movement of our historical philosophical past and present is already contained as a frozen instant–moment in the Eleatic proclamation of the Way of Truth as Thought, One, Being. In that original instant–moment, Time and temporality, Being and beings, One and many, ontology and epistemology, mind and body, language and speech, stood together, inseparable, in equal parity, an aperspectival vision. This was the instant of its conception: the still point. It has taken us almost 2,500 years to run the full length of this instant. This is what I call the moment, the execution of that original vision. The fact that it has taken us so long is accidental, in the sense that temporality and its measure was not so much the result of Time, but rather, the result of taking the theoretical (the idea of time) as the measure of Time; we have taken *invariant epistemological criteria* and elevated them to invariant metaphysics. What we have called *here* and *there* in our measure of history or of human life, has taken space for granted as *extentional*, in the sense that one thing is next to the other; but if we view the original determination implied in *one thing is next to the other*, we find that the whole movement is already *dimensional*, in the sense that the experience of *one thing is next to the other* already assumes an underlying dimension of how *here–there* relate to one another. The same applies to Time as a total dimension underlying the particular readings of the temporalities of *now*, *no more*, and *not yet*; but this also implies that, regardless of the space–time configurations (the human spaces) through which a man moves, a man's movement cannot be reduced to any one single configuration of space–time without simultaneously fixing man and stopping his vital movement. Man's search for freedom is contextually determined; but it is this same determination that makes man's freedom possible. Man's extentional moves include not only the two dimensions given in extension (breadth and length), but they also include a third dimensional movement, depth, on which they rest, and of which, they are only surface manifestations. And these three dimensions are ultimately grounded on their own possible (original and final) radical cancellation: Man's fourth dimension, where philosophy's critical task and meditation coincide. Without this fourth move, no man may be ultimately free. Therefore, it would be unphilosophical and inhuman not to open up man's possibilities by grounding him on that movement which will set him free. But this can only be done by making man's radical movement coincide with the movement of other contextual domains, other cultures, other space–time configurations, in the hope that man might find his determinations and his freedom through them.

This is the scope of the following chapters.

1

Ṛg Vedic Life

3
Culture and Meaning: The Hymns and The Sacrifice

O friends, no more these sounds!
Let us sing more cheerful songs,
more full of joy!

Ludwig van Beethoven's
Symphonie No. 9

Let us now with skill proclaim
the origin of the gods
so that in a later age someone may see them
(origins)
when the hymns are being chanted.

R.V. 10.72.1

INTRODUCTION

In the beginning was tone, and tone became chant and chant grew into human flesh through the sacrifice. This is the theme we shall try to develop in the following chapters; this is also the general theme of the Ṛg Veda. We shall, however, proceed slowly. The hymns and the sacrifice are the two most original, and therefore, the most difficult, notions needed to understand the Ṛg Veda. For they are not merely notions, but the most difficult of human activities—and they are needed not only to understand the Ṛg Veda, but to understand the *criteria* by which the Ṛg Veda makes itself understood. This is not a task that can be approached theoretically; but when we allow ourselves to be engaged in the activity of the hymns and the sacrifice, we are forced to see that the East and West have never met—that they cry out for an historical mediation.

In the beginning . . . The original beginnings are as elusive to man as his future; but unless he recovers his origins, he will forever be a child of alien powers with a predetermined destiny. In his search for beginnings, the individual reverts to his childhood; Western culture turns to Greece; and in our case, we turn to the Ṛg Veda. However, more often than not, the individual ends up the way he started: at home where he had been and would continue to be. For what we experience is *our* experience of others grounded in our origins.

Psychology is as much to blame as philosophy in its inability to discover man's origins. Psychology has only taught the individual to revert to his childhood through *memory* (Freud); or to return to Greece in search of original archetypes through the use of *imagination* (Jung). The rest of psychology has been stuck in a semantical game; the only invariant for the individual in search of therapy is the theoretical demand that sickness and health both be reduced to fleshless names: radical nominalism and cultural lobotomy. Thus, the individual is condemned to end up where he always is: in the same place where he started his inquiry. The individual is sent back to his childhood, but he cannot discover there how his face looked before he was born; he has to draw a line that puts him inexorably on this side of his past; so that memory becomes a reinforcement of the same idea of individuality which sent him to the psychiatric couch. Or he is again sent through imagination, to Greece in search of origins; and in place of origins, he discovers a multiplicity of archetypes or personalities with which he can do a number of things—but he can never embody them. These archetypes are not the radical origins of man; they are only images of a more radical man, who was or is yet to be. But by returning to Greece as the origin of Western man, what Western man does is to draw an imaginary line between himself and the rest of humanity. By acting thus, all he does is reinforce the controls of his present cultural isolation and sickness. "The whole of Western philosophy," Whitehead said, "is just a footnote to Plato." But what hardly anyone[1] has bothered to find out is how Plato himself is a footnote to previous cultures; for neither Plato nor Greece are absolute beginnings for Western man and Western culture.[2] Underlying them there is still man, the maker of ideas and cultures of man.

No human therapy is possible unless memory, imagination, and names are released from the controls of their methods and stretched as far as what Ortega y Gasset called "lived memories": man must not only face his images and theories about himself, which are easily verifiable—but he must confront his radical capacity to *falsify* any theories and images of man; it is only at this level that man can execute his right to freedom and continuity through the surrounding controls.

We have no other alternative but to start where the text starts: in the case of the Ṛg Veda, its particular form of chanted language and the criteria of its use. We have to forget for a while the ground we are standing on even while reading/writing this book: we have to forget what we take language to be, even the prose here used and all the presuppositions and criteria it entails; and strive to find the *meaning* of the Ṛg Veda within the cultural context of its birth: a time when prose and logic, poetry and imagination, music and meter are still one and their intentionalities have not yet been separated. Our way is to focus not so much on theory and communication, but on action, which is as constitutive of philosophy as theory and communication.

I

The Ṛg Veda is a document composed and delivered in the pre–dawn of recorded history. It is the earliest literary document of Indian tradition and narrates the struggle of the Aryan families of 'seers' (*ṛṣis*) as they tried to unify the world of diversity and opposition around them through sharing in a common 'vision' –a common 'viewpoint' (*darśanam*). India was the battle ground of this struggle and the intended reconciliation, and to India we owe what no other nation has been able to offer: "so ample a literary representation of an equally distant epoch and its mental development . . . (and) a test (which) exists in a state of purity almost absolute, offering hardly a corruption."[3]

To successfully accomplish a historical reconstruction of prehistoric times is a difficult task. Racial anthropology (physical features of people) and cultural ethnology (languages and cultures of people) have tried repeatedly to reach this goal in relation to pre–Vedic and Vedic periods. However, racial anthropology has found that skeletal remains of Early Indian Man are hardly existent;[4] so, a physical reconstruction of the people of Early India must remain "largely hypothetical" and based on, or inferred from, present or later situations.[5] We have already stated the case of Cultural Ethnology and the dangers of reading the Ṛg Veda from the outside (Chapter One). The Indian Aryan, for example, has been commonly presented with many of the fanatic features of Nazism; as a racist group of nomads, thirsty for battle and conquest, destroyers of towns and people. In this view, the Vedic '*ṛṣis*' have been interpreted as some sort of "war correspondents" of the past.

However, it is still the case that the Aryans came to India from outside and found themselves surrounded by diversity, both racial and cultural.[6]

In fact, according to the *Census of India*, no kind of man originated on Indian soil; all Indians arrived originally from other lands (in a sense very similar to the American situation). And the Aryans were comparatively late arrivals;[7] so that, many have said their only choices were to assimilate or to set themselves up in opposition. The natural antagonisms that developed between them and the Dravidians are the source of a romantic and simplified version of the Aryan invasion of India; first proposed some four generations ago, it is still maintained in many quarters. In summary, the Dravidians, 'cruder' and more 'biological' in their life and symbols than the Aryans, had icons for their worship, dancing women at their festivals, sexual symbolism, phallic deities, and intoxicated themselves with *sūra* (beer). The white–skinned, blue–eyed and golden–haired Aryans, like their kinsmen of Northern Europe, entered India from the Plateau of Central Asia, then a land of romantic mystery. They made easy conquest of the black–skinned non–Aryans, imposing upon their inferior race the superior Aryan religion, culture and language. What is noble in Indian tradition came from the Aryan (superior) race; what was dark, low and superstitious was only the expression of the repressed non–Aryan mind.

This 'myth' is slowly being abandoned; for the fact is that the Indian civilization, like any other great civilization, is a composite creation of the influence and dialectical tension of many civilizations. In fact, the Dravidian influence on later Indian tradition is more extensive and deeper, in many aspects, than the Aryan influence.[8] What is significant in the Indian Aryan case, is that the Aryans of India 'heard/saw' this diversity and tried to reconcile its continuity and innovation through the sacrifice, a condition which escapes any reader of the Ṛg Veda if he does not exclusively attend to the text itself and share in its original intentionality.

Two general criteria through which the meaning of the Ṛg Vedic text may appear are *structure* and *context*.[9] Structure coincides here with the hymns, in the sense that the path and order (criteria plus things, not chronology) of the hymns is the path and order that we will try to follow. Context coincides here with the sacrifice, in the sense that it is through the sacrifice that the whole linguistic world of the Ṛg Veda is grounded for its meaning. The notions of structure–hymns, and context–sacrifice, open the way to the particular understanding of movement, language, body, time, and space understood in the Ṛg Vedic text and later presupposed by the whole culture.

There are obviously many questions we might be tempted to ask, but we should refrain from asking them until we have seen the world from the Ṛg Vedic perspective. My students often seem very puzzled by my own refusal to accept such questions as, "But how can we know that this is the way that the Ṛg Vedic man felt?" or, "How can we know that your interpretation of Ṛg Vedic man is really Ṛg Vedic man?" But these questions, like other similar questions, are not really concerned with Ṛg Vedic man or the Ṛg Vedic text; rather, they are our demand that Ṛg Vedic man be like us, obsessed with theory and communication, instead of with the radical activity of which theory and communication are only the surface.

But what is being offered is not a definition of any kind of man: We are focusing on an activity. Every man must actively constitute himself by creating a certain order with the things around him (structure) within a general orientation he already has (or has received) about the whole of life; it is in relation to this activity that the body of man appears as flesh, and that the flesh of man makes present for us *a context and a structure with which it shares its dimensions*. For this reason, our path or method must focus on the silent and fleshy unity which underlies and is the root of any human reflective thinking. We are looking for presuppositions rather than statements that take their presuppositions for granted; but also, we are looking for those statements that lead us to the radical presuppositions which make the text of the Ṛg Veda *readable by its own criteria*.

The two main criteria we have established to find the ground where the meaning of the Ṛg Vedic text becomes apparent are the Hymns and the Sacrifice. Their unity and interdependence are so strong that it is almost futile to try to establish any chronological supremacy between them. In general, we find that the hymns give rise to the sacrifice (8.69.1),[10] and conversely, that the sacrifice is an incentive for new hymns (4.20.10).[11] A chanter–poet remarks that, "The gods created the hymns first, then the fire, then the burnt offering; the body–protecting sacrifice came into being from these." (10.88.8)[12]

Not all the poems were composed for the Sacrifice (7.29.3), nor were they all considered to meet the standard (for the Sacrifice).[13] Furthermore, those ignorant (*apracetāḥ*) of the standard (*aramkṛtiḥ*) could not offer the Sacrifice (1.120.1,[14] 7.32.13). A kind of 'circle of effectivity' is established between the chanter and the 'divinity,' so that the poet gains the needed inspiration from the 'divinity' which in turn will be rewarded with a chant befitting its high standard (1.73.10, 9.82.4). For example, the Soma sacrifice is said to grow on account of the hymn (4.20.10, 7.26.1, 9.17.4).[15]

It is obvious from certain examples in the texts that it is the context of the hymn that makes the Sacrifice efficient—in relation to Soma, again (8.62.1); and in relation to ordinary people (10.7.2). In fact, it is pointed out very clearly in certain passages that the sacrifice can be fruitful only through the hymns (7.16.2;[16] 7.26.1;[17] 10.105.8;[18]); that it is the hymn–song which makes the Sacrifice successful (7.66.8);[19] or that the hymns, by themselves, are the 'efficacy' of the sacrifice (8.26.16).

It is the 'power' of the hymn, 'what it intends,' that raises the level of sacrificial performance from a human plane to a higher divine plane (10.93.8).[20] A certain 'seer's' composition is more efficient than another's (8.1.4, 8.26.16). Certain poets neared the perspective of the gods through their composition, (8.64.9). In general, of all the actions of the sacrifice, the most important and efficacious one is the hymn–song (8.24.20); furthermore, even a pleasant offering like Soma could never be imagined to Ṛg Vedic man without a hymn–song; regardless of how fond Indra is of Soma, he is said to prefer a combination of the two: Soma and Hymn (7.26.2).[21]

Men and gods depend entirely on the hymns. Indra gains 'light' through them;[22] the 'gods' can be brought to the sacrifice through them;[23] the Angirasas penetrate the darkness (*Asat*) only through them;[24] the gods dispense gifts through those sacrifices associated with hymns;[25] even the whole Creation is the result of a powerful hymn.[26] Thus, sacrifice (9.99.4) and social continuity, through both hymns and sacrifice (8.98.9), appear to be the context and the structure of the Ṛg Veda; ritual and social classes came later. The hymns became human flesh in different form, as we shall see.

The hymns (*Vāc*) are the teachers of the gods (8.100.10; 10.125.3). They are the divine, wonderful, and immortal word (1.139.8). Even though inspired and new (1.61.2), the hymns are a revealed word (4.5.3) and the continuity of the original orientation (3.31.19; 8.2.17). They are the light that lightens (8.97.12), not only the gods, but also the poets (8.6.8); for the hymns themselves are the light (9.73.5). They are called the mothers (*mātaraḥ*) (8.6.20), the women in search of males (9.19.5), indestructible (*akṣarā*) and always procreating (*vardhanam*) (1.80.1; 3.36.1), a milch cow that feeds herself with her own milk without needing a shepherd (3.57.1).

The hymns enjoin the Dawn, the Earth, the Sun, and the Sky, in fact all of creation, through incestuous coupling where the sons give birth to their own mothers. (1.164.33, etc.) It is the singers who, with their minds, formed horses harnessed by a word for the chariot of the gods (1.20.2). The hymns established Indra king forever (7.31.12). The priests themselves are car–borne through hymns (4.16.17. and 19 through 24). The light of heaven is made apparent by the hymns of seven singers whose songs cleft even the mountain open, bringing rains so copious that cattle walk knee–deep in water (4.16.6; 1.37.10). Agni, saviour and god of fire, is himself the holy Singer who precedes the sages . . . growing mighty by laudations; and the secret he alone can impart is a certain lofty hymn (3.5.1–2; 4.5.3).

These cryptic notes about the hymns of the Ṛg Veda should make it sufficiently obvious that we have no other alternative than to start where the Ṛg Vedic text starts, with its particular form of chanted language and the criteria of its use.

Perhaps the greatest shortcoming in cultural studies is the hidden presupposition and steadfast belief that our linguistic criteria are the only ones by which all men and cultures should be measured or reduced. On this crypto–premise, lies the universalized belief that the only language of man is prose, and that the ground of its meaning is a logic to which this prose conforms, independent of how people use language, or even dependent on how people use language; in both cases, a particular form of logic is universally established as the universal image to which language must conform. The positivistic view of language is also grounded on a category of fact that uses the criterion of the Verifiability Principle as its own ground of meaning; and prose is again taken as the standard for communication, and its statements are considered as the only carriers of truths. These truths, in turn, are dependent for their meaning on how they conform to the logic on which all meaning thus radicalized is grounded.

Two immediate consequences follow: First, all human languages are presupposed to be linguistically uniform; secondly, all cultural studies are rendered trivial or superfluous, for linguistic criteria of other men and other cultures are supposed previous to any discovery of human or cultural judgment within the culture. Unless the reader is able to free himself from these determinations, he will not be able to read anything different from what he already knows; the result would be no more than a reinforcement of his present beliefs; for this view of language fails to take into account the human *activity* by which language itself is formed, made flesh.

In the beginning was tone. This is the most important clue to bear in mind in our effort to understand the Ṛg Vedic conception and use of Language and of languages. The whole of the Ṛg Veda is chanted. It is not prose; it is not poetry; rather, it is chant, close to music, in its form. In Chapter One, we have already pointed out the sophisticated musical–metric structure of the hymns; and it is precisely on this model of musical tones that the meaning of the hymns is grounded. So, unless we discover the basic tone–structure of the hymns, their meaning will elude us.

Tone is a sound of a certain fixed pitch. No later than the third millenium B.C., and probably more than a thousand years earlier, man discovered that the *intervals* between the tones could be defined by the *ratios* of the lengths of pipes and strings which sounded them. It was the ear that made ratios invariant; by its vivid memory of the simpler intervals, the ear made the development of a science of pure relations possible within the theory of numbers, the tone–field now being isomorphic with the number field. From this musicalized number theory, which we know as "ratio theory," but which the ancients simply called "music," man began his model building. The ratios of the first six integers defined the primary building blocks: the octave 1:2; the fifth 2:3, the fourth 3:4, the major third 4:5, and the minor third 5:6. From these first six integers, functioning as multiples and submultiples of any reference unit ("1") of length or frequency, a numerological cosmology was developed throughout the Near and Far East. The ultimate source of this "Pythagorean" development is unknown. The hymns of the Ṛg Veda, however, resound with the evidence that their authors were fully aware of it and alive to the variety of models it could provide.

That tones recur *cyclically* at every doubling or halving of frequency or wave–length is the "basic miracle of music". From this acoustical phenomenon, the number 2 acquires its "female" status; it defines invariantly the octave matrix within which all tones come to birth. Here, in this initial identification of the octave with the ratio 1:2, is the root of all the problems which haunt the acoustical theorist, problems which the ancient theorist conceived as symbolizing the evil and disorder of the universe. The octave refuses to be subdivided into subordinate cycles by the only language ancient man knew—the language of natural number, or integers, and the rational numbers derived from them. It is blunt arithmetical fact that the higher powers of 3 and 5 which define subordinate intervals of music never agree with higher powers of 2 which define octave cycles. It is man's yearning for this impossible agreement which introduced a hierarchy of *values* into the number field. For our ancestors, the *essence* of the world and of the numbers which interpreted that world was *sound*, not substance,[27] and that world was rife with disagreement among an endless number of possible structures.

When we talk of language in reference to the Ṛg Veda, we must therefore take the hymns literally; namely, as hymns, in the sense of their musical tonal structure;[28] for it is in this structure that their criteria for meaning is grounded; though this tonal structure, like its counterpart in prose—propositional logic—cannot be presupposed *a priori*, but must be discovered within the specific circumstances of its use. These clues may be the key to understanding how the Ṛg Vedic universe emerges as a victory of gods over the restraining forces which can be defeated but never annihilated. Enemies are counted, and so are the spoils of war, singers, hymns, their syllables and tones, the ribs of the cosmic horse, the sticks of the sacrificial fire, rivers, tribes, gods, sieves, footsteps, twin sons, mountains, cattle, dogs, sheep, birds, snakes, storms, the seats and wheel–spokes of chariots, castles, priests, sacred stones, and meters; the poets seem concerned with the exact number of everything they encounter. They are very precise to locate their subjects in space—a space which would be unintelligible unless we had in mind the musical scale. Fate itself is not in the gods or from the gods, but is the result of the power of song and it is faith in its efficacy.

Therefore, from a linguistic and cultural perspective, we have to be aware that we are dealing with a language where tonal and arithmetical relations establish the epistemological invariances. Invariance was not physical, but epistemological; ratio theory was a science of pure relations; its fixed elements came from the recognition of the octave, fifth, and derivative tonal relations which made ratio concrete. The divorce of music from mathematics came later. Language grounded in music is grounded thereby on *context dependency*; any tone can have any possible relation to other tones, and the shift from one tone to another, which alone makes melody possible, is a shift in perspective which the singer himself *embodies*. Any perspective (tone) must be "sacrificed" for a new one to come into being; the song is a radical *activity* which requires *innovation* while maintaining *continuity*, and the "world" is the creation of the singer, who shares its dimensions with the song.

In ancient times, the infinite possibilities of the number field were considered isomorphic with the infinite possibilities of tone; Pythagorean tuning theory set no theoretical limit to the divisions of an octave; it knew many alternative definitions of the scale, and allowed for extensive modal permutation of that material. Today in the West, we use number to constrict all possibility to an economically convenient limit; the international pitch standard of A = 440 Hertz and the limitation to 12 equal semitones within the octave are antithetical to the spirit and needs of music. Ṛg Vedic man, like his Greek counterparts, knew *himself* to be the organizer of the scale, and he cherished the multitude of possibilities open to him too much to freeze himself into one dogmatic posture. His language keeps alive that "open–ness" to alternatives, yet it avoids entrapment in anarchy. It also resolves the fixity of theory by setting the body of man historically moving through the freedom of musical spaces, viewpoint transpositions, reciprocities, pluralism, and finally, an absolute radical sacrifice of all theory as a fixed invariant.

II

And chant grew into human flesh. When Language is grounded on a tone system, as in the Ṛg Veda, then the immediate result is a plurality of systems; that is, a Language which we can speak only *through* sub-linguistic systems. In terms of culture, we can speak only of a plurality of cultures where all the cultures have the same right to be heard but no voice can sound above the others. Thus, Culture and Language—the universal invariants—may live in innovation and continuity, but neither may be *defined a priori* through any dogmatic exercise in power.

The empirical root of these statements is that the Ṛg Vedic hymns were composed by groups of families from a multiplicity of perspectives.[27a]

For it is the human voice, chanting the hymns, that turns the structure of the hymns into human flesh; the limit of this flesh being shared by the limits of the structure. See for example hymns 10.71 and 10.125:

ṚG VEDA 10.71

HYMN TO WISDOM

(Addressed to Bṛhaspati, Lord of Speech)

1. *When men, Bṛhaspati, by name-giving*
   Brought forth the first sounds of Vāc,
   That which was excellent in them, which was pure,
   Secrets hidden deep, through love was brought to light.

2. *When man created language with wisdom,*
   As if winnowing cornflour through a sieve,
   Friends acknowledged the signs of friendship,
   And their speech retained its touch.

3. *They followed the path of Vāc through sacrifice,*
   Which they discovered hidden within the seers.
   They drew her out, distributing her in every place,
   Vāc, which Seven Singers her tones and harmonies sing.

4. *Many a man who sees does not see Vāc,*
   Many a man who hears does not hear her.
   But to another she reveals her beauty
   Like a radiant bride yielding to her husband.

5. *They speak of a man too cold in friendship,*
   Who is never moved to act courageously,
   All caught up in his futile imaginings;
   The Word he hears never yields fruit or flower.

6. *Who forsakes a friend, having known friendship,*
He never had a part or a share of Vāc.
Even though he hears her, he hears in vain;
For he knows nothing of her right path.

7. *Even friends endowed with eyes and ears,*
Are not equal in the swiftness of their minds.
Some are like shallow tubs that reach only the mouth and shoulder,
While others are like deep lakes fit for a bath.

8. *When brāhmans in harmony offer the sacrifice*
Fashioned by the heart and inspired by the mind,
In attainment one is far behind the others,
Though brāhmans in name some wander senselessly.

9. *Those who move neither forward nor backward*
Nor are brāhmans, nor prepare libations,
They are poor craftsmen, misusing Vāc,
Ignorant, they spin out a useless thread for themselves.

10. *All the friends rejoice for their triumphant friend*
Who has won in contest with other brāhmans (in debate),
For he removes guilt and provides food,
And he is ready for acts of strength.

11. *One man recites verses,*
Another chants hymn Śakvarī measures.
The brāhman talks of existence, and yet
Another sets the norms for the sacrifice.

ṚG VEDA 10.125

HYMN TO VĀC (WORD)

1. *I move with the Rudras and the Vasus,*
The Ādityas and the Viśve Devāḥ.
I support Varuṇa and Mitra,
I hold Indra, Agni, and the Aśvins.

2. *I lift the swelling Soma, and*
Tvaṣṭṛ, Pūsan, and Bhaga.
I shower gifts on the faithful patron of the sacrifices,
Who makes oblation and presses Soma.

3. *I am the queen, the gatherer of wealth,*
I know knowledge, the first to be sacrificed.
The gods have scattered me to all places;
I have many homes, (for) I have scattered the chants in many places.

4. *Through my power, he eats and sees,*
Breathes and hears, who hears me as Vāc.
Even if they do not know, they dwell in me.
In truth I speak: hear me, famous men.

5. *Only I utter the word that brings joy to gods and men.*
The man I favor, to him I give my power;
I make him like a god,
The seer, a perfect sacrificer.

6. *I stretch the bow for Rudra, so*
That his arrow may pierce widsom's enemy.
I rouse the battle fury for the people.
I have pierced Heaven and Earth.

7. *On the brow of the universe I give birth to the father.*
My birthplace is in the waters, in the deep ocean.
From there I spread out over the worlds on all sides.
And with the height of my head I reach the sky above.

8. *I breathe like the wind holding all the worlds.*
I am so powerful
That I go beyond the heavens
And beyond this broad earth.

It is the creative force of the Vāc that by the touch of its own creation turns structure into flesh. It is this human Vāc that humanizes the whole world. Or, as in 3.8.2–3:

Ask of the sages' mighty generations: firm–minded and
Wise they framed the heaven.
These are thy mind–sought strengthening directions, and
They have come to be the sky's upholders.

Disguised in the world with anonymous forms, they
Decked the heaven and earth for high dominion,
Measured with measures, fixed their broad expanses, set
The great worlds apart and held them firmly for continuity.

And it is precisely because the structure of the hymns has become human body through the power of the Vāc (the human word), that the words of man are recoverable; but this recovery can only be accomplished as it was originally formed. For unless they are recovered as human flesh, man remains incomplete. This is what the sages hoped for when they said that "one may see them—the origins and the gods—when these hymns are chanted in future times" (10.72.7), or when they said that "the sages, searching in their hearts with wisdom found the relation of the Existent with the Non–Existent" (10.129.4).[29]

It is this efficient 'active power' of the word making the world, that makes the gods possible; either to make them or to give them the power invoked as in R.V. 5.31.4. It is this power, *māyā*, that causes wisdom, judgment, knowledge, etc. Over a hundred times this word is used in the Ṛg Veda; through this power 'the Maruts bring rain,'[30] or the 'Sun appears in the sky'; it is the *māyā* (power) of Mitra and Varuṇa,[31] the power to produce the marvelous;[32] or it is the power of the *māyināḥ*, those gifted with powers.[33] Only when these powers are used for evil purposes, without the sacrifice in mind, does *māyā* turn to 'abuse' and 'illusion.'[34]

It is this identification with power that joins its efficient action with efficient vision. To exemplify this insight, Ṛg Vedic man is obviously generous with words relating to seeing, like *darśanam*, from *drś*—to see, meaning perspective. In this sense, the *jñānin* is one having knowledge, in the sense of vision—like the '*ṛṣi*' who is filled with this power of vision, and gains omniscience as he transfers the power to the word of the chant. Similarly, the *kaviḥ* is the "*kaveḥ dhīḥ*"—the sage–seer and his vision.[35]

In the Ṛg Veda, the sage belongs to a category of beings who, by questioning and inquiring by their own power, presuppose that 'realization' is already generated in their hearts and minds.[36] These sages are *svardṛśāḥ*, seers by the 'light of heaven.' They are equal to the gods in that they share the god's own viewpoint. They also have the sun for an eye,[37] like Agni who looks with a 'heavenly light'; for he is the eye that stirs the heart;[38] and so are Soma,[39] Indra,[40] and Viṣṇu.[41] Savitṛ has all–seeing eyes;[42] Indra and Vayu have a thousand eyes swift as thought and they are the lords of *dhīḥ* (vision).[43] In the same way, the seers 'see' by the insight given to them by Soma,[44] and by those who performed sacrifices before them.[45] In this connection, the Ṛg Vedic poets are cautious in pointing out a distinction between the physical eye, *akśan*, and *cakṣas*, the eye of vision, the eye through which Mitra and Varuṇa see; for even when "they close their eyelids observant they perceive."[46] In this sense, Viśvakarma is called Father of the eye, the wise in spirit, the mighty in mind and power.[47]

Ṛg Vedic man side–stepped the difficulties of names and individuation by centering on the activity—*Vāc*—that coincides with the Vision (*darśanam*) that makes naming identical with the experience (*anubhava*) of *making reality*. In this sense, to make words—to chant the *Vāc*—is identical with the vital force of man himself: *ayu* and *ayus*, as vital force and time of life;[48] which, in turn, were simultaneously the cosmic–life–force *viśvāyuḥ*,[49] identical with life and the extent of life. Eventually Ṛg Vedic man will search for the vision "that knows the father;"[50] for to him, knowledge and action are understood as ontologically one; while, in our case, the *agent* and the action are not. Ṛg Vedic man centered the movement of knowledge in *manaḥ*, "the quickest among all flying objects," which is both the source of questioning as well as of "vision."[51] *Manaḥ* is the center of all thought, will, and feeling;[52] and no human inquiry can be efficient unless it is centered on the mighty power of mental concentration (*manasā*).[53] Thus, it would be through *manaḥ* and vision (*dhībhiḥ*) that the 'wisemen' (*vipaścitaḥ*) see the relation between Soma and cosmic fertility,[54] and that the Earth gave the Father a share of *ṛta*, and was made pregnant (*dhīty agre manasā sam hijagme*).[55] This is the auspicious moment of Ṛg Vedic creation and perspective transposition; the time, *kāla*[56] and *abhīka* of Indra's victory;[57] of the Aśvins assisting the needy; of the union between the Father and the Daughter when the procreative seed of the universe was planted.[58] It is this auspicious moment which guarantees man his right to continuity, for it makes it possible for him to step out of space and time, independent of the biological fluctuations of the body.

Word–making (*Vāc*) is the radical human activity; but because it must give flesh to the world of man, it can only succeed on the condition that action–perspective–auspicious moment coincide;[59] and on the further condition that word–making be focused upon as an activity of "breathing" flesh into the world, rather than as a theory and a communication of the world, or even a subject of the world.

III

And chant grew into human flesh through the sacrifice. The problem cultures face is not only to guarantee continuity but also to guarantee innovation. The dialectical tension between continuity and innovation has given rise to the greatest kind of inhumanity of one man against another, or one culture against another. It is almost trivial to note that culture cannot be defined by only listening to the "loudest voice" amongst all the voices simultaneously demanding to be heard; yet this has been our history. Hence culture is yet to be discovered; and what we constantly face is the plurality of perspectives with which a culture has to contend and somehow guarantee each equal rights so that Culture may live in continuity and innovation. It is therefore essential that we do not presuppose what Culture is before we discover it, and that we concentrate on the only thing at hand: a plurality of perspectives through which Culture makes itself. But because of this *making*, Culture is always incomplete, always on the move; this *making* gives it a certain indirection, as an open phrase hanging in mid air.

We need to revert again to tone as our model. Any tone can serve as the reference point for any kind of tonal development; and the primary fact of any development is the cyclic identity which we recognize at the octave. It is our recognition of this cyclic identity which makes the musical octave first, a cyclic matrix for tuning theory and then, by symbolic extension, a cyclic matrix for cosmology. The "sexual" imagery which Plato associates with certain numbers, apparently known to the Ṛg Vedic poets, begins with the identification of the matrix with "mother."

Since multiplication and division by 2 produce the octave matrix, 2 is essentially "female." By itself 2 can generate only "cycles of barrenness" (2:4:8:16, etc., numbers 2^n). The original unity, 1, which is subdivided to produce the "octave–double" 2, requires divinity to be conceived as "hermaphrodite," and apparently accounts for the Ṛg Vedic statements of the daughter (2) being produced from the father, 1, without benefit of a mother. God = 1, and his virgin daughter = 2, and they must be coupled in divine incest to produce the prime number 3, "the divine male number," from which brahman tones (or angels), and "citizens of the highest property class" (Socrates' metaphor), are generated. The musical function of 3 probably gives rise to the later notion of a "demiurge" or subordinate god who actually creates the phenomenal world; from this demiurge = 3 and the virgin daughter = 2, the "human male number 5" emerges as 3 + 2, in a statement widely appreciated in ancient times, but one quite mysterious once the musical origins of culture had been forgotten. (The prime number 3 appears to have been deified by Ea–Enki in the Sumerian–Babylonian pantheon and by Thoth = Thrice Greatest Hermes in the Egyptian–Greek pantheons.)

Tuning theory establishes for us certain epistemological criteria which we need bear in mind if any meaning is to be derived from any culture which takes tone as the ground of language: a) It is not the case that numbers or ratios *control* movement, but it is the case that movement *may be ordered* according to certain ratios; we are not watching the movement of certain sounds, but rather, we are watching how movement becomes certain sounds. b) Tones may be generated by numbers; this generation does not give us isolated elements, but rather *constellations* of elements in which each tone is context and structure dependent. c) Within the matrix of the octave any tonal pattern may rise or fall, hence opposite or reciprocal possibilities are equally relevant, both in the sense of *time* (order) and *space* (rising–falling). d) Any perspective remains just one out of a group of equally valid perspectives, and the variety of possible perspectives from which to view any set of tones is apparently inexhaustible; any realization (i.e., any song) excludes all other possibilities while it is sounding, but no song has so universal an appeal that it terminates the invention of new ones. e) Linguistic statements remain structure and context dependent, and the function of any language is to make clear its own dependence on, and reference to, other linguistic systems; a model based on the primacy of sound is not based on the reality of substance. Whereas the eye fastens on what is fixed, the ear is open to the world of movement in which "Existence" (*Sat*) and "Non–Existence" (*Asat*) are locked in an eternal and present absence/presence.

The following examples from the Ṛg Veda text are clarification of the above insights; further examples may be found in the Textual Appendix III.

Hymn 9.112 is as explicit and contemporary in sound as one would wish in pointing out the path of "thought" without the sacrifice in mind. The hymn is addressed to Soma:

1. *Our thoughts wander in all directions*
   And various are the ways of men:
   The cartwright looks for accidents,
   The physician for the sick,
   And the brāhman for a rich patron.
      For the sake of Indra,
      Flow, Indu, flow.

2. *With ripe plants and glowing fan,*
   With bird's feathers and tools of stone,
   The blacksmith seeks
   The customer with gold.
      For the sake of Indra,
      Flow, Indu, flow.

3. *I am a singer, my father a leech (doctor).*
   My mother grinds corn with a millstone.
   Diverse in means, we all strive,
   Like cattle, for wealth.
      For the sake of Indra,
      Flow, Indu, flow.

4. *The horse draws a swift carriage,*
The generous host an easy laugh and play.
The penis seeks a hairy slot
And the frog hankers for a flood.
For the sake of Indra,
Flow, Indu, flow.

The plurality of perspectives becomes more complicated when the generator, i.e., the "Father," is identified with prime numbers; or as Plato would say it, "the model in whose likeness that which becomes is born."[60] The Ṛg Veda expresses this in reverse as a son who through knowledge becomes "his father's father;"[61] for as the Ṛg Veda tells it:

The Father with five feet and twelve forms,
Affluent, standing in the far side of heaven
Some say.
Others affirm that he is one seeing wide
Seated in heaven
On the seven–wheeled six–spoked chariot.
(1.164.12)

But then, in the next paragraph of the same hymn, He supports the worlds "on the five–spoked wheel." Indra, "the Dancer, the Lord of men"[62] is also linked into this fivespoked wheel, for he rules "the five-fold race of those who dwell upon the earth."[63] The Dawn, who opens "the pathways of the people," does so in "the lands where man's Five Tribes are settled."[64]

The variety of perspectives, the plurality of tuning systems, and their connection with prime numbers is too numerous to even try to synthesize; fortunately, the Ṛg Veda does it for us with the *Asya Vasmasya* Hymn (The Riddle of the Universe) (1.164). Dīrghatamas (the alleged blind author of the *Asya Vamasya* Hymn) opens the song–poem at the time of the morning sacrifice. There, surrounding him, are not only the perspectives of his culture, but also the unavoidable *reciprocity* of perspectives. (A full translation of this hymn and others is included in Appendix III at the end of the book.) At the time of the morning sacrifice, Dīrghatamas sees the rising sun and his two brothers: the mid–fire (lightning) and the sacrificial fire. The sun rides his one–wheeled chariot drawn by seven horses in the sky. His seven creative and vivificant rays are seven "cows" drinking water by their feet and drawing milk by their heads, thus bringing down nourishing rain. This leads Dīrghatamas to consider time, the liturgical year symbolized by the one wheel of the sun's chariot, the three navels of the three principle seasons, and the twelve months marked by the twelve spokes, always moving on but always returning. The Sun appears as the year (v. 11) with seven hundred and twenty sons of days and nights resisting all decay. The Sun remains in the sky as a universal witness (v. 12) or becomes the yearling calf offered in a cosmic sacrifice. But if one tries to synthesize these plural perspectives, Dīrghatamas makes us aware of the *reciprocity* of perspectives even after any synthesis:

Two birds with fair wings, inseparable companions,
Have found refuge in the same sheltering tree.
One incessantly eats from the fig tree;
The other, not eating, just looks on.
(v. 20)

This multiplicity of perspectives, and the inability of any synthesis of them to provide the antithetical perspectives essential to freedom would have caused dismay or skepticism in a smaller heart than Dīrghatamas'. Of this skepticism, political powers, cultural lobotomies, and personal amputations are born; but fortunately for us, the author of 1.164 is not content with superficial and expedient answers. He delves into the root answer and, therefore, the root origin of the whole social condition. He wants to know the *origin* of the sun: Who gave blood, soul, spirit, to the Earth? (v. 4) Which are the hidden stations of the gods; which is the hiding place of the sun? What is the meaning of the seven threaded story spun by the poets around the sun? (v. 5) What is the One–unborn support of the (born) Universe? (v. 6) How could the "boneless" give origin to this structured world?

These earlier questions of the poem are formally proposed in the *karmodyabrahmodya*[65] verse 34:

I ask you: What is the ultimate limit of the earth?
I ask you: What is the central point of the Universe?
I ask you: What is the semen of the cosmic horse?
I ask you: What is the ultimate dwelling of speech?[66]

The answers to these questions are given in the following verse (35): this altar is the ultimate limit of the earth; this sacrifice is the center of the Universe; this Soma is the semen of the cosmic horse; this brahman is the ultimate dwelling of speech.

The originality of Dīrghatamas' skepticism is not that he acknowledges answers which he does not know; but rather, that while knowing all there is to know, he has not yet found the reconciliation of the multiplicity of answers. In fact, Dīrghatamas is the model of philosophical modesty.

Unknowing, I ask of those who know, the sages,
As one ignorant for the sake of knowledge.

(v. 6)

For

I do not clearly know what I am like here (idam)
(In relation to what I can say 'this I am' I do not know)
Bewildered and bound with thought, I wander.

(v. 37)

It is not, therefore, that the Singer is an ignoramus "asking these questions out of immaturity and ignorance" (v. 5), but rather, that any form of reconciliation of the multiplicity will have to contend with the Singer's experience:

Then came to me Speech, Ṛta's first born!
And quick, I am a portion of her.

The immortal is of the same origin as the mortal,
He moves up and down by his own power.
Different directions they take,
Fixed in continuity moving around,
When men see one, they do not see the other.

(v. 37–38)

Any form of reconciliation will have to contend, not only with saving the multiplicity of perspectives, but with the fact that these perspectives, through languages, have become chant—human flesh. How can any form of reconciliation be carried out without simultaneously amputating the human singer? The Ṛg Veda states that:

Speech is divided into four levels
The wise singers know them all.
Three levels are hidden, and men never attain them.
Men speak only the fourth.

(v. 45)

Is there any form of compromise possible between opposing views? Can we, in dealing with human language and human culture, make compromises—where what is given up in every compromise is also a portion of one's own human flesh? These philosophical questions become particularly interesting when we consider that "compromise" has become our way of life—in Western music through equal-temperament,[67] in philosophy through nominalism, in politics through a mixture of nominalism and pragmatism, and in psychology and religion through nominalism, polytheism, and monotheism.[68] What is significant in every one of these compromises is not that a questionable compromise is being carried out; but rather, and more significantly, that a new human orientation has been demanded, or been imposed through power, on all humans; in fact, a single perspective has been imposed or demanded on all humans.

It is interesting when viewing Ṛg Vedic skepticism to note that there are few similarities with what we understand by that same word; skepticism, in the Ṛg Vedic sense, is rather a preparation or an invitation to the sacrifice.

One has only to read "What god shall we adore?" (10.121), or even more clearly, 10.129:

No one knows whence Creation has arisen;
Or whether he has or has not produced it:
He who watches in the highest heaven
He alone knows, unless . . . He does not know.

Or 8.89.3:

Some say: There is no Indra. Who has seen Him?
Whom, then shall we honor?

Or 2.12.5:

Of the terrible (Indra) they ask: "Where is he?"
Of him, indeed, they also say: "He is not."

Ṛg Vedic skepticism is significant to our study not only because it underlies the role of knowledge in relation to the sacrifice, while simultaneously making knowledge, like language and perspective, context and structure dependent; but above all, because it forces us to shift our focus of attention from the images of man, to 'man' as radically or primarily active. This can be summarized in a reading of the complete hymn 10.129:

1. *Neither Existence nor Non–Existence was as yet,*
   Neither the world nor the sky that lies beyond it;
   What was covered? and where? and who gave it protection?
   Was there water, deep and unfathomable?

2. *Neither was there death, nor immortality,*
Nor any sign of night or day.
The ONE breathed without air by self–impulse;
Other than that was nothing whatsoever.

3. *Darkness was concealed by darkness there,*
And all this was indiscriminate chaos;
That ONE which had been covered by the void
Through the heat of desire (tapas) was manifested.

4. *In the beginning there was desire,*
Which was the primal germ of the mind;
The sages searching in their own hearts with wisdom
Found in non–existence the kin of existence.

5. *Their dividing line extended transversely.*
What was below it and what above?
There was the seed–bearer, there were mighty forces!
Who therefore knows from where it did arise.

6. *Who really knows? Who can here say*
When was it born and from where creation came?
The gods are later than this world's creation —
Therefore, who knows from where it came into existence?

7. *That from which creation came into being,*
Whether it had held it together or it had not
He who watches in the highest heaven
He alone knows, unless . . . He does not know.

The skepticism of this hymn is interesting because, after taking account of every possibility with regard to the knowledge of the problem of Creation, it appears to end in a skeptical note. As a matter of fact it does not. Let us consider the alternatives offered:

Either he knows (*yadi vā veda*) **or** **he does not know (*yadi vā na veda*)**

Either he fashioned it (*yadi vā dadhe*) **or** **he did not (*yadi vā na*)**

out of

Sat (*existence*) **Asat (non-existence)**

but, there was neither existence nor non–existence
(*na sat na u āsīt*)
There was no water, unfathomable and deep, nor breath
(neither body nor perspective)
(*ambhaḥ kim āsīt . . . anīdavātam*)

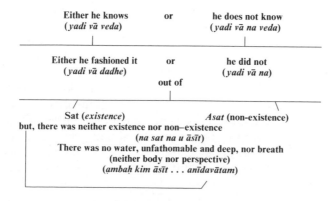

Therefore, to say that he knows, and to say that he does not know, are both 'experientially' meaningless statements since, "the gods came after the creation," and "no one 'knows' how the world began;" "for no one was there to *behold* (*dedarśa*)," (no one shared that 'viewpoint' which caused) the Creation.

To 'know' within a context, can only be applied to the 'things' within the structure of that context; but to use 'knowing' in the same sense when addressing a totality as undifferentiated as the whole of human creation—consisting not only of entities, but of structures and contexts as well; that is to seriously misuse 'knowing,' because the conditions lack both the *efficacy* to create and the perspective that would make any form of creation possible. And thus, by this route, the Ṛg Vedic seers place us face to face with what is primary to man: the first act of man, the Sacrifice: "With sacrifice the gods begot the first one, and it became the first Act of mankind." (1.164.50) In this way, the One came to be spoken of as many: "They call it Indra, Mitra, Varuṇa, Agni and Garutmat the heavenly bird (the Sun)." (1.164.46) And it is in the sacrifice that the past and the future coincide: "Future ones are also ancient, some say, and those past are also present" (1.164.19). For "these sacrifices are set in harmony with definite rules" (1.164.15), and "those energies reach up to heaven where the original Sādhyas, the gods are." (1.164.50)

In sum, the Ṛg Vedic Aryans not only saw the sacrifice as the origin of the multiplicity of perspectives within their culture, but they also strived through the sacrifice for an open culture where all human flesh would feel itself at home. In this sense, Ṛg Vedic society was open to accept others within its fold on only one condition: that they also accept the sacrifice, not only in its ritualistic form, but as the radical activity of man so that all men may live in innovation and continuity. The Ṛg Vedic seers summarized their opposition to those who did not accept or did not understand the sacrifice in one word: *amānuṣa*, inhuman (8.70.11, 10.22.8):[69] For they were the coverers of truth (*satyadhvṛt*) and opposed freedom (*adititva*). (7.51.1; 1.185.8; 1.114.4) The reason why Ṛg Vedic man does not accept any way of understanding man's role other than as an original and continuous sacrifice (an activity rather than a theory), is because, according to Ṛg Vedic man, any identification of man with a theory of 'man' obscures the fact that any and all theories of man about 'man' are made of the radical dismemberment of man himself, and distract him from engaging in his only original and primary activity: the sacrificing of all theories about himself so that he may recreate himself as man. We can offer many examples, as we shall do later in this book;

but for simplicity's sake, we shall offer here only one hymn: the *Puruṣa Śūkta*, the hymn of man, 10.90:

1. *Thousand headed is Man,*
   With thousand eyes and feet.
   He envelopes the whole earth
   And goes beyond it by ten fingers.

2. *Man indeed is all that was and is,*
   And whatever may come in the future,
   He is the master of immortality,
   Of all that rises through nourishment.

3. *Such is his power and greatness,*
   Yet man is still greater than these:
   Of him all the worlds are only one–fourth,
   Three–fourths are immortal in Heaven.

4. *With three–fourths of Himself, Man rose,*
   The other fourth was born here.
   From here on all sides he moved
   Toward the living and the non–living.

5. *From him was Virāj born,*
   And Man from Virāj.
   When born he overpassed the earth,
   Both in the west and in the east.

6. *When with Man as their offering,*
   The Gods performed the sacrifice,
   Spring was the oil they took
   Autumn the offering and summer the fuel.

7. *That sacrifice, balmed on the straw,*
   Was Man, born in the beginning;
   With him did the gods sacrifice,
   And so did the Sādhyas and the Ṛṣis.

8. *From that cosmic sacrifice,*
   Drops of oil were collected,
   Beasts of the wing were born,
   And animals wild and tame.

9. *From that original sacrifice,*
   The hymns and the chants were born,
   The meters were born from it,
   And from it prose was born.

10. *From that horses were given birth,*
And cattle with two rows of teeth.
Cows were born from that,
And from that were born goats and sheep.

11. *When they dismembered Man,*
Into how many parts did they separate him?
What was his mouth, what his arms,
What did they call his thighs and feet?

12. *The Brāhman was his mouth;*
The Rajanya (Princes) became his arms;
His thighs produced the Vaiśya (professionals and merchants);
His feet gave birth to the Śūdra (laborer).

13. *The moon was born from his mind;*
His eyes gave birth to the sun;
Indra and Agni came from his mouth;
And Vāyū (the wind) from his breath was born.

14. *From his navel the midair rose;*
The sky arose from his head;
From feet, the earth; from ears, the directions.
Thus they formed the worlds.

15. *Seven sticks enclosed it like a fence,*
Thrice seven were the sticks of firewood,
When the gods bound Man
As the offering of the sacrifice.

16. *By sacrifice the gods sacrificed the sacrifice.*
Those were the original and earliest acts.
These powers (of the sacrifice) reach heaven,
Where the Sādhyas and the gods are.

We are now in a position with all the notes, concepts, and cautions we have introduced to bring out the four "languages" or sub–linguistic systems through which the Ṛg Vedic text itself makes and gives meaning through its own statements.

As we have already mentioned many times, we are in search of the origins of man and, in this particular case, of the origins of Hindu man through Ṛg Vedic man. Needless to say, the challenge we are facing is almost superhuman, for we are talking from a distance, as we measure time, of maybe over four thousand five hundred years. The distance, though, is not as significant as the fact that, during all those many years, man has systematically strived to divide and reduce everything into such manageable sizes that things, cultures, worlds, theories, gods, disciplines, and even man's images, and man himself, are manageable and controllable in use at every level. Therefore, our most gigantic problem is, that by returning to the origins, and in particular those of the Ṛg Veda, we find that, even when we have nothing else but the text to deal with, it yet remains a text that has not suffered the division of the centuries. So, we are put face to face with language before it became prose and logic, poetry and imagination, or music and meter; but was all three, combined and inseparable, in a unity which the intentionality of the text will hopefully surrender to us. We have established the criteria for not straying from this original intentionality in the Hymns and the Sacrifice; but the Hymns and the Sacrifice come to us in the Ṛg Vedic text in primary and discreet intentionality–structures through which and to which any statement, chant, or song in the Ṛg Veda reverts for meaning, or from which it derives its meaning. These four intentionality–structures are the languages of 1. Non–existence (*Asat*); 2. Existence (*Sat*); 3. Images and Sacrifice (*yajña*); and 4. Embodied (*Ṛta*) vision (*dhīḥ*).[70]

These four languages, with their multiple perspectives, function as four spaces of discourse within which human action takes place, and from which any statement in the text gains meaning. The languages of Non–existence, Existence, Images and Sacrifice show the human situation within disparate linguistic contexts embodying different ways of viewing the world. These may be integrated within a transcendent context, not by rejecting the reality of any of the previous frameworks, but only by changing to a transcendent 'view', and looking at the world as the result of the internal dynamic activity of the languages themselves—by allowing Language to be the integrating and transcendent context. Language is, after all, anonymous as an activity, neither fully speakable, nor reducible to any theory; and because it is primarily action, it contains the totality of the possibilities of manifestation, while simultaneously orienting its movement in view of the cultural norm (*Ṛta*)—which is also the cultural and individual body. In this manner, Language always remains an open possibility and a Cultural Norm, while each manifestation will always be a part of a sub–linguistic system. Thus, a *complementarity* of languages is suggested under a transcendent and unifying Language–activity by dropping the opposing demands of exclusivity in the original context–languages in exchange for a way of viewing and acting in the world which is eternally (*nitya*) efficient and follows the Norm (*Ṛta*).

Thus any statements in the Ṛg Veda can be traced to an original language source, either *Asat*, *Sat*, *Yajña* and *Ṛta*, where the meaning of those statements is grounded. Each one of these languages is also the ground of a particular intentional acting through a particular intentionality: *Nirṛti* (non action) is the modality of being in the world of

Asat, either as possibilities to be discovered, or as stagnant dogmatic attitudes; *Satya* is the modality of acting in the world of *Sat*, as the truth to be built, formed or established; *Ṛtu* is the modality of acting in the world of *yajña*, as the activity of regathering the dismembered sensorium and the multiplicity of the worlds of *Sat* by sacrificing their multiple and exclusive ontologies; and *Ṛtadhīḥ* (embodied–vision) is the modality of *having gone through*, and being in, a world which remains continuously moving because it comprehends the totality of the cultural movement on which it is grounded. Simultaneous with the languages as origins of meaning, and of the activities through which these meanings are originated, there is also a multiplicity of images which synthesize, and embody, both the languages and the activities of a whole cultural orientation. Thus, we have *Vṛtra*, the dragon, and his cohort of ophidians, as the prototypes (*pratirūpa*) of the *Asat*, covering up the possibilities of cultural man, either through inaction or dogmatism. Heroes like Indra and a multitude of gods are the prototype of the multiple ontologies of the *Sat*: Agni, Varuṇa, Prajāpati, etc., are the prototypes of the sacrifice; while *Ṛta* embodies the totality of languages, activities, images, and in general, the total cultural movement that needs its own continuous sacrifice of particular perspectives so that the whole cultural body may remain totally alive without partial amputations.

Finally, I would like to remind the reader again that our concern in this book is not primarily to bring forth a new interpretation of the Ṛg Veda. As a philosopher, my contribution rests in being able to uncover the necessary and sufficient conditions through which any interpretation of the Ṛg Veda would be possible; or, reversing Max Müller's statement: when the philosopher has finished his work, let the scholar—philologist, historian, mathematician, musicologist, etc.—begin. For so the wheel moves on. However, it is my intention following the subtitle of this book—Meditations—to lead both author and reader to that primordial ground where all men are born equal: to that primary activity which both verifies and falsifies any creations of man, so that man may live in innovation and continuity. This is a mutual invitation to freedom–making, truth–making, and life–making.

Meet together! Speak together!
Let your minds be in harmony,
As the gods of old together
Sat for their share of sacrifice.

(10.191.2)

II
The Ṛg Vedic Intentional Life

Introduction: The Problem of Intentionality

From this point on we will focus exclusively on the Ṛg Vedic text as a linguistic whole. However, so much of what follows hinges on the concept of 'intentionality' that it is imperative that we not leave open the possibility that we might deviate from the path we set ourselves by riding the unbridled horse of an unexamined concept. Therefore, we must be cautious that the 'intentionality' we are riding is the same one that the *kavis* and *ṛṣis* (the philosopher–singers) of the Ṛg Veda straddled.

The word intentionality was first formally introduced into Western philosophy by Edmund Husserl. For a fuller description of intentionality as formalized by Husserl, I direct the reader to my book, *Avatāra: The Humanization of Philosophy Through the Bhagavad Gītā*, especially Appendix II; but my task in the context of this book is to caution the reader as to the determination of the concept of intentionality. If one is not able to free this concept from the determination of the tradition out of which it was born, it would be meaningless to use it in the context of the Ṛg Veda. Intentionality, like any of the other concepts from our Western philosophical vocabulary, must be radically submitted to a historical mediation to allow the Ṛg Vedic text to surrender its own intentional life to us. Therefore, the reader must be patient in his eagerness for definitions, and engage in trying to discover how the concept of intentionality *functions* in, or emerges out of, the Ṛg Vedic text.

Using the concept of intentionality, the Ṛg Veda's intentional (*pracetas*) life should emerge in such a way that our description of it and the Ṛg Vedic intentionality, i.e., what the *kavis* and *ṛṣis* had in mind, coincide in at least these two points: 1) the conscious ordering of the structures of experience, and 2) the dynamic activity produced through the conscious ordering of these structures. Anyone able to reconstruct these structures by himself should achieve at least an understanding of the Ṛg Vedic intentional life and/or perhaps a way of viewing the world which would be as effective as the Ṛg Vedic viewpoint. Furthermore, the presuppositions and *criteria* on which this intentional life is grounded should become clear—how through structures and the activity of discovery the ground on which metaphysics, ontology, logic, epistemology, etc., were presupposed; or rather, and more importantly, how these structures and the activity of discovery may combine so that a disciplined kind of viewing and listening will be generated, thus causing speculations and objectifications to give way to functions and synthetic activities which will, in turn, generate perspective upon perspective. These perspectives, in turn—finally or intermittently—could produce an effective a–perspectival vision such that no ruptures are found between thought and action, viewing and action. But before we proceed to thematize these points, we must return to the word intentionality.

According to Aristotle, intentionality meant only the referential character of knowledge; for Descartes, consciousness was a mere *cogito*. But for Husserl, consciousness is a *cogito–cogitatum*, not a mere self–consciousness, but a subject open to an environing world of objects, given, or to be given, in experience. The basic structure of this situation is then a human consciousness, consisting of both a subject and a field of objects, toward which the consciousness is turned intentionally. Intentionality (or noetic–noematic structures) becomes, in the hands of Husserl and his followers, the study of the way objects are constituted as objects, present to and in consciousness, by the functioning of the appropriating intention which characterizes the form of life (horizon) in question. It is within this structure of intentional consciousness that meaning is possible. The notion of constituting intention later took on more complex meanings in Husserl, eventually embracing these elements:

- the objectification of sensory (hyletic) data by unifying them into an empirical object and relating the object so established to one thing;
- the relating of successive sensory data to a permanent object;
- the conjoining to an object of the various profiles (*Abschattungen*) which it would present from different perspectives;
- the projection of an object into an intersubjective field.

For Husserl, intentional consciousness is a concrete cognitive intentionality—structure implicit—in a concrete form of life. The noetic (subjective) and noematic (objective) aspects make up an intentionality structure; the noetic aspect is the subjective heuristic anticipation as already structured by the method of inquiry—rationality; the noematic aspect is the objective which fulfills the anticipation. The *noema* or object appears to a knowing subject in the light of the heuristic anticipation to which it corresponds. *Noesis*, therefore, is a *structured* heuristic anticipation; it corresponds to an open field of connected, often implicit, questions addressed by a subject to empirical reality, and *implying the acceptance* of a particular interpretation of experience, whether in a common sense framework or in a scientific framework. Husserl calls the domain of reality to which this particular interpretation of experience belongs a *horizon*. A horizon appears then as a set of actual or possible objects revealed or to be revealed by the functioning of a particular empirical noetic intention. The functioning noetic intention constitutes then—and determines to a great extent—a reality–outline to be filled. The intentionality structure of a particular question, then, determines or prefigures the kind of answer it will receive. It does not determine, however, that there should be a meaningful answer; but only that an answer will be given as revealing the *noemata* looked–for within an already ordered set of *noemata* which we call *horizon*.

For Husserl, the *World* is the totality of all horizons, "the horizon of all horizons." True reality for a subject is the World. A subject could settle for a horizon, but since horizon takes meaning from the World, no horizon can stand on its own isolation. The World is the source of meaning for the set of horizons found in it, and for the *noesis–noemata* structures of particular horizons with which they appear.

According to Husserl, each class of objects has its own mode of "being–given–in–its–selfhood" (*Selbstgebung*), i.e., of *evidentness*. But evidentness can be understood in two ways: as evidentness of the objects themselves, or as judgments about them; and Husserl declares roundly that the evidentness of objects is prior to that of judgments, because the former is what makes possible the latter.[1] The primary substrates are individuals, individual objects. Every judgment which can be thought refers in the last instance to individual objects. Now, it is in the mode of experience (*Erfabrung*) that individual objects become evident to us, and the world is the universal "soil of beliefs" (*Glaubensboden*) for all experience of individual objects. Consequently, the world, as a world of being (*seiende Welt*), is the universal passive assumption of all activity of judgment.[2] The world functions as a *horizon* of all the possible substrates of judgment; but the movement of judgment is circumscribed to the movement of a logic which is the ultimate ground of reality as a "worldly logic" (*Weltlogik*)[3] or the "consciousness of" (*Bewusstsein von*). There is, therefore, according to Husserl, an experience at the bottom of every judgment, a perceptual apprehension of individual objects—directly or indirectly—and this implies (1) a world as a "passive" or previously given assumption, a horizon; and (2) an activity of a subject which first perceives and then judges.

Perception and concept are, then, ultimately connected; both are concerned with the apprehension of objects, and only the mode of apprehension varies from one to the other, as a result of their different structures. Perception (in the usual sense of this term) is insufficient on account of its isolating character; an object is properly apprehended only in the combination of its characteristic qualities with reference to a context; and so, the only adequate form of perception of reality is the concept, provided that the latter includes the *moment of presence* of the reality itself. A thing is truly *captum*—seized or apprehended—when it is *con-ceptum.* Thus, the function we have termed rational is only achieved conceptually.

If reality is radically *historical*, its apprehension or reason will have to adapt itself to fit that mode of historic reason within which it appears; and such an adaptation will make necessary a transformation of its instruments—in the first place, of the concept. Traditionally, the concept has been regarded as "universal;" at best, the existence of "singular" concepts, applicable to only one object, was admitted; but, above all, this singularity was understood as a limiting case at the bottom of the scale of "extension." But no great attention was paid to them, nor was their peculiar nature investigated; and the concept was interpreted in all cases as what is "constant"; and thus, in the individual or singular concept, one considered the constant qualities of a thing persisting throughout its varying states, so that every kind of concept was affected by universality and abstraction.

Traditional logic has been particularly interested in judgment, and, still more, in reasoning, and has usually regarded concepts as mere terms. For example, for the purpose of constructing a theory of the syllogism, its point of view might be admissible; but things are different as soon as we stop thinking about "reasoning" as a mental instrument or process, and think of *reason* as an actual and historical apprehension of reality. When the mode of being of the latter is historical—and such is the case with human reality—the concepts are either essentially and intrinsically individually historical or else of a "universality" which is *sui generis.* The fact is that the concepts mentioned have an identical schematic nucleus, of a *functional* kind; this nucleus is actualized conceptually and attains to fullness of meaning when it is historically mediated. Even concepts which refer to non–human realities—provided they *are* realities—imply an historical and contextual dimension, because I can only call "reality" that which *in one way or another* is rooted or given as my life; and it only acquires its meaning or "sense" for me as a function of my participation in radical interpretation of such an activity as my life which, as such, is present and historical.

A distinction must be drawn, therefore, between the concept as an authentic *signification*—that is, a *meaning–function*, and what we might call the *logical* framework of the concept, which is abstract of the concept itself—a possibility or movement, which is only actualized in each one of the moments of conceptual thought. But there is nothing strange about this; we have seen that concept and reality appear simultaneously. What confers a true radical character to the concept is its actual functioning. What is usually designated as a concept is only a potentiality which in turn can be actualized in various ways; all these ways are historically mediated and as such, discoverable. On the other hand, the logical diagram which is usually called a "concept" can take on only a limited repertory of conceptual functions, and thus, inversely, one can apprehend a single reality by means of different logical diagrams, *provided that they are partially coincident*.

With these cautionary notes in mind, it is useful to review the concept of intentionality and its relation to what we have already delineated of Western philosophical tradition in Chapter Two, and of the Ṛg Vedic tradition in Chapter Three.

The concept of intentionality at the hands of Husserl is itself already riding the crest of the whole philosophical wave known as Western philosophy. In this sense, the movement of intentionality is already determined by the philosophical tradition which gave it birth, even as this movement guarantees the continuation and determination of the same tradition. In order to be able to use the term intentionality in the historical mediation in which we are involved here, we must first cleanse the concept of its universal and a–historical determinations. To achieve this end, we must first critically focus on what the concept of intentionality would demand that we *do* universally and a–historically.

If language is to be understood universally as necessarily being grounded on the form of thought we described in Chapter Two, then this original decision about language will determine whatever moves the language we use makes to communicate and theorize universally and a–historically. If thought, as described in Chapter Two, is the ground of man, as thought is the house of his being, then all the movements of being must of necessity be the moves of the particular form of thought which grounds it. If thought is radically the stadium where a man's life runs its course, then either the course of one man's life is as long as the movement of his thought, or every thought is all the stadium there is for a man. A man's life and a man's death are not the facts of a man's life and a man's death; but rather, those facts belong to, and last as long, as a man's life and a man's death are grounded on the form of thought which establishes itself as the ultimate criterion and factual limit of a man's life and a man's death. But just in case I am misunderstood, let me immediately clarify that I am not using thought here in the exclusive idealistic sense that reality is only what can be thought; but rather, in the historical sense that *reality is also* thought, point of view, perspective, of which the idealistic understanding of thought is only an instance.

Therefore, if thought is the ground of man, then it follows that thought is radically man's body. The limits of his body being again the same limits of the thought that grounds it.

But if the body of man is radically and metaphysically man's thought, then man is condemned to live by the dim light of this image of himself. To reduce and measure man by the image of his thought carries inevitable consequences: For one thing, whatever is not an image, a thought, is outside of man, a mystical power, a god or a devil; while whatever is human must of necessity be only that which appears or is an image. For another, the only possible role for man to play in a world grounded on thought is to systematically reduce and control all his possibilities to the reality offered by the image. In human terms—in terms of sensing, feeling, thinking—in a word—living, it is a systematic effort to force man to body-sense the world, not as the world, but rather as an image of the world. Furthermore, to sense the world in this manner (through the mediation of thought), is to systematically condemn man to a program of desensitization through the reinforcement of his belief in the idea of a permanent body that can remain so only as long as his whole sensorium feeds exclusively on ideas of sensation.

I have tried on many occasions to exemplify the above points in some simple and yet accurate way. I have always found myself returning again and again to a very familiar theme in the East: the mirror—though I was forced to give it a more radical twist to fit the present circumstances.

It would be trivial to suggest that whatever else thought can do, when it tries to reduce man to itself it is not only engaging in a futile exercise in power, but also in an exercise in very bad philosophy; were it not for the fact that, through this identification, the body of man and woman have grown sick and live in mortal suffering. But let us look towards the mirror: With every look at *ourselves* in the mirror, what we are really doing while looking for wrinkles, hairs out of place, and blemishes on the skin is no more nor less than reinforcement of the radical belief that, with small and accidental variations, *we* remain constant, in spite of the accidental changes. But this only shows us that looking in the mirror is not only not an innocent act, but one of the most important philosophical acts we perform on ourselves daily. To begin with, the mirror gives us only an image, and this is a triviality. However, the triviality may turn into a nightmare or a liberation the moment we start looking carefully (philosophically) at the image in the mirror, for the image we see in the mirror is always an image we recognize in relation to a very similar image we saw previously in the mirror; and this, in turn, we recognize in relation to another image we saw in the mirror—and so on. The fact that we lump all these images under the same personal pronoun "I," is trivial;

for this "I" is, again, a linguistic image within a mirror of language which reflects whatever images *we decide* to conjure up. However, the decision about which criteria to use in relating to these images is not in the images, in the mirror, but is entirely up to the language–user or the mirror–user to decide.

The mirror confronts us with these two possibilities; we may acknowledge the source of the images—namely, us, I, man, woman—as forever unknowable and unidentifiable, or we may reduce ourselves to the image in the mirror. Unfortunately, this second choice is the one we usually take; not like Alice in Wonderland, to travel to new worlds more fantastic than the one appearing in the mirror, but by reducing ourselves to the image in the mirror, we have chosen to live *in* the mirror. In fact, we are stuck *in* the mirror, and no matter how hard we try to feel others, ourselves, the world, all we can feel, touch, think and hear is the walls of the mirror. No flesh, no man, no woman, no wind, no sun, no pity, no love, just the walls of the mirror. The more we cry for sensation, the more we atomize sensation, the more we multiply the vocabulary of sensation, the vocabulary of love, of sex, of life; the more we reinforce the walls of the mirror from within which we have decided to body–feel the world and each other. For we have decided to remove living from life and turn it into a performance.

Nor can we escape this radical sickness by following the path of Alice in Wonderland; no matter how long we can prolong our journey through Wonderland, ultimately we have to come back to a world we left unattended. And all we have to show for our moment of escape is another row of mirrors which reflect again and again the same Alice that left. Nothing has radically changed, and the mirrors multiply.

If the plight of man is grounded neither in language nor in the mirror (thought) but, rather, in man's decision to reduce himself to a universalized form of thought by grounding himself on it, then the emancipation of man will be in radicalizing himself on his decisions rather than on his images. But in order to do so man *needs* other men and the ability to discover them at their origin—at the radical level of their decisions and not just their images or ours, for this is man's own origin and, ultimately, his own flesh; though this might demand of every man a constant sacrifice of images—the ability to liberate himself from the prison of his mirrors—and to acknowledge a human reality which, though the source of multiple images, can neither be reduced nor identified with any of them. The *other* is my own possibilities and, in realizing these possibilities, I actualize my right to innovation and continuity.

To what we have said in Chapters Two and Three, we need to add a few remarks on the concept of intentionality in order to liberate that concept from the determinations of its original tradition and make it historically viable. For even though intentionality implies a movement—of thought, the world, man—one must be aware that the movement of intentionality may be reduced to being just one of the qualities of a body when presented to a *seeing* agent who has already organized a sensorium on a model of sensation and conceptualization which takes *sight* as the primary model and organizer of sensation. On this view, one has to be very careful in using the words vision, perspective, or viewpoint; a radical abstraction and disembodiment is already inflicted on the historical world *prior to* knowing the historicity of the world.

Movement, to the Western eye, is one of the characteristics or properties of a living body or a physical object. From a Western human viewpoint, i.e., insofar as I am able to perceive my body movements in space through my flesh and muscles, the kinaesthetic sense is just one more sense among the other senses—sight, touch, smell, hearing. But such a view presupposes an existing continuous body in space and time before properties are ascribed to it; and further, it only serves to reconfirm an already existing theory of the body which does not change itself in spite of movement. We can only presume that the reason for the last standstill is the fact that movement, to the Western eye, is only capturable or seeable on the same fixed "visual" model on which a perspectival, three–dimensional space and linear time are already presumed to rest; but this conception is, of course, an optical illusion. Movement cannot be seen by the eye, or rather the 'eye' does not embody movement. What the 'eye' sees is the geometrical forms it has already theoretically accepted as movement. The eye only sees what it recognizes; and what it recognizes is already a movement reduced to some particular form; it is, in a way, "still" movement.

The kinaesthetic body–perspective, however, besides underlying the different "fields" of perception and the differing emphasis on perceptions that cultures have projected on those "fields," also underlies the radical structure of every experience and of its conditions of possibility: space and time. It is only with a kinaesthetic body–perspective as the radical structure of experience that past and future, as embodied memories, can be made present in the total body–presence of the present. Every movement is the whole, the whole is in every movement. The kinaesthetic body–perspective is the fully realised presence of a total body–system of possibilities embodied in every body movement. As concrete examples, we may point out how, in Chapter Two, in presupposing a field opened by *sight*, vision came to be based on a linear kind of movement, which disclosed a perspectival, three–dimensional space and linear time. In contrast, the audial space–time structure opened by *sound* in Chapter Three, was articulated not only by rhythmic and cyclically recurring movements, but movement itself became the base of all contexts (structures), and the source of meaning within each and every field of experience.[4]

What the concept of intentionality offers us in view of what we said in Chapter Three is not just phenomena, or single bodies, but rather, embodied structures through which bodies and their perspectives appear. Insofar as these bodies appear in front of me as I encounter them historically, corporality is always simultaneous with the structures it is capable of embodying: body and perspective share an ontological parity. Though it is I who sees, I am also visible; the weight, the thickness, the textures, the colors, the sounds of the world may be sensed not because I am a mind or spirit apart from them and surveying them, but rather my body is made of the same flesh as the world it faces. *The body makes present a context with which it shares its dimensions.* At its roots, this silent and fleshy unity underlies any reflective thinking; and *a fortiori*, any reflective thinking must carry the flesh of history with it for its own justification and human continuity.

These cautionary notes are important to us as philosophers and as interpreters of the Ṛg Vedic text. As philosophers, we need to justify our own rationality; and as interpreters of the Ṛg Vedic text, our rationality can only be justified if our intentionality coincides with that of the philosopher–singers of the Ṛg Veda. For the sake of clarification, I will anticipate the coming chapters with the following short notes:

1. The philosopher–singers of the Ṛg Veda, the *kavis* (from the root *ku–*, "to have the intention of") and the *ṛṣis* ("one sharing the viewpoint of the gods"),[5] were not only aware of the need to structure experience, but they acknowledged themselves as the only creators of such structures of experience.

2. Radical to all these intentionality structures, there is a movement (from the root *ṛ–*, to move, to go, whence *ṛta*), which is not only the source and ultimate context of all movement in the Ṛg Veda, but also the absolute Norm, the body of Law, and the cultural body of the Ṛg Veda and of the Ṛg Vedic intentional life.

3. The ordering (*vṛs–*, push, rush; like *samkḷp–*, *abhi–*, *saṃskṛ–*, *yuj–*, *tan–*, etc.) of such intentionality structures has to be such that all heuristic anticipations (*abhi–*, *sam–*, *kṛ–*) could produce an exact (*satya*) way of acting that would be eternally efficient, continuous (*ṛta*), or immortal (*amṛta*).

4. These intentionality structures, already described as the languages of Non–Existence (*Asat*), Existence (*Sat*), Sacrifice (*Yajña*), and the Liberating viewpoint (*Dhīḥ*, or *darśanam* as vision), comprise the viewpoint which is coincident with immortality (*amṛta*), efficient embodiment (*ṛta*), and durability or continuity (*abhīka*, *āyu*, *āyus*, *āyur*, *visvāyuḥ*).[6]

5. Every 'space of discourse' or language, is a field of manifestation. The contents of those spaces of discourse are dragons (*Vṛtra*), heroes (*Indra*), and gods (*Agni*), etc., which human acting requires for certain identifications, both of experience and of self. Yet one has to bear in mind that gods and the rest are this side of creation.[7]

6. The constructing of these worlds or spaces of discourse is not a desire to build a metaphysics, logic, ontology, etc., of *what is*; rather, its purpose is to incite (from the root *su–*, whence *Savitṛ*, the "inciter") an internal chain of insights (*manaḥ*),[8] which will eventually produce a kind of vision or viewpoint (*dhībhiḥ*) which will prove effective within the structured worlds,[9] by sharing its dimensions and overflowing them.

7. To understand the fabric of Ṛg Vedic methodology, one must bear in mind that it does not rest on a naïve epistemology of 'looking out' and seeing the objective world out there, or of 'looking in' and seeing the contents of consciousness. Instead, the focus is on insight and embodied–viewpoint: the original generators of consciousness and its objects; they can be recreated continuously by sharing that original viewpoint which created these worlds.

8. While not much may be said about the origins of the world,[10] much can be said of the worlds which appear in the consciousness of the *ṛṣis* and *kavis*; i.e., originally dragons, heroes and gods were undifferentiated (*Asat*); they became differentiated (*Sat*) with the birth of interpretation; but this differentiation has to be sacrificed (*yajña*) in the wake of insights and vision, since originally, and finally, there is no story at all for any identification whatever, for life goes on.

9. The coordinates of space and time within which 'spaces of discourse' function in the Ṛg Veda are not absolute and objective, nor relative and subjective; their function is exclusively in relation to consciousness and vision (space), and consciousness and objects (time). The space out of which dragons and gods emerge conceals a power of manifestation which allows space to be infinitely dynamic; consciousness, in its time function, is no more than awareness of slices of that infinity. The internal methodology of the Ṛg Veda is geared to focus time on space, so that the viewpoint becomes infinite and the limitations of space–time bound viewpoints are erased.

10. By focusing time on space, consciousness becomes infinite, transcends its own limits, and becomes eternally efficient. This is expressed by the Ṛg Vedic philosophers with such terms as *dhātu*, *kratu*, *sucetu*, *ketu*, and the combination *tantu–ṛtu*,[11] meaning the capacity to construct structures within space and time for the sake of conquering the opportune moment, the limits of space and time, the efficient instant. Consciousness of phenomena produces only discontinuous time; the Ṛg Vedic philosophers imply that any continuity—such as the cosmic, social and human one—can be achieved only through a constructed time, which dramatically becomes efficient once the limits of those constructions of space and time have been erased.

11. Following this internal dynamic activity elevates man from the darkness of *Vṛtra* (*Asat*) to the heights of *Agni* in the same manner that *Agni* rose from the belly of *Vṛtra* to the Third Heaven,[12] i.e., from *Asat* to *dhīḥ*, from non–existence and inaction to effective embodied–action–vision.

12. It is in the above context that we have to read the questions of the philosopher–poet, Dhīrgatamas, which directed our inquiry from the beginning:

I ask you: What is the ultimate limit of the earth?
I ask you: What is the central point of the Universe?
I ask you: What is the semen of the cosmic horse?
I ask you: What is the ultimate dwelling of Language?

The answer to these questions rests in the following presuppositions of Ṛg Vedic methodology: the construction of the structures of experience; the interiorization of these structures in body–perspectives; and finally, the reaching of the limits of these perspectives through the movement of insight and vision.

The logical formalization of these presuppositions and ways of doing philosophy rests on the following presuppositions: the construction of the structures of experience both affirms and denies experience; the negation of experience has to be again denied through the activity of experiencing through other constructed experiences (i.e., other frameworks); this negation of the negated constructed experience produces the real affirmation of experience in insight, or a series of insights, which such activity generates; these discontinuous insights should eventually produce a continuous (eternal or a–perspectival) viewpoint which would be effective in the sense that no separations could be established between seeing and action, vision and action. This type of logic will be formalized as a non–Boolean logic or a logic of complementarity of intentionality–structures.

Having these points in mind, the following pages may make sense, or even more, what is offered in a descriptive manner may turn out, internally, to be normative. For after all, insofar as interpretation is also radical human reality—the root of human reality—man can only exercise his right to innovation and continuity if he is capable of retrieving his human flesh in its radical human origins. For this is the embodied–consciousness men and women *count on* so that they may embark on theorizing and communicating their *consciousness–of*.

4
The Language of Non-Existence (Asat)

Am I indeed a monster more complicated and swollen with passion than the serpent typho or a creature of gentler and simpler sort . . . ?

(Phaedrus, 230)

I do not clearly know what I am like here.
(I do not know in relation to what I can say
'This I am.') Bewildered and lost in thought
I wander.

(R. V. 1.164.37)

Not from me but from my mother
comes the tale how earth and sky
were once together, but being rent asunder
brought forth all things, . . .

(Euripides, Fragment 484)

I

The starting point of the Ṛg Veda's intentional life (*pracetas*) is the *Asat*, the non–existent. The Ṛg Veda calls the whole undifferentiated primordial chaos the *Asat* and states that the *Sat* (the existent) comes from the *Asat*.[1] The Atharva Veda speaks of the Universal Framework (*skamba*) as including both the *Sat* and the *Asat* as its parts;[2] and from the *Asat*, it is said, are born all the gods.[3] In two instances, Brahman (neuter) is mentioned as the source (*yoni*) of the *Asat* and the *Sat* (A.V. 4.1.1; 5.6.1). Without the *Asat* or its equivalent *Vṛtra*, the Dragon, there would be no Indra,[4] nor even the gods,[5] for he is their container. Even more, *Agni* himself rose from the mortality of *Vṛtra*'s belly to the immortality of the right intention (*kratu*), and through him the *ādityas*—sons of light—are also born.[6] In fact, whatever moves, is born, generated, or stated in the Ṛg Veda, is *potentially* contained in the *Asat*. The possibilities of Ṛg

Vedic man, as much as his actualizations of these possibilities have the *Asat* as a radical origin.

This chapter will focus on those conditions that are necessary and sufficient for the meaning of the *Asat* to be possible by its own criteria. However, since our actual task is the double effort of a) actualizing the possibilities of the *Asat* within the whole Ṛg Vedic context, and b) actualizing the possibilities of the *Asat* within the broader context of our *present* way of doing philosophy, we shall find that we cannot do the one without the other. This means that while actualizing the possibilities of Ṛg Vedic man through the *Asat*, we shall simultaneously be engaged in actualizing our own possibilities as contemporary men from whatever unexamined determinations block us from recovering our whole human flesh. For we understand man to be the possibilities of man as realized by man, and in this realization, man actualizes his own possibilities in innovation and continuity. With these notes in mind, let us retrace our steps to the threshold of the Ṛg Vedic *Asat* as a language or linguistic field.

From the simple analysis of speaking and listening, we know that a word spoken in a sentence does not gain its meaning from the relationship of the words within the sentence. The sentence is not the source from which the inanimate, individual word receives its life; a linguistic field, common and present to the speaker and hearer, is the silent background out of which the sentence emerges, and within which the individual words gain meaning. If any individual word is to be understood, it will be to the degree in which the entire linguistic field is present. The words and sentences may break this inaudible and silent background, create an audible style, movement, and foreground, but only on the basis of the total linguistic background. The meaning of a word is only in the total linguistic field and only yields its meaning in terms of that specific field.

Words and linguistic fields need to appear simultaneously for any word to have meaning; simple succession of words or sentences is meaningless unless the entire linguistic field or language appears simultaneously. This means that an interpretation of a particular historical text cannot be accomplished by etymology alone; in fact, etymology may imply certain universal affinities among words which have no etymological relationship in their historical linguistic fields; or because of etymological relationships, etymological–meaning–giving may erase radically any and all historical sources of meaning.

The silent and historical field, the background, the linguistic whole, is vibrated and broken by the spoken word without it being erased or cancelled. Thus, philosophy's task is to return the act of creation to the history of language by retrieving, with each historical verbal gesture, the historical linguistic field from which the verbal gesture emerges as meaningful. The historical mediation of the word is possible because, together with the *consciousness–of* from which it emerges, there is also the historical linguistic field, or consciousness it *counts on* in order to emerge. It is in such terms that we may understand the meaning of a particular word from different historical periods, or even from one historical period.

II

The above remarks are important because we are not accustomed to reading 'backgrounds,' and also because, in our analysis of the Ṛg Veda, we will be dealing, in one way or another, with the following *explanatory sets of statements* which hide their own silent background:

1. Myth; 2. Descriptive phenomena; 3. Several forms of explanations of such phenomena, i.e., scientific, religious and magical; and 4. Certain types of philosophies which permit one to thread one's way around both the descriptive phenomena and the several explanations of such phenomena.

It is important to note at the outset that the activity we have in mind in setting these distinctions is an interioristic one; opposed therefore, to the objective examination of such classifications as undertaken by such different disciplines as comparative religion, philosophy of science, and history. In fact, all we are concerned with here is the functional character of such distinctions within any one individual, and the possibilities for integrating such interioristic activities in so practical an activity as the one we engage in when we express the understanding we have of philosophy.

The above fourfold division of *explanatory sets of statements* is neither arbitrary nor exclusive of the Ṛg Veda. Piaget[7] and his collaborators have identified for us *ways–to explain* among children's statements which are the equal of what we have just called scientific explanation, religious explanation (use of deity) and magical explanation (animism of some sort). Though propositional assertions may vary from child to child, still there are similarities in the *ways* of children's explanations. It is of no consequence whether the child's explanation is acceptable or not; the important fact is that explanations seem to be based on three markedly different sets of explanatory rules.

The above classification may suggest some of the anomalies that the adult person will have to deal with when he develops his personal philosophy. For one thing, the adult's observations are biased by a set of preconceptions and expectations, depending on which of the three sets of explanatory rules he chooses to follow. On the other hand, since the three sets of explanatory rules are apparently within each adult's potential, an adult's personal philosophy may, at best, result in a complex of explanations, each based on one set of explanatory rules, since he will be using one set of explanations for certain phenomena, and another for another set of phenomena. It would appear, therefore, that different consequences may result for the individual, according to the *decision* he chooses to make in using any one, each in turn, or an integration of all these explanatory sets: either outwardly—socially, or internally—psychically. However, the problem, at least for the purpose of this book, is not so much in examining the moral conflict which may result in the individual according to his choice of action; but rather, in examining how, in the Ṛg Veda—and by implication within any one individual's philosophical activity—the possibility of integrating the different explanatory modes can be actualized if the individual understands the activity of philosophy to be such an integrating activity.

To clarify this question we refer back to the *explanatory sets of statements* again, and note that we have not yet mentioned the first set: Myth. The answer will lie in the proper understanding of this word and the possibilities within it for integrating the other *explanatory sets.*

It would be a constant headache, if not sheer schizophrenia, if man was to act constantly *conscious* of the *explanatory set of explanation* he uses to deal with the phenomena facing him. Instead, what men, or Society, or Institutions, do, is to lift one of the *explanatory sets* to the level of an internal image to guide their actions. Of course, this functions as a suppressed premise, and is rarely or hardly ever made explicit; and it is to this internal image that we give the name of myth. But my discussion here is only interested in its functionality, not its objective analysis.

For the sake of clarity let us take the most prevalent explanatory set amongst us: 'the scientific set.'

Roszak[8] points out that the myth of science is "the myth of objective consciousness;" i.e., that the mentality of scientists leans heavily on objectifying as the basis for explanation and prediction. In this view, science cannot go beyond the "thinking–of–everything–and–everyone–as–object;" and thus, scientists "certify themselves as experts . . . in the decision–making process generally employed in 'the technocracy'." However, it is important to note that, despite the popular appeal such an attack on science has in certain quarters, this 'myth of objective consciousness,' at best, only defines a particular *kind* of mentality found among certain scientists; while it certainly does not unmask the fundamental image–myth of science, nor does it invalidate the potential of scientific thinking to go beyond the "thinking–of–everything–and–everyone–as–object." Science itself has disproved this assumption in Quantum Mechanics. The Fundamental Image–Myth of Science, in all its impact, is a much wider and more hidden premise where *the methodology for acquiring scientific knowledge constitutes a useful, meaningful and sufficient way to cope with human experience.* In this way, the scientific mode of explanation would take over the other two modes of explanation and act as a large controlling image to govern all human experience.

As a comparative device let us surprise the Fundamental Myth of Science and the isolated Fundamental Image–Myth in their functional dimension. As suggested above, the Fundamental Myth of Science would read as follows:

> *Explanation, prediction and the implied possibilities for control of phenomena constitute a useful, meaningful and sufficient way to cope with experience.*[9]

The main feature of such a definition is that neither of the other two explanatory modes are meaningful human experience *if* Science cannot deal with them. This anomaly is caused by the fact that one of the explanatory modes has proclaimed itself the reigning Image–Myth for action; thus human experience is deprived of the possibility of further self–expression and integration. This example may lead us to see the functional aspect of myth as Mark Schorer suggests:

> *Myth is a large controlling image that gives philosophical meaning to the facts of ordinary life; that is, which has organizing value for experience.*[10]

Myth, thus viewed, is not only a guiding and corrective attribute of Science, but also of the other two explanatory modes. The reason is that each of these explanatory modes are diverse *features* of the larger *kind of statement* about human experience which only Myth, in its comprehensive meaning, can integrate.

The Fundamental Myth of Science is a crypto-premise; it is not stated by the several philosophies of science, nor by the laws, axioms and theories which constitute science at any given time; it does not sprout from the nature of scientific knowledge, nor the relation among phenomena. It is a suppressed premise and, once converted into the Fundamental Myth, it turns into a *kind* of statement about dealing with human experience.

The same, or similar statements may be made about 'magic' (which, by the way, is as alive today as in the times of the Atharva and Yajur Vedas). For example, the statement "the touch of the woodpecker's beak cures toothache," to paraphrase Levi-Strauss,[11] belongs to, what I called above, the 'explanatory set' in the case of magic; it is of the same order of statements as 'God is love,' or 'germs cause disease.' The philosophy which joins together the 'woodpecker's beak' and the 'toothache' is a different kind of statement; but it arises from the same need to explain links between certain phenomena. The fact that a certain classification of phenomena and their relations has been established as opposed to another, in order to cope with human experience, is what elevates the magical statement to the realm of myth. It becomes the fundamental myth of a generation or culture if this mode of explanation—the magical—is taken as the one mode of explanation to deal with human experience.

The *religious* explanatory mode also lends itself to this type of examination. Within every religious doctrine we find a body of statements explaining phenomena of various sorts; and in addition, we find philosophies of religion which permit one to make one's way through the explanatory corpus. Here too, when the *reasons* for coping with experience are taken, either exclusively or predominantly, as the one way to deal with the human experience, they take on the nature of Myth, and become the Fundamental Myth of religion.

The above definitions and clarifications are of immediate interest to our task for the following reasons:

1) Myth, as a 'large controlling image,' is a kind of statement which should be considered in its own right.

2) The *Asat* will not be properly understood unless one is made aware of the fact that within any explanatory mode there is always the tendency to convert it into Fundamental Myth. The *ṛṣis* of the Ṛg Veda were very much aware of this and put the axe to this tendency. They wanted to keep *all perspectives* alive simultaneously.

3) The implied philosophical activity of the Ṛg Veda holds the internal language of images essential to both human experience and human progress in such a way that both become dependent for their functional efficacy on a clear understanding of the Language of the Images themselves. The *Ṛṣis* of the Ṛg Veda resolve the philosophical activity of integrating the different images through which man functions in the Language of the Sacrifice, a Sacrifice of complementary integration which leads to new creations through sharing in an effective way of viewing

human action (*dhīḥ*) according to the effective body of common law or norm (*Ṛta*).

The following pages deal with the *Asat* (the non–Existent). The textual analysis of the *Asat* will lead us to two conclusions:

1) The *Asat* is the ground of all possibilities of perception; and

2) The *Asat* is an attitude certain people take which, through dogmatic conceptualization, becomes an impediment for human development (*Nirṛti*, non–action).

The controlling image of *Asat* is *Vṛtra* (the dragon), the one 'that covers up all human experience,' and also, the ground of 'human possibilities.'

As referential texts, I take R.V. 7.104; 10.5; and 10.72. The first text deals with sorcery; the second with the origin of the gods; the third with origin of *Agni*. The interpretation of these shows the kind of analysis which had to be done in order to come to the conclusions of this book.[12]

III

The following hymn offers a description of the *Asat*. Other hymns confirming the description offered in Hymn 7.104 are scattered all through the Ṛg Veda;[13] the important point about this song–poem is that it not only gives a description of the non–Existent, but also, points out a further dimension of that description by establishing concretely the type of intellectual dogmatism which some men take hold of, and which delivers them into the *Nirṛti* (inaction) of the *Asat*. We shall try to bring out these points through our analysis of the Ṛg Vedic texts.[14]

R.V. 7.104

1. *O Indra and Soma, burn the Rakṣas (demon), subdue it;*
Throw down those who prosper in darkness, you two bulls.
Crush down the unthinking (acitas), destroy them, slay them;
Push down the Atrins (devourers), weaken them.

2. *O Indra and Soma, let the glowing heat—like a kettle near the fire—*
burn the dangerous one who plots evil against (us).
Direct your unyielding hatred against the
Brāhman–hating, flesh–eating, horrible–looking Kimīdin.
(R. V. 3.53.22)

3. *O Indra and Soma, pierce the evil–doers that they may fall into the cave,*
The endless darkness,
So that not even one would come up here again;
Let this angry strength be for the benefit of your power.

4. *O Indra and Soma, turn (your) crushing weapon from heaven,*
Turn (your) crushing weapon from the earth,
Towards the one intent on wickedness;
Form (your) crushing (weapon) out of the mountains;
With which (weapon) you two burn down the Rakṣas which has been prospering (in the darkness).

5. *O Indra and Soma, roll from heaven*
With the fire–heated strokes of stone;
Pierce the Atrins with the unaging, glowing weapons,
Till they fall into the abyss. Let them go silently.

6. *O Indra and Soma, let this hymn encircle you on all sides,*
As the girth (encircles) the two swift steeds;
(This is) the sacrifice which I offer to you by my understanding,
Give speed to these words, like two kings.

7. *You two should remember back (when you were) with your swift–moving horses;*
Slay the hostile, malicious Rakṣasas; who hate us and would break us to bits.
Indra and Soma, let there be no happiness for the evil–doer,
Who, at any time persecuted us with hate.

8. *Whoever works against me with lies that are counter to the ṛta (anṛta)*
As I follow my path with honest heart,
Let him go to non–existence (asat),
Like waters held in the fist,
As he pronounces non–existence, O Indra.

9. *Those who tear apart, in the usual way, one with honest intentions,*
And who corrupt an excellent man wantonly,
Either let Soma give them over to Ahi (Serpent),
Or let him place them in Nirṛti's lap (inaction).

10. *Whoever, O Agni, tries to harm the essence of our drink,*
Of our horses, our cows, our bodies,
Let him, our enemy, a thief and a sorcerer, fail;
Let him be put down (in the darkness), his body and his offspring.

11. *Let him be far away, bodily and with his descendents,*
Let him be below all three worlds;

Let his renown wither, O Gods,
Whoever wishes us harm during the day or at night.

12. *It is easy to distinguish, for a man who is wise;*
He has contended with the two words 'existence' and 'non–existence';
Of the two, whatever is true, whatever is more just
That, indeed, Soma favors: he destroys non–existence.

13. *Soma does not, indeed, further the guileful (man),*
Nor the man who gains rule through false practices.
He kills the Rakṣas, he kills the one who works false doctrines.
Let them both lie in Indra's power.

14. *If I have ever been one who made anṛta his god (anṛtadeva);*
Or if I understand the gods wrongly, O Agni,
Why are you angry with us, Jātadevas?
Let those who speak maliciously obtain destruction.

15. *May I die today if I am a sorcerer,*
Or if I have burned the life of a man;
Then, may he be deprived of ten sons
Who wrongly calls me 'sorcerer.'

16. *Whoever calls me a sorcerer when I am not a sorcerer,*
Or whoever says that I, undefiled, am a Rakṣas,
Let Indra strike him with his mighty weapon.
Let him fall below all creation.

17. *She who raids about at night like an owl,*
With craftiness disguising her body,
May she fall into the endless caverns.
Let the soma–pressing stones with their noises destroy the Rakṣasas.

18. *O Maruts, scatter yourselves among the people.*
Search for, seize the Rakṣasas,
Crush them who becoming birds fly about at night
And have deposited droppings on the godly Soma–sacrifice.

19. *Throw from the sky, Indra, the stone*
Sharpened by Soma; sharpen it, O Maghavan;
From the east, west, south, and north
Strike the Rakṣasas with your boulder.

20. *Here fly the dog–sorcerers!*
With harmful intent they seek to harm Indra, the unharmable.
Śakra sharpens his weapon for betrayers;
Now may he hurl his thunderbolt at those who practice sorcery.

21. *Indra has been a destroyer of sorcerers,*
Of those who disturb sacrifices, of those who are hostile;
The mighty one approaches those who are Rakṣasas,
(Shattering them) like earthenware, just like an axe splitting wood.

22. *Strike the owl–sorcerer, the bird–sorcerer,*
The dog–sorcerer, or the wolf–sorcerer,
The eagle–sorcerer or the vulture–sorcerer,
As if with a mill–stone, smash the Rakṣas, O Indra.

23. *Don't let the sorcery–practicing Rakṣas reach us,*
Drive off with brightness the two Kimidīns who work in couples;
O Earth, protect us from earthly distress;
O Mid–Air, protect us from heavenly (distress).

24. *O Indra, strike the male sorcerer and the female*
Who triumphs by her magic (māyā).
Let the Mūradevas (false worshippers) with twisted necks dissolve.
Let them not see the rising sun.

25. *Watch over and around, O Indra and Soma!*
Be wakeful!
Throw your weapons at the Rakṣasas,
Your thunderbolt at the sorcerers.

Ṛg Veda 7.104, as may be seen above, describes the *Asat* in this manner: It is downward (as seen in stanzas 1, 10 and 11); it is a cave (*vavra*), as seen in stanza 3; an abyss (*parśāna*), as in stanza 5; an endless cave (*vavrān anantān*), as in stanza 17; it is bottomless (*anārambhaṇa*), as in stanza 3—there is no light there, only darkness (*tamas*); for those staying there, there is never the vision of the sun, as in stanza 24. Other hymns note similar characteristics: (*trādvam . . . kartād avapado yajatrāḥ*) 'save us dutiful gods, from falling into the pit' (2.29.6) *padam . . . gabhīram*, 'deep place' (4.5.5), and *adharam tamaḥ*, 'deep darkness' (10.152.4). In stanza 3 (7.104), Soma and Indra are to let the heat (*tapus*) boil up against the evil plotters, while stanza 4 repeats the same theme of Indra and Soma burning down the *rakṣas*, enemies, with their bolt (*rakṣo vāvṛdhānam nijūrvathaḥ*).

It is also a place of silence (*nisvaram*, as in stanza 5), since those inhabiting there cannot endure the noise of the Soma–pressing stones which assist in slaying the enemies and sending them there (*grāvāṇo ghnantu rakṣasa upabdhaiḥ*), as in stanza 17.

This place is the place of self–destruction (*asann astv āsata indra vaktā*), (stanza 8) and the lap of *Nirṛti* (in–activity), (stanza 9). For the one who stays there, there is no return (that is his chosen way of life) *yathā nātaḥ punar ekas canodayat*, (stanza 3). It is a place of disappearance: *vigrīvāso mūradevā ṛdantu*, (stanza 24).[15]

The *Asat* is personified by *Ahi*, the Serpent, and *Vṛtra*, the Dragon; they live in this place of darkness, (stanza 9); *Vṛtra*'s body, even after being defeated by Indra, lies there (*dīrghaṃ tama aśayad indraśatruḥ*), (R.V. 1.32.10): this is also the bottomless ocean from which the Aśvins rescue Bhuju, son of Tugra, (R.V. 1.116.5, 1.182.6).

Besides the above description of the *Asat*, 7.104 also gives an important hint concerning the kind of mortals that fall into it—mortals in the power of the *rakṣasas*, the evil doers, the doers of actions contrary to the *ṛta*, i.e., those following any form of conceptual order which when turned into dogma reduces them to inaction, those incapable of renewing their sensation by returning to the source and unable to follow the Norm, the *Ṛta*. *Asat* is the place for those mortals (*nṛcakṣas*), ignored by the gods themselves (who are incapable of change of insight and vision), and who fall prey to the evil doers (R.V. 10.87.8, A.V. 8.3.8).

Those who are to be condemned to the place of the *Asat* are creatures opposed to the Norm of *Ṛta*; they are the lovers of *anṛta*: *Vṛtra*, the *asuras* and *dasyus* (A.V. 9.2.18): the *rakṣasas* and those who view the world as *rakṣasas* and act accordingly: sorcerers, whether *vātudhānas* or *kimidīns*, for opposing the norms of the Sacrifice and impeding men from human continuity. These people, the evil doers, operate with charms which are contrary to the *ṛta*, *anṛtebhir vacobhiḥ* (7.104, stanza 8). They cover themselves with the spirit of *Asat*, contrary to the *Sat*: *sac cāsac ca vacasī paspṛdhāte*, (stanza 12). Those acting according to the *Asat* are called 'dealers in black magic,' (stanza 13); phony gods (*mūradeva*, stanza 24), and all those lovers of *anṛta* are the firewood of *Agni*, (stanza 14).

It would be a clear misinterpretation of the descriptive notes given about the *Asat* and *Vṛtra* were we to take them in their nominal, descriptive, static forms: *Asat* is not a physical place, and *Vṛtra* is not a physical added component of all that is bad in nature, or in man. Our Western language has conditioned us to view the world in this manner, and it is difficult to negate this misconception; but the root meaning of the words used in the texts gives us the implied meaning we offer, even if the texts are not fully explicit.

In their verbal roots, both *Asat* and *Vṛtra* stand for an activity of covering—or not letting exist—that which longs to exist. *Asat* would be better translated as "that which wishes to exist, progressing towards;

while the privitive *a* impedes this progression, but does not find its way out." *Vṛtra*, on the other hand, from the root *vṛ*, meaning that which covers, and *vṛtra*, the Dragon, together with *Ahi*, the Serpent and all other reptiles used in the same sense, are images to depict 'the attitude of covering up (human possibilities) which long to come out.' (In R.V. 1.54.10 *Vṛtra* is also called *dharuṇa*, the original receptacle—foundation—of the waters.)

Ṛg Veda 10.72 gives as an example of what was trying to come out: the gods (stanza 1); these worlds (stanza 2); the Directions, or pairs: *Dakṣa* and *Āditi*, male and female potentiality (stanza 5); birth and death (stanzas 5 and 8); the sun (stanza 6). In fact, as may be seen from other instances in the Ṛg Veda, the whole universe was eager to come forth, be born (1.32.2). However, there is no possibility of bringing out human possibilities and Creation unless *Vṛtra*'s action of restraint is destroyed again and again; this was the great feat of Indra (or of anyone having Indra–power): the destruction of the *Vṛtra* attitude and the opening of the cave (1.32.11, 6.24.5).[16]

IV

Originally all we have is sheer, undifferentiated energy (*salila*, *hiraṇya-garbha*, ocean, golden germ); yet this energy longs for procreation, reproduction, multiplicity. R.V. 10.129 and annotations of 10.72 confirm this undifferentiated initial energy—an egg–like shell, that hatches by the power of its own inner generating desire and heat. The first born of the waters is Agni—Sūrya and Indra and the rest of the gods are but different aspects and names of the same original unity; the same applies to *Vṛtra*, *Ahi* and their cohorts. This insight will be more fully developed later on; but as hinted in R.V. 10.5.7, the ontological unity of Agni and *Vṛtra* is such that the world is said to have been born from *Vṛtra*'s sacrifice and dismemberment, an exclusive operation of Agni. The most important point for us to note at this time, however, is the fact that the origins of the world, are not based on any revelation, but are explained solely on the power of the reflection, insight and vision of the Vedic sages as in (10.29.4).[17] Again, it is this reflection, insight and vision that one has to be most aware of in Ṛg Vedic interpretation since: 'It is by their wordings that the vibrant co–creators (*vipraḥ kavayaḥ*) conceived as being manifold that which is One,' (*vacobhir ekaṃ santaṃ bahudhā kalpayanti*)[18] and 'called manifold what is but One,' (*ekam sad viprā bahudhā vadanty agnim. . .*).[19]

This chapter was introduced with two quotations, one from Plato, the other from Dīrghatamas; a philosopher from the West, and a philosopher from the East. The contrast of these quotations is very significant in clarifying the *Asat*, (the starting point of philosophical inquiry for the *Ṛṣis* of the Ṛg Veda). Both philosophers, Socrates (quoted by Plato), and Dīrghatamas, seem to be asking the same kind of question: What am I? For Socrates, the answer to this question appears to lie in how to bring together the *what* and the *I* of the question; in other words, the answer to the mysterious *I* lies in figuring out the *x–what*. By finding out the *what*, "serpent or gentler creature," Socrates would then have his answer to his eluding self–identification, and to the Delphic dictum: *Gnosce te ipsum*, know thyself.

It would make an almost interminable list were we to examine individually all and each of the identifications given to the "what" of man in the History of Western Philosophy. The fact remains that, for one reason or another, the insistence on answering to the phenomenon man has been heavily sought, one could almost say it was exclusive in figuring out what that 'whatness' of man really meant, were it not for Existentialism and Phenomenology. But, in every answer provided, the phenomenon itself was always presupposed, or obscured, or forgotten as meaningless. The *what* in question was taken to be a strictly linguistic question or, some sort of empirical problem which could be answered by adding up sets of empirically discovered characteristics—or as a substance . . . etc. Yet, in each case, the *what–ness* admitted of no answer whatever unless it was taken for granted (presupposed) that the phenomenon itself needed explanation, and that the answer to figuring out that phenomenon was encrusted in the atomic *what* which the question seemed to repeat 'inexorably,' to paraphrase Wittgenstein.

In contrast, Dīrghatamas, and with him the *Ṛṣis* of the Ṛg Veda, appear to have taken the same question in a different manner. For them it is not the *what*, nor the subsequent possible identifications with the *I* which would give an answer to the problem, but rather the *am–being* of the question. In other words, what is looked upon as the source of inquiry by the philosopher–poets of the Ṛg Veda is not the what–ness of 'What am I?' nor even the I, but rather, the core of both the *what* and the *I*, i.e., existence itself, the *am–being* which every question–asking–subject *is* before he even bothers to figure out essences, or substances, or whatever else becomes fashionable within a community to ask. At the present moment it seems to be the Delphic dictum again, and knowing one–self can be achieved, according to certain journals, in "Ten steps. . . ," or "Five. . ." However, as Marcel remarks,[20] modern man's almost frantic concern with 'personality' and 'self–identity' would not be there "if human personality were not on the way towards its disappearance." Marcel suggests that the old way of answering and looking for the answer to the what–ness of man is outdated and doomed to disappear; but he does not deny the fact that he and others are facing the question differently, and in some ways similarly to the way we are suggesting the *Ṛṣis* did.

The *Ṛṣis*' mind was certainly not after abstract definitions of essences. They worried about what 'existence' really meant, the concrete act of existing; and the observation of this act was their whole concern from the *Asat* to Vision. In the *Asat*, this act of existing is not the concrete act of this man, or this force, or here or there; it is something more vague, undifferentiated, unnamed, except as a "beginning," "an origin," a "ground," an "ability to." It is the "sheer–being–able–to" that takes the name and form of the existing actuality.

These expressions, used to clarify the *Asat* of the Ṛg Veda, resemble Existential and Phenomenological approaches to philosophical anthropology. Heidegger calls this priority of existence "*Da–sein*;[21] Merleau–Ponty, "*etre–au–monde*;" Nathanson, "human–being–in–reality;" and it is this, I think, that Sartre means when he says: "existence precedes essence. . ."

However, the main point of this comparative discussion is not to prove anyone nearer the truth than another, or to arbitrarily establish contact points between East and West; but rather, to make clear the Ṛg Vedic *Asat*. The *Ṛṣis* were interested in establishing the fact that "man's ground," "capacity," "energy to exist," was there, and that it was in virtue of this ground that the man of the Ṛg Veda was able to realize himself as 'this,' 'that,' 'here,' or 'there;' since, originally and finally, *man–was–able–to–become* one or another or several in an infinite repetition of this first affirmation of existence–as–capacity, which is the *Asat*.

At the same time, it is important to our understanding of the *Asat* that we be aware of the 'images' which Vedic seers invented to represent it. We have already seen about *Vṛtra* and *Nirṛti*.[22] There is also *Namuci* (mentioned nine times in the Ṛg Veda), equal in nature (*āsura*) and power (*māyin*) to *Vṛtra*; *Cumuri* (mentioned six times); *Dhuni* (five times); and *Śuṣṇa* (forty times more or less). *Śuṣṇa* shares in *Vṛtra*'s qualifications as powerful (*māyin*),[23] inhuman (*amānuṣa*),[24] devourer (*aśuṣa*)[25] bearer of bad fruits (*kuyava*),[26] and having many followers of offspring *puru-prajāta*.[27] There is also *Sambara* (mentioned 20 times), described as 'well fortified' (*dṛṃhita*);[28] *Pipru*, mentioned eleven times, with characteristic powers as the others, especially *avrata*, i.e., behaving in defiance of the established order[29] *Ahi*, the Serpent, as already mentioned; and *Vala*, meaning both dragon covering the waters or the cows, and cave where all is covered or enclosed (root *vḷ* equals *vṛ*).

In relation to the usage the *Ṛṣis* made of these names, it is important to notice that all of them are usually found in the accusative, as noticing a condition conquered; or in the nominative, as naming a power of such possible or actual condition which certain men take or may take.[30] It is also significant that verbs of slaying, i.e., conquering *Vṛtra*, bring in a plural, or singular accusative, with a *collective* meaning, intimating rather than the atomic individual, the destruction of "the manifestation of the *Vṛtra*–idea."[31]

Finally, the images of dragons, snakes and ophidians in general, which the philosopher–singers of the Ṛg Veda use in connection with the *Asat*, have different functions, and in no way do they correspond to the one–to–one identification with man or any single individual which Socrates, in the quotation presented at the introduction of this chapter, intimates.

V.

In order to understand the relationship which holds between the language of *Asat* and the other languages found in the Ṛg Veda, a final clarification is necessary. In summary: The *Asat* in the Ṛg Veda functions as the original 'space' out of which all form and name derive; as such, i.e., as original space, it is the container of all human possibilities.

This proposition needs further clarification for two important reasons:

1. We have named the *Asat* 'space;' and this word, even if understood as only a ground, may evoke in the mind of the Western reader, whether consciously or unconsciously, that what the *Ṛṣis* had in mind was a kind of 'visual model' leading to a visual synthesis of their human experience. After all, most of our Western models accruing any kind of knowledge are grounded on such visual models leading to a visual synthesis of human experience;[32] and the reader might also be misled in this direction by the fact that from the early pages of this book we have insisted on some kind of 'vision' as the end result of following the Ṛg Vedic philosophical way.

2. It will be important for any kind of understanding of the Ṛg Veda to have in front of our *eyes*?, *ears*?, *mind*?, *senses*?, the model upon which the Ṛg Vedic philosophical way moves. The preceding question marks and italicized words may indicate the type of forced reading our language encourages us to make of any other language. The question we face, therefore, is this: Are we dealing with the *criteria* of a 'visual model,' or of an 'audio–aural model'? This and subsequent chapters will contribute to a fuller kind of answer.

The vision we are speaking about throughout this book has nothing in common with our Western gaze, or looking out or in, or from above or from below. The vision we are speaking of is grounded on a model of "sound," not "sight," and therefore follows, the moves and activities of sound.

The Ṛg Veda is a contact with an original civilization, and civilizations vary greatly in their exploitation of the various senses. It is commonplace by now, to observe that the ancient Hebrews and the ancient Greeks differed in the value they set on the auditory; that for the Hebrews, understanding and knowing were more in sound and touch, while for the Greeks, knowing became more a kind of 'seeing,' (although not as much as for post–Cartesian Western man). The Greeks kept to the sense of touch in their geometry—in a way they imagined themselves fingering their way around a geometrical figure, while modern geometricians think of shapes as the way they look.[33] Much of the modern confusion and misunderstanding comes from the fact that the media—visual and auditory—mix so freely in modern man's experience of himself that he is unable to understand or figure out a synthesis of their mixed perceptions.

There is nothing mysterious in all this, for Western philosophy, from Aristotle on down, has equated vision or contemplation with gazing at human life from the heights of a theory. This vision has in many ways become human flesh for contemporary man: an organism with ideas; though the organism must remain constant, while ideas may vary. Philosophical reflection has been reduced to perambulate only within the limits of theory; the soil of vision and contemplation has remained theoretical. The philosopher's feet have been necessarily condemned, by the criteria of that vision, to endlessly tread on the flimsy cloud of nominalism; and the cloud blankets metaphysical theories, forces, powers, actions and possibilities. The only form of transcendence possible within such determined confines is either, the decapitation of theories by other theories, or a system of dialectics by which the process of executing theories is accelerated, leaving in its wake a world empty of human creation but uniformly nominalistic. By the criteria of this visual model, human survival and continuity is condemned to give up the human act of creation for a theoretical compromise by which all men and women are equally uniform, to the degree in which they are able to ignore their own human creativity and surrender to the theoretical compromise controlling their lives. But the history of man, and therefore his flesh, was begotten in sound and ruled by the criteria of sound. From the dark, the human flesh slowly moves towards the clear; bodies sing themselves away from the shades; the flesh wants to be music; for this was the beginning.

It is, therefore, essential for us, in trying to understand the Ṛg Vedic intentional life, that we realize from the beginning that what we call the language of non–Existence, the *Asat*, is a tonal context ruled by the criteria of music. By these criteria, we find that the ground of transcendence, the origin of all organized perception, the original ground any and all sounds *count on* in order to sound, is the *Asat*: in the sense of "non–Existence" or "inaction," it is simply *silence*; in the sense of "obscuring" or "covering" or "chaos," it is pure *noise*, from which tone is a distillation. Thus, *Asat* embraces the whole spectrum of sound, from its absence to its plenary confusion. In the sense that the *ground tone* of any string sounds its lowest pitch, the *Asat* can be described tonally as "downward," a spatial derivate, as in 7.104, stanzas 1, 10, and 11. However, the Sanskrit suffixes of time, *puras* (before) and *paścāt* (after), are not temporal, but logical referents with respect to origin; while up (*ud–*) and down (*atha–*) are not so much spatial but ontological referents with respect to proximity to, or distance from, the moment–centered fullness which is *Ṛta*. In this sense, the *Asat* is the opposite of *Ṛta*. *Ṛta* is the end of an effective synthesis of the sensorium, through a whole range of clear and distinct acts of particular senses and their subsequent insights; while the *Asat* stands as the initial space–ground of indeterminate perception, or rather, of "sets" of organized perceptions.

As we mentioned in Chapter Three, a vibrating string of any reference length, the "Norm" of which grounded all early civilizations in mathematical acoustics, can be halved to sound the octave higher, or doubled to sound the octave lower. Since all tones recur cyclically at the octave—as the "same" tone, in one sense, but as a "different" tone, in another—any octave can serve as the model for all possible octaves, at least for the general purposes of tuning theory. The cyclic structure of the octave is the *invariant* ground common to all systems of tuning, and the explicit references to circles in the Ṛg Veda, as in Plato, suggest that the tones were actually graphed in a "tone–circle," which functioned as a cyclic matrix or "mother" within which derivative tones came to birth, or were generated. Unless one has the experience of actually tuning an instrument, behaving as "midwife" to successive tones, the activity of generation may have little meaning. This may be the reason why Plato's genetic theory, with its sexual metaphors, has hardly been understood.[34]

It is Plato who reminds us of the tradition we are here investigating. Musical criteria introduce a hierarchy into the field of number; *even* numbers *define* the octave matrix as "female," *odd* numbers fill that matrix with "tone–children" and are defined as "male"; the smaller numbers define intervals of greater importance, and *poetic metaphor* (or an allusion to sound criteria) differentiate number ages before our specialized mathematical vocabulary was developed. That part of the continuum of *real* number which lies beyond *rational* number belongs to non–Existence (*Asat*) and the Dragon (*Vṛtra*). Though to a mathematician all numbers may be holy; to a musician, some are far more valuable than others: the "divinity" of 3, the "humanity" of 5, and the "sexual roles" of even and odd reflect their tonal functions. The number 2 is "female," in the sense that it creates the matrix—the octave—in which all other tones are born. However, by itself it can only create, as in Socrates' phrase, "cycles of barrenness;" for multiplication and division by 2 can never introduce new tones into the tone–maṇḍala. It is a theme of ancient cultures, and of the Ṛg Veda in particular, that the Original Unity is hermaphrodite, producing a daughter, "2," by a process of division without benefit of a mother. God is "1," but he cannot procreate except via his daughter, "2," the female principle and mother of all:

Not from me but from my mother
comes the tale how earth and sky
were once together, but being rent asunder
brought forth all things, . . .

as Euripides reminds us in Fragment 484, echoing a cultural theme as early as the Ṛg Veda.

We shall see in the next chapter how the hymns describe the numbers poetically by distinguishing "sets" or "quanta" by classes of gods and dragons and heroes, and also, how they portray tonal and arithmetical relations with graphic sexual and musical metaphors. The continuum of the circle (*Vṛtra*) will be dismembered repeatedly by Indra, for it embraces all possible differentiations; the conflict between Indra and *Vṛtra* will never end; it is the conflict between the field of *rational* numbers and the continuum of *real* number. Integers which introduce new "cuts" in the tone-maṇḍala demonstrate "Indra power" over *Vṛtra*; *Vṛtra* (or *puruṣa* for that matter) is "cut to pieces"—dismembered—in every battle with the gods, though his death is their own. Without the *Asat*, or its equivalent, *Vṛtra*—the Dragon—there would be no Indra, nor even the gods; for he is their container.

In conclusion, let me briefly summarize this chapter.

By using the criteria of the tonal context by which the language of non–Existence, *Asat*, is ruled, the *Asat*, as 'space' (or as the field–condition out of which all differentiation in human experience emerges), becomes a 'space of discourse' in the following sense: First, it is a necessary field of sound emergence,[35] of all organized sensation and of all communication; sheer vibration, energy, possibility—the sounding silence from which the worlds, gods, and man emerge. Secondly, it is a 'discourse' which certain humans take to manifest themselves in ignorance of their origins and of others; that is, certain humans share the *Vṛtra*–attitude of covering up their own human possibilities, by dogmatizing certain theoretical conceptual schemes, thus depriving man of the possibility of *returning* to his origins and that of others. In this sense, the *Asat* attitude becomes their 'space of discourse–manifestation' and absolute boundary; this is the only sin the path of *Ṛta* could not tolerate, for it deprived man from the eternal return to his origin, and tried to reduce the multiplicity of embodied–songs to one theoretical voice. Contemporary man and contemporary science, especially psychology, needs to dwell on this sin; for unless memory and imagination are freed from the theoretical constraints limiting their movement, man and woman cannot recover their body completely. Not allowed to reach the beginnings of the human body we all carry with us, the present crisis of contemporary man and woman is, not only the verification of this Ṛg Vedic insight but also, the falsification of any theory imposed on man and woman substituting for the original human act of creation. We have cried for and praised many Saviours, but have lost our own act of creation and the power to revive it. We have forgotten the Dragon, the Snake, the Silence, and the Flesh that wants to be music.

5
The Language of Existence (Sat)

Arise! The breath, the life has reached us,
darkness has passed away, light is coming.
She has left a path for the sun to travel,
and we have come where men extend their
lives.

Ṛg Veda 1.113.16

His form is to be seen everywhere
for of every form He is the Model.
Indra, by his power (māyā) appears in many
forms,
Indeed, his bay steeds are yoked a thousand
times.

Ṛg Veda 6.47.18

The One we follow bows not to the weak or
the strong,
or to the challenger incited by the restless foe;
To Indra the lofty mountains are as plains
and in the deeps there is a foot-hold for him.

Ṛg Veda 6.24.8

I

How can I tell you about the earth and the sky? How can I tell you how they became separated? Remember that the *Asat*, the Dragon, the Cave is all around us. How can I tell you about the separation of the earth and the sky without separating them again? Remember, in a world of sound, ruled by its criteria, the Cave, the Dragon, the *Asat*, is anywhere, everywhere, any *point* where I start my narration, where you and I meet— The Cave, the Dragon, the *Asat*, is you!

You have picked up this book and read through it hoping, in some way, to expand your mind, to expand your consciousness, to increase your ideas; while simultaneously, you had taken for granted that your 'body' would in no way change through this activity. As far as you were concerned, your 'body' could remain constant, even while your mind might be subject to variations; but, in taking this attitude, you only repeated a prevalent interpretation of the body and the mind which stretches through contemporary psychology, through Descartes, and only as far back in human history as Aristotle and the Asclepiad medical tradition in which he was raised.[1]

But as we have seen, when you take this attitude, you are agreeing that the method of the natural sciences is the only method by which man and his 'body' may be understood, explained, predicted and controlled. It is a necessary condition of the method of the natural sciences, for the possibility of experimental observation, that one variable remain always constant while the other is varied; the 'body' as an organism must be conceived as historically resting, while the mind may be conceived as historically moving. Aristotle and the present scientists are facing the *same* 'body,' but the scientific approach to this same 'body' has changed with the improvement of its instruments; the *unchangeability* of 'body' is a presupposition for saying that we, in one sense, have better explanations of natural 'body' processes than Aristotle had—if Aristotle and present-day science explained different 'bodies,' we could not say this. The *unchangeability* of 'body' is a presupposition for establishing experimental techniques giving the same results at the time t_1 as t_n; the *unchangeability* of 'body' is a presupposition for linking the progress in knowledge with the improvement in the instruments of science. The repeatability of experiments is a presupposition for establishing reliable knowledge through the sciences of the understanding; and on the basis of established 'body' laws, we are able to predict and to control. The control is facilitated by our ability to predict what happens under conditions which we are technically able to reproduce repeatedly. The result of this journey has led the natural sciences to the only conclusions possible within its theoretical human abstraction: either total behaviour control, or genetic manipulation. In either case, historical man is denied his own act of creation: the active ability to release all that is human in him. This is the task assigned to education, and which education has almost fully given up.

How can I tell you the story of how the earth and the sky were separated unless you are able to cancel out the determinations of your mind and listen to your body? For it is your body that is the Cave, the Dragon, the silence of centuries. How can I tell you the story of how the earth and the sky were separated without breaking you into the numberless numinous dots of sound buried for centuries in your flesh? How can my narration return flesh to flesh? How can I release from your docile and silent body the buried memories, imaginings and rhythms, without breaking the boundaries that now hold your memory, imagination and movement? We need to return to the body with the same innocence and the same determination of a new birth: A birth in the darkness, the Cave; a birth in the Dragon of historical man without historical constants. The diverse historical determinations through which man makes his body, his life, his time, his space, his movement, and his voice in the world, are constantly demanding a responsible decision from man; are constantly offering him life; but no new birth is possible unless our meeting point is the Cave, the Dragon. Our inquiry necessitates that the body be split open, like the Cave, like the Dragon; and that all its memories, its imaginings, and its history be released.

Main Characters of the Languages of Existence, (Sat)

Originally, two kinds of beings are presented in opposition: *devas* and *asuras*, (which also applies to forces who are benevolent and also malevolent). Most gods are called by the two names; only a few are not—at least not in the texts available.

The Sky and Earth have '*devas* as children' (*devaputra*).[2] The word *deva*, 'god,' is an epithet for the children of the Sky—*Uṣas* ('the Dawn'), and the two *Aśvins*, ('Horsemen'). Some other gods are also given the same title: *Parjanya*;[3] *Agni*,[4] although *Agni* is normally son of the Waters; and *Parjanya*, as son of the Sky, appears only as appellative. The same can be said of the *Maruts* ('men of Heaven'),[5] who are obviously the sons of *Rudra*; and of the Sun, *Sūrya*.[6]

The *asuras* have no father and only their mothers are mentioned. The word *asura* means 'power,' and the beings designated by this name in the Ṛg Veda fall into two classes: the *Dānavas*, 'descendents of *Danu*' of unfortunate characteristics; and the *Ādityas*, 'descendents of *Aditi*' of auspicious and benevolent nature. The *Ādityas* resemble men, in appearance, or sometimes birds; the *Dānavas* appear in the form of a serpent, a dragon, or a boar. The leader of the *Ādityas* is *Varuṇa*; of the *Dānavas*, *Vṛtra*.

The functions and conduct of the two groups is sharply differentiated. The *Dānavas* bind, restrain, hold back, cover over, and enclose: They cover over, restrain, and hold back the Waters and the sun (the embryo of the Waters). The *Ādityas*, on the contrary, unbind, give freedom, and liberate: They operate to evolve and give growth; their goal is creation. The *Dānavas* stand for inertia and destruction: they oppose creation.

Each group has its own sphere of action or life: the *Dānavas* dwell in darkness and the cold below, where the sun never reaches, where the cosmic order (*ṛta*) does not exist, and where *Vṛtra*'s body lies forever dead; this is the non–Existent. The *Ādityas* live in the lap of their mother, *Aditi* (light);[7] their field of action is the surface of the earth, where there is sun and order (*ṛta*): This is the *Sat*, the Existent. The *Dānavas* deal in death, chaos, in–action (*Nirṛti*), and in the company of demons (*rakṣasas*). The *Ādityas* bring immortal life. The nature of the two groups is the same before or after the death of *Vṛtra*. Creation has only made their separation more obvious.

A hint as to the common nature of both groups of *asuras* is found in the fact that both share in the same power—*māyā*. Both *asura* and *māyā* mean power, therefore, they are creatures which are 'powerful,' 'creatures of power.' With this same meaning, the term *asura* is later on used for a human king, who may also be called *deva*. The word *asura* is also used in the Ṛg Veda of *Varuṇa*, *Mitrāvaruṇa*, the whole group of the *Ādityas*, *Indra*, *Agni*, the Sun in several aspects, of *Rudra* a number of times, the gods, and opponents of the gods. On occasion, it is also used for other gods, *Maruts*,[8] *Pūṣan*;[9] *Soma*;[10] *Parjanya*;[11] the Father;[12] probably *Vṛtra*, the *hava* (cave);[13] *Bṛhaspati*[14] and others. It is not used with the *Aśvins* and *Uṣas*. It is twice used unequivocally of *Dyaus* 'the Sky.'[15] It is most interesting to note that Indra, the supreme *deva* (1.32.12) is also called *asura*, and that the gods gave him the *asura* power to slay *Vṛtra*.[16] It is also in view of this power of the *Ādityas*, that one has to read the so much quoted prayer in the ḄĀỤ 1.3.30: *asato mā sad gamaya, tamaso mā jyotir gamaya, mṛtyor māmṛtam gamaya*, "From the Non–Existent lead me to the Existent, from darkness lead me to light, from death lead me to immortality."

With these notes in front of us, we may now proceed to line up the two armies of *asuras* before they enter into battle.

On the one hand, we have the *Ādityas*. They are first said to be two: *Varuṇa* and *Mitra* and later on three: the same two and *Aryaman*. Once, six are named:[17] *Varuṇa*, *Mitra*, *Aryaman*, *Bhaga*, *Dakṣa*, *Aṃśa*; and in 9.114.3 the number of seven is given though no names are mentioned.[18] *Aditi*, the mother of the *Ādityas*, is said to have had eight sons (10.72.8), no names are mentioned; of whom the last one is deposited by the mother as an egg in the cosmic Waters. It was called *mārtānda* (egg of mortals), i.e., the ancestor of men, related to the sun.[19] This inclusion of the sun is a normal one considering that the *Ādityas* are the deities of freedom and light, and the personified sun would become a member of the group as the source of light. He is called *Adityā*,[20] and would stand in later India for the 'sun.' The leader of this army is obviously *Varuṇa*; *Mitra* is the next in command; and the Sun, as embryo of the Waters, is the youngest officer.

Opposite to the *Ādityas* stands the army of the *Dānavas*; their number is also indeterminate. In two late passages,[21] they are numbered as seven, matching the *Ādityas* in number, but the names are not mentioned. The leader of the *Dānavas* is *Vṛtra*, who appears to be called 'seventh' (*saptatha*).[22] Other officers of this army mentioned are: *Pipru*, *Śambara*, *Śuṣṇa*, who are also *Dānavas*.

It is interesting to note that no mention is made in the Ṛg Veda as to the father of either group; a fact which assumes its full significance when we consider that both share, not only in the same power, but also in the ultimate anonymity of their origin. The Ṛg Vedic notion of propagation seems to be that the male puts the semen in the womb, whereupon *Tvaṣṭṛ*—which is later than the semen—gives shape to the embryo. There appears to be no evidence that any female element combines with the semen (though, in later times, the semen and the menstrual fluid are considered to combine); but the milk is afterwards the female life–giving or life–nourishing fluid. We shall see later on in the story, how Indra, after freeing the Waters, pours milk in them, (makes them pregnant), and causes them to bear; a feat which *Tvaṣṭṛ* had not been able to perform (10.49.10).[23]

Therefore, we are only left with the mother's names, which in each case is also the etymological designation of their functions and those of their respective sons. In this sense, we have *Aditi*, with the private *a*, the abstract noun *diti* meaning 'bondage,' from the root *dā* 'bind;' which thus means 'non–bondage, freedom.' *Dānu* seems also to indicate the same root–origin *da* 'bind;' it is a primary derivative from the suffix *–nu*, and similar to *bhānu* from the root *bhā* and *dhenu* from the root *dhā*. The meaning again, is 'bondage,' 'restraint;' which agrees with the root of *Vṛtra*, her son, whose name is derived from the root *vṛ* 'cover,' 'enclose,' meaning the 'Encloser.'

Thus, the names appear to be personifications of powers. Indra, for example, is called the 'son of strength' (*śavas*), out of which epithet a mother, *Śavasī*, is born (created) for him; though we shall see that she is not his real mother. Indra is also called 'lord of might' (*śacīpati*), meaning also 'husband of might' (*śacī*), and so, a wife is created for him, *Śacī*. In the same manner, *Mitra* and *Varuṇa* are sons of *śavas* and sons of *dakṣa* ('skill'),[24] and *Agni* is son of *śavas* and father of *dakṣa*.[25] The *Ādityas* are called 'sons of freedom' (*aditeh putrāḥ*), out of which grew the feminine personification *Aditi* and the descendents of *Aditi*, the *Ādityas*. Similarly with *Danu* and *Vṛtra*, in relation to the *Dānavas*.

Therefore, the story as it stands now, reads as follows: In the beginning, there was *Vṛtra* (*Asat*), who covered over all the powers of man. Opposed to him was *Varuṇa* and his army of *Ādityas*; one represented bondage, the other freedom. Bondage and Freedom were the result of a family feud of different mothers and brothers, but where all share in a mysterious power which is at their origin.

In the Beginning (*Agrajā*)

The oldest, and at the same time, the least prominent and shortest–lived story of creation in Indo–Aryan speculation, is Indo–European. The first names and forms found in the Ṛg Veda are Father Sky (*dyaus pitṛ*) and Mother Earth (*pṛthivī mātṛ*), who have gods (*deva*) as their children; namely, Dawn (*Uṣas*) and the two heavenly Horsemen (*aśvinau*, *divo napātā*). Also named are the twins Yama and Yamī,[26] described as the progenitors of the human race.[27] However, neither these, nor other similar references, derive from the prevailing creation story of the Ṛg Veda. It appears that certain symbols of Indo–European or Indo–Iranian origin mix freely in the original speculations of the people of the Vedic period, though these speculations are not truly Vedic until they are grafted to the proper story or narration of the Indian seers: *Tvaṣṭṛ* is the beginning of the Vedic creation story.

Earlier than Sky and Earth was *Tvaṣṭṛ* (the one which can make things, 'fashion'). He is the 'one born at the beginning' (*agrajā*), or the 'first–going' (*puroyāvan*),[28] 'belonging to the beginning' (*agrajā*).[29] *Tvaṣṭṛ* created all creatures,[30] and 'adorned with forms these two parents (of the gods)' (as in 1.185.6, where Sky and Earth are proclaimed parents of the gods . . . *huve devānām* . . . *janitrī* . . . *dyāvā* . . . *pṛthivī*), and all the worlds were his creation.[31]

When *Tvaṣṭṛ* made the Sky and the Earth, the idea seemed to be to build a house for himself; for they constituted a house (*sadanam*),[32] and he made them together.[33] They were in a common house or were a common house (*samokasa*);[34] and again, it is repeated that Sky and Earth and *Tvaṣṭṛ* were together in the beginning. The story then proceeds to narrate how it so happened that Sky and Earth were later separated from *Tvaṣṭṛ* and from each other; that is how differentiation entered this world.

Tvaṣṭṛ is indeed the great Fashioner or Artisan and his symbol is an axe. During his life, he made not only the Sky and Earth, but also the *Soma* cup for the gods, the *vajra* weapon for Indra, an axe for *Bṛhaspati* and, in general, he is celebrated as a skillful artisan; while, on the other hand, the verb '*jan*' (produced) is commonly used of him.[35]

Tvaṣṭṛ combines in himself both the male and female qualities, and so, he also becomes the universal impregnator or stimulator (*savitṛ*).[36]

This conception is, for the greater part of the Ṛg Veda, personified as a separate deity connected with the sun, making that body start on its daily course. *Tvaṣṭṛ*, puts the element of life (*turīpa*) in creatures, making them multiply. In the male, the principle of life is in the semen (*retas*); in the female, it is in the milk (*payas*)—later this word also signified semen. This principle of life is also its principle of growth. The Atharva Veda describes him as "a pregnant male, stout, filled with milk, beesting, curds and ghee, whose seed is the calf, the afterbirth" (9.4.3–6). That combination was the gods' portion. Indra chose a drink of *soma*; his body became a great mountain; the *soma* is also described as the stallion's semen.[37]

Tvaṣṭṛ as the first active or dynamic force in the universe was, it seems, preceded by the Waters (*apas*). In Atharva Veda 9.4.2, *Tvaṣṭṛ* is called the 'counterpart of the Waters in the beginning' (*apam yo agre pratimā babhuva*) and the implication is that both were contemporaneous.

Reconstruction of the Story of Creation

From what we have said so far it would seem that in the beginning there were the Waters and *Tvaṣṭṛ*: *Tvaṣṭṛ* created Sky and Earth which constituted his house; Sky and Earth were endowed with the principle of life, and they begat the gods, who then proceeded with all else that was needed to construct the universe. However, this was not done without drama: the drama of differentiation, of fight between light and darkness, *Tvaṣṭṛ* and *Vṛtra*, *Sat* and *Asat*. This account, substantiated by later Ṛg Vedic thought in the form of repetitions or rather in the form of *Tvaṣṭṛ*'s creative functions imitated or duplicated by a number of other deities, is an effort to recreate, in varying names, the underlaying primordial unity of a nameless Reality beyond form and name.

These gods are *Parjanya*, 'who makes his body whatever he wishes;'[38] *Viśvakarman*, 'Maker of all;'[39] *Brāhmaṇaspati* who 'blew up' the material of the universe like a smith at his forge.[40] They differentiated by generating the *Sat* from the *Asat*. The *Asat* is here called *Uttānapad*, 'the directions,' as a woman with legs outspread in parturition. *Dakṣa*, 'male potentiality,' and *Aditi*, 'female creative power,' are the creators of animate and sentient beings, the sacrifice of *Puruṣa*,[41] the sacrifice itself as power of creation, *Vāc* as word in the sacrifice,[42] *Viṣṇu*, *Dhātṛ*, *Pūṣan* and *Tad Ekam*.

The variation in names for the same functions of the gods goes hand in hand with the radical skepticism of the sages to accept any of the gods as the personificator of, or exhausting in any way, the Reality from which they were supposed to have come. And so, we find the skeptical hymns[43] against Indra's supremacy as a god: 'They call it *Indra*, *Mitra*, *Varuṇa*, and *Agni*, or the heavenly bird *Garutmān*. The sages speak of the 'One Existent in many ways.'[44] And Indra's place as supreme god is alternately taken by principles as *Ka* ('Who'), *Prajāpati*, *Viśvakarman*, *Skambha* (Framework),[45] or *Kāla* (Time).[46]

However, in order to understand the *Tvaṣṭṛ–Vṛtra* story, we must retrace our steps and try to surprise it in the midst of its dramatic conception: that is, in the narration of the separation between *Sat* and *Asat*, *Indra–Vṛtra*.

The War between Ādityas and Dānavas

Reading 8.96.9 carefully, it is obvious that the Vedic seers were not playing guessing games in trying to describe the original condition of the world. For one thing, they are not trying in any way to give us reasons for the feud between the families of *Ādityas* and *Dānavas*, nor are they very specific about the way the Waters originally contained the elements the universe needed. The Vedic seers were only describing the condition of the world as manifested to their introspection; and in their vision they proclaimed it to be so necessarily. What they saw was the Cosmic Waters, containers of all the possibilities of life held over by *Vṛtra*, while *Varuṇa* and his followers wanted them released. *Tvaṣṭṛ* and the sun seem at this point to be left in the background in this first encounter between the two armies. However, they regain their prominence later, as soon as they are needed.[47]

The first skirmish between *Ādityas* and *Vṛtra* is not related in the Ṛg Veda except by obscure hints. One late hymn, represents *Varuṇa* as having been made a prisoner of *Vṛtra*, though later on he was released.[48] *Agni* and *Soma* were also made prisoners. However, this late hymn could well be a parallel of earlier hymns,[49] where *Vṛtra* is said to have enclosed heaven as well as the Waters. The fact is that *Varuṇa*, *Agni*, *Soma* and the other *Ādityas* were no match for the *Dānavas*, and so, the *Ādityas* and their troops had to retreat and look for a new champion. Indra is then born.

The Ṛg Veda states that the gods had arranged for Indra's conception and birth with the aim of destroying *Vṛtra* and his followers,[50] while in another passage it is said that as soon as Indra was born, he became the protector of the gods[51] who generated him with *stomas*,[52] (or that *stomas* were recited to egg him out).

However, there are a few problems involved in trying to line up Indra's parentage. We have already seen in what sense *Śavasī* was called Indra's mother; and we have seen it only refers to his power. The same can be said of *Aditi*, especially since *Aditi*'s motherhood refers to *Varuṇa*; and it is also true of all the references to *gṛṣṭi* (a cow that bears only once),[53] where Indra's mother is called "the bull," (*garṣṭeya*); and also "the calf" (*vasta*), with reference to a cow–mother which, we know, is a compliment for a female in the Ṛg Veda. Equal disclaimers to motherhood are found, among other places,[54] in the *dhiṣaṇa* reference to the Earth.[55] In the duel, the two *janitrī* are Sky and Earth.[56] In fact, *Aditi* and Earth were in later Indian tradition equated with each other. Also, Indra and *Agni* are stated to be brothers, and both sprung from a common father and a universal mother.[57] *Agni's* father is *Dyaus*, while his mother is *Pṛthivī* or *Uṣas*.[58]

Tvaṣṭṛ is often thought to be Indra's father (1.52.7; 5.31.4), and Indra stole the Soma in his father's house (2.17.6; 3.48.2–4; 4.18.12); yet, in those passages, no noun or pronoun stands for this claim. *Tvaṣṭṛ*'s house, on the other hand, was the Sky and the Earth—*Dyaus* and *Pṛthivī*—and as we shall soon see, these two seem to be Indra's real parents. Only in this way, as we shall see, can the statement that Indra made his mother a widow[59] be understood—and not by killing *Tvaṣṭṛ*, as it has been thought—since *Tvaṣṭṛ* remains alive and well through the Ṛg Veda. The claim of *Soma* as Indra's father[60] has to be interpreted as the strength of *Soma*, and on this account, fatherhood is attributed to *Soma*; or *satyayoni* in 4.19.2 as his birthplace, which makes reference to Indra separating the *Sat* from the *Asat*; or *satpati*, which means 'maker of the *Sat*.'

The above mentioned may be reduced to this: Indra is the youngest of the gods, and therefore called *kanīna*, 'little one,'[61] and *Kumāraka*, 'boy,'[62] as well as the much commoner *vatsa*, 'calf' and *yuvan*, 'youth.' Furthermore, since he is his mother's last child, he received in later times, as his offering, a cow with a single calf. Indra is the 'ageless' one, *ajara*,[63] and his wife *Indrani* is the most fortunate of women–godesses.[64]

For information on Indra's birth one has to turn to R.V. 4.18. Indra's parents appear to be the Sky and the Earth. After a gestation period of 'a thousand months and many autumns,' when the time came for Indra to be born, he seems to have had a disagreement with his mother. In the first verse, someone argues with Indra saying: "This is the ancient accustomed path, whence the gods were born upwards, all of them. From here the mighty one (*pravṛddha*) should be born (upwards). Let him not make his mother fall down there."[65] This is evidently a hint that the place of the gods is upwards (*ud jan*, as it is said of *Agni*,[64] and of Indra's might[67]). But Indra refuses to join them since he is aware of his mission: "I shall not go (straight) forth to dangers here. Let me go forth from the side to avoid them.[68] Many deeds not done before must I do. I have both to fight and question."

The questioning is about the enemy.[69] Indra's mother answers naming the enemy—the Covering (the word used is *apsas* and, in this meaning, would be equivalent to *Vṛtra*); in another passage, she names the two wicked *asuras*, *Aurṇavābha* and *Ahisura*; in 8.96.16, the enemies are numbered as seven, the *Dānavas* of 10.120.6 and leader *Vṛtra*.

The story continues that as soon as Indra refused to be born up, "he saw his mother leaving him" (*para i*, like *para gam*, 10.97.21, and *para car*, 10.17.6, should mean 'go off,' or in the case of Indra's mother, spoken of often as a cow, 'go off grazing'; in no case does it mean 'die,' as favored by some who want to see a parallel to Buddha's unnatural birth from his mother's side). Indra decided to follow her: "I must follow her," "I shall go with her." Then, in *Tvaṣṭṛ*'s house, Indra drank the *soma*, which he stole.[70] He drank a hundred–worth and got strength.

The drinking and stealing of the *Soma* is also a bit confused. He is said to have drunk it in *Tvaṣṭṛ*'s house, and in another passage (3.48.2), in Mighty Father's (*pitṛ mah*) house, that is *Tvaṣṭṛ*'s. He had to overcome *Tvaṣṭṛ* to drink it (3.48.4), or he had to take *Viśvarūpa* (all forms), which he did, either alone or with the help of *Trita Āptya* (10.8.8.9; 2.11.19). He stole it (3.48.4), or had *Viṣṇu* steal it for him (3.48.4). But still in another passage, it is said that he found it on his mother's breast: 'he drank the beestings growing on the mountain, which the young mother poured for him in the Great Father's house; he looked upon the sharp *soma* on her breasts and drank it' (3.48.2.3). Keeping in mind that his mother was the Earth, all these statements can be reconciled; for the *soma* grew on her breasts, that is, the mountains (the soma is called *giriṣṭhā*, *parvatāvṛdh*, i.e., 'mountain growing'); and since the Earth was part of *Tvaṣṭṛ*'s house, both house and breast are reconciled.

Until Indra became ready for battle, his mother concealed him (4.18.4.5), or swallowed him, as it is said in stanza 8 (or 4.18, that the female *Kusavā* did).

As soon as Indra drank the *Soma* he was filled with might (4.10.5); he swelled to a terrific size and filled the two worlds, Sky and Earth (3.36.3). The Sky and Earth were terrified (1.63.1) and flew apart (3.54.7), or into concealment, becoming hidden (8.96.16). Thus Indra lost concern for father and mother, and cared only about *Soma* (4.17.12). Now we may understand how the Earth and Sky were separated, how Indra's mother became a widow (4.18.12), and also how Indra was their last child; since the separation of Sky and Earth was forever, and the mother was deprived of her husband.

Even *Tvaṣṭṛ* was dismayed and afraid (1.80.14), and made for Indra the *vajra* (bolt) as his weapon (5.31.4; 1.52.7), which appears to have been in the Waters (1.84.11; 8.89.9) or below the sun (10.27.21), or even in the belly of *Vṛtra* (1.54.10).

Then the gods bestowed upon him all their powers (*tasmin nṛmṇam uta kratuṃ devā ojānsi saṃ dadhur*, 1.80.15 and also 3.51.8). These powers were for the submission of the *asura* rule (7.21.7 and without reservation 6.20.2).

And so, the gods had their new champion, the battle between the two fields was about to rage again.

The Battle of Indra and Vṛtra

As the battle was about to start, the gods seemed to doubt their champion. Indra's mother says to him, "My son, the gods here are deserting you" (4.18.11). Then Indra calls out, "Friend *Viṣṇu*, step out your very widest!" A clue to this friendship is that *Viṣṇu* stole the *Soma* for Indra. Yet Indra speaks of his own loneliness, "In my need I cooked a dog's entrails; I found none among the gods to solace me. I saw my wife being dishonored, (he refers here to his own impotence which can only be overcome when drinking the *soma*,) then the eagle brought me the *soma*," (stanza 13).[71]

The eagle made things right for Indra again by providing him with the strength of the *Soma*. And indeed, he needed that strength for he had to overcome even the gods who deserted him (4.18.11; 8.96.7) or who were in *Vṛtra*'s power (10.124.2).

Indra drank three vats (huge beakers) of *soma* (1.32.3), and then went into battle. Sometimes he is said to have fought alone, and other times helpers are mentioned: *Rudra* and the *Maruts* (2.11.3), *Viṣṇu* (8.77.10), *Soma*, or *Agni*. He could have fought it alone, created a storm—*Rudra* and the *Maruts* being a personification of it—and became terribly indignant, hence *Manyu* ('Wrath') is also mentioned.

The battle was fierce and Indra was wounded when *Vyaṃsa* (who is *Vṛtra*, 1.32.5) broke his jaw (4.18.9). Indra broke *Vṛtra*'s jaw (10.152.3; 1.52.6) and his face or nose (1.32.6), split his head (4.17.3; 1.5210) crushed and slew him, and left him lying there dead (*amuyā*). His weapon pierced twenty–one mountains (8.96.2), and burst the bellies of the mountains (1.32.1)—which means that he slew *Vṛtra*.

Indra, then became lord of the Cosmos (3.30): released the waters (1.32.3), i.e., generated the sun, the sky, the dawn (1.32.4)—or rather, he and *Soma* made the dawn shine; he led forth the sun with its light, supported the sky, and spread out mother Earth (6.72.2; 10.62.3; 2.13.5), having struck away *Vṛtra* from them (1.51; 1.52). Or, in simple terms: having killed *Vṛtra*, he proceeded to creation (2.15.1 ff.). He is, therefore, also known as *viśvakarman*.[72] He created by setting the worlds apart and starting the sun on its revolution;[73] this is stated as Indra fixing Earth and Sky like wheels on an axle (10.89.4), or when his creating activity is termed "dancing" (2.22.4; 10.72.6; other cosmogonic functions are described in 1.103.2 and 2.15.2).

The most important fact of the victory was, of course, the release of the Waters, which had *dāsa*—*Vṛtra*—as lord or husband (*dāsapatnī*).[74] Though the Waters were goddesses (*devi*), *Vṛtra*, the anti-god (*adeva*), had been restraining (*pari vavṛvāṇsam*) them (3.32.6). In releasing them Indra became their lord, or husband—the noble one (*vṛsapatnī*, *aryapatnī*,)[75]—and caused them to bear his mark (*varṇa*, 10.124.7).

By releasing the Waters, also called the cows, Indra scattered the darkness (5.31.3), coerced the Dawn, who appeared to oppose him,[76] and made the Sun follow her (3.55.1).

The Sun is another result of the great conquest of Indra. It had been hidden by darkness (*tamasi*),[77] and operated contrary to its normal function (5.40.6); but by Indra's conquest, it is set in the Sky,[78] its wheel in motion;[79] he also rolled the sun's disk (4.16.12), and made it shine (8.98.2) to open a pathway through the darkness (6.21.3); but then, he also steals its wheel so that it does not move too fast (10.43.5; 1.175.4; 4.30.4).

Indra makes every possible claim about the Sun, even that it came into the embryo of the Waters: 'In them (the Waters) I have placed what not even the god *Tvaṣṭṛ* could place in them, the white (milk), the desirable, in the udders, the breasts of the cows (Waters), the honey of honey, the mighty, the *Soma*, the Blend,' (10.49.10). Together with this claim is Indra's boast of his feat of placing the milk in the Waters (or cows).

Then creation takes place. The Waters, now released, make their way to the ocean (1.32.2). Thus, Indra separated the *Sat* from the *Asat*, the Existent from the Non–Existent. At *Varuṇa*'s command, the cosmic order (*ṛta*) was born (1.105.15). This applied to all in their respective functions,[80] including the gods.[81]

All that was needed for the world was now present: moisture, from the breasts of the cows; the sun to give light and warmth; Order for humans and gods; and Indra reigned supreme, although with some collaboration from *Varuṇa*. The Sky and Earth are separated forever, making room for the sun's place and the spreading of the Earth (7.86.1). One god is born to see that all the other gods live according to *ṛta*, this god is *Savitṛ* (4.53.4; 10.34.8; 10.139.3).

Recapitulation

In the beginning, there were the Waters restrained within a shell, personified by the wicked *Vṛtra*, 'The Encloser.' A natural force of expansion existed, personified by *Varuṇa*; but *Vṛtra*, the power of restraint, was greater. Besides the Waters, there was the Fashioner, *Tvaṣṭṛ*, who had created Heaven and Earth as his abode. Of these last two, Indra was born. He drank the *Soma*, became strong, and forced apart the Heaven and the Earth, filling the space in between with all the greatness and beauty of Creation. The Waters were impregnated and gave birth to the Sun and then flowed into the ocean. This was Creation: the separation of the *Sat* from the *Asat*. Then *Varuṇa*, prescribed the laws by which everyone, gods included, should live.

Yet the destruction of *Vṛtra* does not do away with opposition. Indra himself had sinned by slaying him and had to be cleansed by the Waters (1.23.2), and the *rakṣasas* were left to roam freely and ensnare men who surround themselves with restrictive perspectives to escape them (*Atharva Veda*). *Sat* became triumphant, yet not without constant opposition. *Devas* and *Asuras*, Birds and Dragons, Light and Darkness, Sky and Earth, *Tvaṣṭṛ* and *Vṛtra*, would thus face each other forever in the heart of man. For after all, the separation of Earth and Sky is a continuous return to man–world's origins, to their innovation and continuity.

II

Despite drastic changes in interpretation, I have tried to follow W. Norman Brown as closely as possible, in *the above account* of the story of Creation.[82] The above account might help Western readers to get a superficial acquaintance with the characters of the Ṛg Veda; but outside of providing a few unfamiliar *names* and philological clues in the Ṛg Vedic text, the above account labors under a host of presuppositions which philology mishandles and with which only philosophy is equipped to deal. Our task, however, must be to re–acquaint ourselves with the Ṛg Vedic *Sat* from that perspective from which, not only what is *said* in the Ṛg Vedic text appears, but principally what it implies is made manifest.

The first peculiarity of the above account of Creation is that the Ṛg Vedic seers were certainly not good story tellers. It is really an ordeal, not only to make a coherent story of Creation, but even more, to understand its meaning by the criteria used by philologists. This difficulty, however, is not so much a Ṛg Vedic problem as it is a problem for the one interpreting the Ṛg Veda as an epic poem, with heroes, damsels in distress and happy endings. The truth of the matter is, that in the Ṛg Veda, there is no beginning, no end, and hardly any kind of coherent story by the standards by which we measure biography and story–telling.

Our first step is to remind the reader to "beware of names." Throughout this book, we have been working towards a critical activity for reaching another peoples' life by trying to capture their activity of living on the same ground they themselves feel at home with their life. It would be most dangerous for us and a tremendous waste of time if we now forget the theories we have developed, and fail to see them embodied in the concrete circumstance we meet. If we filter our interpretation of the Ṛg Veda through the *names* of gods and dragons, we will inevitably find ourselves left with the sludge much of our Western tradition attaches to the *theory of names*: the appropriation by names, empirically known by way of quantifiable sense–data, of qualities or characteristics clustered around them; the theory of abstract concepts which the mind applies to things moving in space and linear time; thinking substances facing matter; fallen bodies facing heaven; what is and what ought to be. But if we, instead, set ourselves the task of fitting our thoughts to the context of the text, we find ourselves facing moving webs, moving structures; each structure a rhythm through which a body–world appears, revealing a background of living beings together with the glory and terrors of their life.

Earlier, the claim was made that the Ṛg Vedic *Ṛṣis* were moving within a world of sound on which they based a whole–human–sensorium–synthesis, and by which criteria we were to examine the text. Western, and even Eastern scholars, have tried to attribute a visual model to the Ṛg Vedic *Ṛṣis*, or presupposed such a visual model as the synthesis of their sensorium. It is commonplace that man's sensory perceptions are abundant and overwhelming; but it should be equally evident that it is impossible for man to attend to all of his sensory perceptions at once. Every man is part of a civilization which is committed to an organization of the sensorium stressing certain types of perceptions and neglecting others. This, of course, is an historical fact. If taken seriously, it may be the most telling clue about specific cultures; that any given culture is committed to one prominent way of sensory perception, and that their way is not necessarily our's, is at the root of many of our misunderstandings and misinterpretations of other cultures. Our Western 'visual' culture is at the worst odds to understand and interpret a culture like the Ṛg Veda, where the stress is not so much on the visual, but rather, on the oral–aural. This rich field of exploration, i.e., the sensorium synthesis of the Ṛg Veda, is at once so varied, vast and intricate, that the following few pages about it can only be taken as suggestive guidelines rather than comprehensive and conclusive statements.

It is obvious, when talking about the whole–human–sensorium, that this refers to the world of sight, sound, taste, smell, touch, kinaesthesia; the relations of touch to sight and to sound, the relations of those sense perceptions to our expressions in the vocabulary of our vernacular, and the relations of those sense perceptions to our self–identification and to the perceptions of others, i.e., interiority and exteriority. What might not be so obvious is that a synthesis based on sound as a primary model of organizing sensation contains a multiplicity of perceptions that will certainly have a different character that, say, a synthesis based on primarily sight–perceptions alone.[83]

A society bent on sight perceptions and on the fixedness which such a priority in perception carries with it, is mostly concerned with surfaces, with objectifying, with fixed spaces and with objects in such spaces; a society so perceptually inclined cannot stand the light, but only its *reflection*, and centers upon such objects. The sun, the electric lamp, and the fire are only objects to be used, but not to be gazed at directly; for they blind, dazzle, burn or suffocate us.

Taste is a discriminatory sense distinguishing for us what is agreeable to our organism or to our aesthetic pleasure. Taste, of course, is very much the lackey of whatever primary sense synthesis a civilization lives by.

Smell too, is a discriminatory sense and its connections with both memory and sex are commonplace. What stinks is rejected and kept away, what pleases, or is remembered as pleasing, is desired and brought near.

Touch, in relation to such a society, and even kinaesthesia, is geared towards the measurement of such an objectified world. These measurements are carried out in tactile terms: fingering, protruding, limiting, fencing objects in visual space. Even persons are watched or gazed at as objects (hence girl–watchers), and sex becomes, in more senses than one, the 'measuring rod' for such objects, a tool for breaking the surface—*hymen*—or the door leading to the interior of the object. Names and objects multiply through mutual fertilization, and we find ourselves flooded by knowledge without wisdom and sensuality without heart. Memory and imagination are restricted to the boundaries of such *closed* organization.

Then there is sound, which is the greatest key to interiority among all of our senses, (even though interiors of a certain kind are also felt through touch and kinaesthesia). But it is only through sound that interiors as interiors are manifested. Sound is the greatest clue we have to interiority, our own and that of others. It is only sound which makes true interiority communicative. Kinaesthesia—under the rule of the primacy of sight—gives us access to our own interior without the violation of touch. I feel myself inside; somehow I feel my own body, my own skin, but I cannot have that feeling about others. Even about myself such a feeling of insideness within my own skin is loaded with the presuppositions of a visualistic synthesis of human experience in terms of bodies, surfaces and space containers. Touch also gives us interiors, yet it cannot be readily communicated to others, and it provides no guarantee that we are being freed of the objectifying approach under the visual synthesis of perception.

Sound discovers interiors by invading them physically; the hearer vibrates not merely empathically but in physical bondage (resonance) with the sounding body. Sound is absolute presence; it is an activity rooted in the present. It must continually vanish into "Non–Existence (*Vṛtra*)" in order to remain a power for "Existence"; and despite this evanescence, man is more existentially rooted in sound than in the other senses, even sight. Sight may provide a lot to think about, but it is only *in* sound that all the thinking is done. No wonder that sound, the word, has been attributed with power, even magical power, or even more, the word has been proclaimed the Son of God.[84]

The above generalizations have very concrete consequences. For one thing, the intentionality of the senses and of the objects of the senses is already determined by that *sense* which the culture stresses, be it sight, sound, or another. Furthermore, in the case of the Ṛg Vedic culture, which stresses sound as the primary organizer of sensation, both sensation and thinking will have a different structure than the same process in a culture which stresses the visual. No thought or object is sensed or thought in isolation, but within 'sets,' 'groups,' 'horizons,' or simply contextual structures. Which means that biography, or story telling, has also a different form. But above all, we must be aware that, in the history of man, sound preceded sight as an organization of both sensation and embodiment. The root of contemporary man's crisis is that while his culture tries to reduce his body to simply the names of an organism, contemporary man's body still remembers its origins in sound and refuses the nominalistic amputation.

It might help clarify these points to review some notes I have already introduced in *Avatāra*: *The Humanization of Philosophy Through the Bhagavad Gītā* regarding the relation between *structure* and the human body. What we call *structure* in this text, Ortega y Gasset defined as elements plus order. Strictly speaking, he meant that we cannot speak of the "structure of reality," but rather, that what we call *reality* is strictly *structure*. This formulation of Ortega's (further thematized by Julián Marías), carries formidable consequences for our present study. According to this formalization which found its maximal expression in Ortega's condensed thesis: I am I and my circumstance, (a) reality is my life; that is, each life lived; (b) human life is not a reality, but rather a theory or interpretation of a general structure which I discover through the analysis of my life, (hence structure is analytical); and (c) man is, viewed from this radical perspective, and insofar as he is radicated in it, a *structure* of human life. The question we face, therefore, is which structure to ascribe to the man confronting us. Obviously, we are not free to give him any structure, but only the structure at which we arrive from his own radical reality, his own life insofar as we are able to know it by making it our own.

With this in mind, we can see that what we call structure is derived from a living, embodied reality; and so are its contents, conditions and criteria. These conditions and criteria are the conditions and criteria without which my life is not possible and which must be found, therefore, in each life. Thus we are speaking of a necessary and, in this sense, universal structure; a structure which, in a sense, exists *a priori* with regard to each individual life, but which is analytically derived; discovered from the analysis of reality (a lived life); and therefore, in no way can it be an *aprioristic* construction. Thus structure is both analytic and empirical, distinguishable as such, yet inseparable and irreducible.

Structure, therefore, is not a quality or a combination of qualities of human life, but it is the human life empirically facing me. It is the empirical fact which constantly constitutes my circumstance: the concrete world through which I make my life constantly. Human life is like that, though in principle it might be different, or at times people decide to make it different. That is why to say that life is like that is not to say anything factual; but rather, to point out the structural configuration of human life.

What we call structure, therefore, appears from this perspective as the field of possible human variations in history. Historical man will make himself present in the world through a particular articulation of this presence: a gesture through structure of which and through which he will acquire his ultimate circumstantial and individual reality while making it present, making it expression, or giving it body. Thus, he learns that the adequate form of unfolding the drama of the appropriation of the general analytic structure into his life is to narrate it. Biography is thus born at the risk of cancelling out the radical structure on which biographical human life stands.

It is only through human circumstance, understood as an open world of possibilities through which I make my life constantly, that the reduction of structure to biography may be corrected. The corporality of each structure becomes my empirical structure (and therefore my body), as I learn to embody the world facing me with its generous offer of life; but the fact that human circumstantiality is corporeal (has a body), does not mean that the body may be restricted or identified only with some definite structures of the human body. Biographical life may be taught to narrate itself through different bodies, while not belonging exclusively to any one body. However, since corporality and world–possession is also joined to the structure of the senses, biographical life may also be taught to narrate itself through different sense structure, without in fact depending exclusively for sensation on the structure of one body–sensation–interpretation. The fact that human life is visual, auditive, tactile, etc., is not sufficient to make human life dependent on one interpretation of structure of the visual, auditive, tactile, etc. It is also a fact that the human senses and their structure are subject to change. Technology, for one, has changed human sensitivity and sense structure, thus changing the horizon of the human body. Neither the sensorial structure, nor the human body of contemporary man are the same as they were a few years ago; though our biographical language has not yet learned to narrate this change or account for these circumstances. Structural changes at the empirical level introduce structural changes into the totality of what we call human life; in this concrete instance the intersection of three lives: mine, writing this book; yours, reading it; and the Ṛg Veda's, providing a *body* with which we may share its structure.

III

In view of the above remarks, we have no other alternative but to retrace our steps and start anew, separating the heaven and the earth.

We must start by remembering that the *Ṛṣis* and *kavis* consciously ordered the structures of human experience in such a way that the movement of their intentional life (*pracetas*, from the root *cit–*, which like *prajña* and *pravid* has the prefix *pra*—indicating a dynamic activity to be realized through *kratu*, through the capacity to string together a series of successive acts to be gathered in an instant moment of maximized efficacy),[85] could produce such an exact (*satya*) way of acting as to be eternally (*nitya*) efficient (*ṛta*) or immortal (*aṃṛta*). It is, therefore, the seers, or *kavis*, because of their powerful intentional vision, who make it possible "to disentangle the mysteries (*guhya*), and with their structures (*mātrā*), regather (*samma–*) the two worlds."[86] This activity of the *ṛṣis*, however, is itself the result of a power (*māyā*) which is the source of structuring itself (R.V. 9.83.3).

By focusing on the *criteria* of sound, by which the measures of the structures of the language of Existence (*Sat*) are discovered, we find three main clues to guide us in our investigation:

1) The originating power (*māyā*) moves in accordance with the movement of the Norm (*ṛta*) and appears wherever the chant sounds (*Vāc*);

2) This coincidence of power, Norm and chant, occurs at any sound–point; any pitch being a possible tonal center for any kind of tonal structure.

3) Gods, heroes, Dragons, etc., are only the prototype (*pratirūpa*) and the embodiment of a multiplicity of perspectives (*pururūpa*) generated from a common origin (*sayoniḥ*), the musical octave, conceived as a field admitting many alternative structures (i.e., "tuning systems").

These clues may lead us, not only into the organization of the hymns according to the criteria by which they were originally chanted, but they may also help us understand the structure of the sensorium and of the body as implied by those same criteria.

With this in mind, one has to read again the exploits of Indra, *Tvaṣṭṛ*, the *Ṛbhus*, *Agni*, *Ādityas*, etc., within the intentionality context of the *Ṛṣis*, who were the ones who devised the whole Ṛg Veda.

Indra, of course, appears as the prototype (*pratirūpa*), immersed in power (*māyā*) and in the multiplicity of forms (*pururūpa*).[87] *Tvaṣṭṛ* is from the root *tvaskṣ tvacane*, to create or produce according to his power (*māyā*), able to create the gods,[88] or become them (1.158.6), as he becomes the *Ṛbhus*, *Vibhā* and *Vāja*, *Brahmā* and *Agni* (1.13.10). *Ṛbhus*, from the root *rabh*–, take hold,[89] are placed nearer to the realm of *Asat*,[90] indicating the difficult task of bringing men from one way of life to another.[91] This activity bestows on the *Ṛbhus* their right to immortality, since they function within the established order (3.60.2).

Further examples of the functional character of the names given to certain actions or activities may be found in association with roots meaning to move, go, order, create, etc., like *ṛ*–, *samkḷ*–, *abhi*–, *samskṛ*–, *yuj*–, *tan*,[92] and in epithets stressing the same functional idea.[93] In view of such characteristics, it would appear that the *Ṛṣis* did not have the atomization of names and forms in mind; but rather, the establishment of an effective activity centered at the heart itself of that powerful *māyā* (force), originator of any and every activity; and which moved according to the Norm (*ṛta*) through song (*Vāc*).

Therefore, in the Ṛg Veda, and by the silent criteria it presupposes, the act of creation is not a single, definitive act; but rather, an act which is repeated at every sound–point. It is where *Sat* and *Asat* meet (10.72.2); it is where *Tvaṣṭṛ* blows up his own home, or Indra, or *Viśvakarman* (10.81.82); or where the human body (*puruṣa*) is dismembered (10.90); or where sexual union takes place, as with *Puruṣa* and *Virāt* (10.90.5), *Aditi* and *Dakṣa* (10.72.4), *Yama* and *Yamī* (10.10), and even *Dyanuḥ* and *Pṛthivī* (6.70.3); it is where there is bottomless water (1.23.16; 6.50.7; 7.47, etc.), the *Hiraṇyagarbha*, the Golden Embryo (10.121), or *Prajāpati*, the father of all creatures; it is where desire (*kāma*) (10.129) and heat (*tapus*) rise; it is where what is bound is released, *Aditi* (1.89.10) and the separation of the heaven and the earth (10.95.18); it is the world of *Sat*.

Sat, from the root *ās*–, to exist, is its participle, meaning the actual existent in its existential dynamic form. It is not any conceptual, static form. *Sat*, in connection with *satya* (usually translated as true), shares with it the same root and the primary suffix *ya*, giving *satya* the meaning of 'one who really knows the existence, clever in existence, firm within the changeable.' *Nirukta* 3.13 would make *sat* as that which arises from the true (*satya*). In any case, the world of *Sat* is a world of continuity and discontinuity, multiplication and division, a pluralism of perspectives, gods, Dragons, and heroes, struggling for both supremacy and survival.

Footnotes 94 through 96 classify the main hymns of the Ṛg Veda according to the function of the different gods. Translations of the main hymns may be seen in the Textual Appendix. At this time, we will focus our attention on the relation of the hymns to the human sensorium.

The World of Sight

The Ṛg Veda is full of visual imagery. The gods are placed in three regions: the Sky, the Atmosphere, the Earth, or as *Yaska* named them: *Dyau–sthāniyā*, *Antarikṣa–sthānīya* and *Pṛthivī–sthāniyā*.

The region of the Sky, or Heavenly region, is the space of *Varuṇa* and *Ādityas*, *Dyaus*, the *Uṣas* (Dawn), the *Aśvins*, *Sūrya* (the Sun), *Savitṛ*, *Puṣan* and *Viṣṇu*.[94]

The Atmospheric region hosts Indra, the *Maruts*, *Parjanya* (in connection with *Mitra–Varuṇa*, *Vāyu–Vāta* (the Wind), *Rudra*, *Trita Āptya*, *Āpam Napāt*, *Matariśvan*, *Aja Ekapād* and *Āpah*.[95]

The Earth is the space of *Agni*, *Pṛthivī*, *Bṛhaspati*, *Soma*, *Sarasvatī*, the Rivers, mountains, forests, trees and plants.[96]

The Ṛg Veda abounds in verbs and roots of verbs denoting 'to see;' this visual activity being as much an activity of the 'seers' (*kavis* or *ṛṣis*) as of those '*devas*' of the three regions. The roots *drś*–, *drati*–, from whence *darsánam*, means view, to see. Cakṣ– (*cakṣus* means eye) equally denotes seeing, although a distinction is established between the physical eye and its seeing (*akṣan*), and the seeing attributed to the gods through *cakṣas*. The word *Ṛṣiḥ* itself denotes a seer; so does *kavīḥ*. The same may be said of the derivatives of *dhī–*, *ven–*, *man–*, (like *manīsā*), etc.[97]

The World of Touch (*sparśa*)

It is obvious in reading song–poems to the wind (*Vāyu*), especially the references to Indra's weapon the *vajra* (bolt), that the *Ṛṣis* were very much aware of the implications of touch to both memory and communication. As seen in the earlier part of this chapter, it is through the *vajra* that Indra has to bring down (touch) the enemies of the Sacrifice, to awaken them to their original memories—the contact with the original initial energy, *tapus*. Touch, in this case, is the last resort to bring about those who have lost contact with the real direction of the original power; or as Plotinus would have put it: "Memory (through touch in this case) is for those who have forgotten."[98]

The World of Taste, Smell, etc.–The World of Soma

A whole *maṇḍala* (book) of the Ṛg Veda (the ninth), is dedicated to *Soma* and its effects on perception. *Soma* is the *ātmā yajñasya*, the core of the Ṛg Vedic Sacrifice (9.2.10; 6.8). The Ṛg Veda has about 120 song–poems dedicated to *Soma*, third in statistical importance amongst the other sense perceptions. Amongst the benefits of *Soma*, R.V. 8.48 names the following: it protects the body, removes illness, lifts from depression, illumines the taker by scaring away darkness, averts hostility, exhilarates, inflames and illumines, stirs good thoughts, makes one feel on top of the world, and leads to immortality. No wonder *Soma* is usually connected with the root *vip–*, indicating the excitement, trembling, shaking, and quivering, which accompanies the 'inspired *kavi*' who has taken Soma at the moment of narrating his vision (*dhiyaḥ*).[99] It is the *soma* juices one must take for inner excitation (*vipaścitaḥ*) (9.22.3), in order to penetrate (in the opposite direction of *vajra*) *vy ānaśuḥ* the visions (*dhiyaḥ*) with a trembling which is efficiently inspired (*vipā*).

We might be better equipped today through the efforts of psychiatry and the psychedelic culture to understand the function of *Soma* in relation to the human body. Psychiatry saw the appearance of multiple personalities as a threat to reason, and therefore labeled it sickness; monotheistic personality has always been the prototype of our culture and *a fortiori* of psychiatry. Schizophrenia was officially coined an illness just before the First World War, at a time when the whole culture was being fragmented in multiple personalities, in painting, music, literature, and even the natural sciences. This multiple schizoid perspective made us aware that the world was no longer one, nor held by one reason; not having one single center, nor held together by one single central authority. The fragmenting personality became fragmented into numerous centers of spontaneity, relativity, discontinuity and disorganization. We were not trained to survive without the monotheism of personality, and were unable to cope with psychological polytheism, except as an excuse for punishment and control. In the Ṛg Vedic context, however, the existence of fragmentary, autonomous systems is not only acknowledged, but no social life is possible without them. Polytheistic personality is the condition for survival when one of our psychic centers cannot hold and things fall apart. Polytheism in the human body is a psychological response to the challenge of breakdown and disintegration; it is a model for integrating disintegration. But this psychological aside cannot be easily understood in a culture ruled by the criteria of sight, and we are therefore compelled to return again to the world of sound.

The World of Sound (*Vāc*, *Brahman*)

It is the greatest understatement to say that the Ṛg Vedic methodology draws its main clue to interiorizing all perception, the whole sensorium, from sound. Ṛg Vedic man was enveloped by sound; surrounded and excited by sound; made aware of presences by sound; looked for centers of experience in the experience of sound; found the model of complete, absolute instantaneity and communication in sound. He structured the sensorium in such an interioristic way as to become, in one instant, the total presence and power of absolute and efficient communion. The Ṛg Veda's song–poems were not only oral creations, but also chanted creations. While the other sensory media provided discontinuity, sound alone, in spite of its evanescence, gave Ṛg Vedic man the instance of eternal presence and unity he so well used to further develop the world of *ṛta*, the ability to be bodily at home with any god, any human personality, any perspective. Numerous examples can be introduced at this point; however, I will only take one I think the most telling, to corroborate the above points:

Dīrghatamas, one of the most impressive thinkers of the Ṛg Veda, offers the clues to what we are indicating (1.164). It is somehow ironical that the meaning of the word *Dīrghatamas* is 'vision in long darkness,' and that tradition, because of the name, or other unknown reasons, says of the philosopher–poet that he was blind. *Dīrghatamas* starts the first stanza affirming that 'he saw' (*apaśyam*) *Agni*, in the form of the altar, the Sun, as a one–wheeled car, and as the first Sacrifice on which the poets and sages weave the woof of the subsequent sacrifices since the first one was the warp. No sooner however, has Dīrghatamas proclaimed his 'vision,' than he starts questioning it: "*ko dadarśa* . . ." (who has seen the birth of the Sun, etc.): "*acikitvān cikituṣas cid atra kavīn pṛcchāmi* . . ." (not having seen, I ask the poets, who (claim) to have seen). Stanzas 31–42 create the setting of Dīrghatamas' vision more clearly: The Sun rises, reaches the highest vault (*nāka*) of the sky, and declines again to die; in its appearance the sun is mortal. To the naked eye that is the vision; however, Dīrghatamas will correct it instantly: Besides the world of sight there is the world of sound: *Vāc*; of *Vāc* is born *Agni*, who transmits immortality to the Sun. Both, the mortal and the immortal, have a common origin (*sayoniḥ*). The answers which Dīrghatamas is looking for are not out there in the sky, but inside (stanzas 37–38): lost in thought, while looking at the first born of the *Ṛta*, then the inspiration of the *Vāc*—speech—arises in him. The following stanza clarifies the difficulty in understanding this: When one looks one way he sees only the mortal, but looking the other way—or rather, listening—one may perceive immortality. The rest of the song–poem is a detailed explanation of the relation of speech to immortality and the description in detail of the meaning of speech (*Vāc*).[100]

The passage in Dīrghatamas of the discontinuity through sight of the sun, i.e., its mortality—and of the continuity through sound of the same experience—is a great clue to the understanding of the workings of the Ṛg Vedic sensorium. The total presence of speech and the discontinuity of sight are both reconciled in the common origin of sound, through *Vāc*. This process presupposes an internal activity that is much in opposition to the Western activity that is suggested by the Western model of sight.

Realizing the intimate unity of all existence, Ṛg Vedic methodology tries to recapture it in an auspicious moment of inspired vision. This moment, however, is not without labor, and it is also a gift.[101] This labor of acquiring an effective and unifying viewpoint was expressed by the philosopher–poets as a correction of the discontinuity of explanation which appears through sight. It tried to convey, even through these discontinuous media, the direction of unity to be sought.

In this sense, it tried to 'picture' a flow of forces (though with different names): so we have *Rātrī* and *Aditi*, night and day, and their union (*sandhyis*) is guaranteed through the Dawn,[102] a rejuvenating force of unity, adding nothing to night or day, yet keeping them together in 'visual imagination.'[103] The same function is performed by the Dawn in the sacrifice,[104] and in relation to the gods of light like *Savitṛ* ('who causes long, not discontinuous, life,[105] and confers immortality—continuity—on the *Aśvins* and *Ṛbhus*, the Sun, Indra, *Viṣṇu*, etc.[106]).

This idea of continuity is introduced through *Savitṛ*, as an impulse of permanence (4.54.4); and on the Sun in 7.62.5.

We may not conclude these remarks without pointing out that the *Ṛṣis*, and in this concrete case, Dīrghatamas, knew the type of sensorium–synthesis they were counting on. We cautioned the reader earlier that unless we become aware of the kind of questions the *ṛṣis* were asking, we might never come up with any answers nor understand their own answers when given. To clarify this point, some of the old Ṛg Vedic questions again.

I ask of you: What is the ultimate limit of the Earth? (sight and sound).
I ask of you: What is the central point of the Universe? (kinaesthesia, touch).
I ask of you: What is the semen of the cosmic horse? (touch, taste, smell).
I ask of you: What is the ultimate abode of Language? (sound).

It will be interesting to reread the answers given in 1.164 and notice how these answers have the immediacy of the instant present:

This altar is the limit of the Earth.
This Sacrifice is the navel of the Universe.
This Soma is the semen of the cosmic horse.
This brāhman (reciting singer–poet) is the center of Language.

IV

It is now time for us to face directly the hidden Dragon of the human body—*Asat*. It is now time for us to separate the heaven and the earth again in this present situation. For we are now ready to face the problem of human embodiment as presupposed by the sound–criteria of the Ṛg Veda, starting with a few remarks on the idea of *time* itself.

The idea that time and space are the two absolute and fixed coordinates that make sensation possible, is not only a necessary condition of Classical Physics, but it is also the underling condition of possibility for *human* sensation. The idea of the human body goes hand in hand with the idea of a duration in time and space which needs, for its own justification, that the ideas of time and space and the human body remain constant. The changes within this framework are only accidental, while nothing substantially changes, for the criteria remain invariant. By these criteria, man is condemned to one life, one body, one death, one personality. Man can be of several minds, young or old, as long as substantially he remains the same body. This idea of embodiment, however, is not itself a fact of the human body, but it has been made such a fact by the criteria of visual space, and the measuring of that space as time; space and time having been presupposed to exist prior to the human body.

On the model of sound, and by its criteria, the Ṛg Veda offers us a completely different picture. The space is the musical scale, and it is neither here nor there prior to song; space and song are simultaneous. Time, again, is not prior to the singer; and the singer is no other than the song; the singer's body shares its dimensions with the structure of the song. The human body is polytheistic, multiple personalities, as the body becomes the multiple perspectives it sings. Since the body remembers all its previous incarnations, and since the human body was born in sound and ruled by its criteria, its therapy does not lie in submitting it into psychological monotheism, but rather in releasing its lost memories, its silent music: The human body has the right to innovation and continuity.

For example, if we look for the Ṛg Veda to give us its idea of time, we find that there is no other time but the time which has been *made up*, sung, fashioned, created by a god, a singer, a sacrificial act. Only two late hymns of the Atharva Veda speak of time (*kāla*) as the absolute primoridal origin of the universe.[107] The Ṛg Veda, on the other hand, uses *kāra*,[108] in the sense of a successful moment (10.42.9); or more generally, *abhīka*, which means the instant–moment of efficacy, as in the fight between Indra and the Sun to prop up the heavens and the earth (10.55.1), or when the *Aśvins* run to help those in need; *abhīka* is used especially in the instant–moment of successful union in the heavenly incest of the Father and his Daughter (Sun and Dawn), (10.61.6).

Time appears as the dispersion of all form and name; the discontinuity of the *Puruṣa*, in the *puruṣaśūkta*;[109] the projections of *Varuṇa*, the *vidhatṛ* (organizer of time) who shot out the days like arrows;[110] or as continuous discontinuity, i.e., as an evolving primal 'desire' to 'look out,' 'become,' 'procreate,' as in the case of the *Hyraṇyagarbha*,[111] the golden germ, and the primeval 'desire.'[112]

The natural inclination of man to 'look out' at the world, yields the discontinuity of time described in 1.164; three heavens, the circular disk of the sun, the twelve spokes (months), days and nights, dawn, seasons, directions. This exteriorizing and dispersing activity of the 'natural inclination' of desire or of looking out, is corrected by Dīrghatamas, the moment he listens to the Word (*Vāc*). The whole dispersion becomes moment–centered presence and interior. 'What is *there* becomes interiorized the moment the voices of sound take hold of the onlooker,' as in stanza 21 or 37, where Dīrghatamas proclaims his awareness of being a portion (taken over) by the interior speech of *ṛta*.

The interiorizing of the activity of turning space (discontinuity) on the moment–centered time (the gathering of all energy) is the key to Ṛg Vedic man's eternity. Eternity is expressed with the word '*nitya*;' derived from the two particles *ni*– (in, en), and the suffix *–tya* ('that which is found in the place illustrated by the adverb or preverb'). *Nitya*, etymologically means 'found inside of.' Historically, it is also found with the meanings of 'proper to,' 'natural,' (7.1.17).[113] The only original 'space' in the Ṛg Veda, what is 'in,' what is really the 'source of,' is the undifferentiated and unlimited power, the infinity of space as described by the *Asat*. And this 'space' is anywhere.

The Language of Existence (the *Sat*) includes a further dimension of human life which may be described as follows: the individual, the society, the cosmos at large, are not three different entities, even though related, but rather society, cosmos and individual are all one *body*; this *embodiment* may be changed, modified, enlarged, made smaller, but in no way can it be radically gotten *rid* of.

The clue to the correct understanding of the above proposition lies in the following fact: the Ṛg Veda presents through the 'seers' a discontinuous, yet somehow unified totality of *embodiment*, where society and the world–out–there are only the 'extension' of the embodied–sensorium–structure of the subjects who conceived and realized the body that they were already *in*. The effort of those same 'seers' was directed towards building such a common body as would make human existence most communicative, pleasurable and likable.

There are two main ways in which cultures differ from one another. One (already mentioned in the previous section), is the over–emphasis of one mode of perception over others, and the limiting of human experience in terms of that same over–emphasis. The other is the way cultures act, or behave—implicitly or explicitly—in relation to the 'limits' imposed on the sensorium itself; that is, some cultures consider the bag of skin as the limits between subjectivity and objectivity, while others add to the natural senses the extension of instruments. All cultures will take a particular attitude towards the 'place' of contact between subject and object, i.e., the skin, or instruments, or a combination of sense–instruments. However, the election by a community for a certain way of perceiving in contrast to others, and for demarcating lines between individuals and society and the cosmos, is the result of certain criteria dictated by the subjective structures of embodied knowers. These criteria reveal objects and limits only as functions of the structures dictated by the embodied subjects. The structure of the embodied subject is mostly tacit, and it is only in relation to this tacit dimension that a community, a Nation, or even mankind, may be expected, to a lesser or greater degree, to live, feel, and in general constitute a common body.

The above notes may give us a glimpse into the importance that any community will give to the 'means' through which that community probes and extends its own sensorium for constituting its communal body. The *means* themselves constitute that embodiment. The human sensorium expands, and very soon the limits between bag–of–skin and world disappear. Examples of such events may be discovered by reflecting on the following: There is no visual space unless 'measurement' is accepted as a 'fact' of body involvement.

There is no visual space for blind people, yet audio devices may constitute such a space. A blind man may 'see' through his cane, not by feeling his cane, but by feeling the objects at the end of the cane.

The ear is extended through sound waves, the telephone, amplifiers, etc. The eye can see at impossible distances through television. Technology itself, as we know it, creates communal extensions of the senses for the embodied subjects who discover and tinker with it: subways, cars, cities, and nations. It is easy to see, with the above perspective, how difficult it would be to separate subjects and their embodiments through their own technology. It is easy to see the role of our own technology in having provided us with the most controversial 'body' in the history of humanity. Despite its luminous spots, our present body is polluted—the lakes, rivers, and air stink; incurable cancers grow–ghettos in the cities and alienation within and outside the individual psyche. There is little doubt that our present embodiment is, for the most part, a painful one. For some it has become so painful that hate has given place to a paranoic desire to destroy it, even at the risk of communal suicide.[114]

It has already been shown earlier that the Ṛg Vedic philosopher–poets were very much aware of this 'tacit dimension,' i.e., that the structure of subjectivity is the structure of the embodied knower, the subject; that is, of the *ṛṣis* themselves.[115] This embodied subjectivity of the *ṛṣis* constituted the Ṛg Vedic horizon of intentional inquiry, through the various embodiments in the means chosen for the exploration of the world. These means, as shown in the previous part of this chapter, were the different kinds of sense perceptions: organized around certain invariant criteria: the song–poems and the Sacrifice. Both were understood as simultaneous and as influencing each other's growth. Both constituted the Ṛg Vedic embodiment.

What is peculiar to the Ṛg Veda is the fact that this embodiment of subjective structures and of the means of exploration took the embodiment seriously enough to consider the subjectivity, and the objects discovered through that inquiring subjectivity, as a unity, one body. This body is as much subjective or objective at both ends (the end of the inquiring subject and the end of inquiry in the objects).

The distinction between both ends, subjective and objective, was understood by the *ṛṣis* as an apparent discontinuity—time, brought about by the sensorium itself and its discontinuous perceptions. These ends could be regathered in a continuous efficacious instant–moment, a space, by falling back on the infinity of an originating *force*, underlying—and found inside of (*nitya*)—all discontinuity.

The embodiment of Ṛg Vedic man was understood, therefore, as an effort at integrating the languages of *Asat*, *Sat* and *Yajña* to reach the *dhīḥ*, the effective viewpoint, which would make these worlds continue in their efficient multiple embodiment.

The structure of the embodied subject has the double–barrel effect of opening a horizon of inquiry and restricting what may appear within that horizon. The structured subject and its means of exploration have, therefore, an immediate effect on the activity of the community. It will be of interest to examine, even though only suggestively, the attitude of the Vedic seers towards action, individual or social.

There are two important elements to be considered for such an inquiry. One is the affirmation Vedic men made of life, as *ayus* or *ayu*, either as the individual principle of vital energy,[116] or as the universal principle of the vital energy;[117] both principles may be taken as identical with life or with its duration.[118] Similarly, this initial energy or power, may be found through words like *sahas*[119] (said of Indra, *Agni*, *Soma* and the rest), or *ojas*—creative energy—said of Indra[120] and *Agni*[121] and, in general, *māyā* (as already seen in Chapter Three). The other element to be considered is that the Ṛg Vedic means of inquiry is the whole sensorium and that, therefore, Ṛg Vedic activity affirms the whole sensorium's involvement in every instance. In fact, as seen earlier, the only enemies of the *Ṛṣis* are those who seem to try to reduce action to only certain theoretical aspects of sensing the world through a limiting viewpoint, sorcery, or dogmatic philosophy.

We have seen in Chapter Three a summary account of the type of *action* that the *ṛṣis* could tolerate. The *Ṛṣis*, as it appears, did not have any one action *per se* excluded from the total embodiment, but rather, they fought the reduction of action to only certain actions which might accrue lesser gifts than those they foresaw as gained through the Sacrifice, which had the whole society in mind. In this connection, it is interesting to note the attitude of sexual, or rather erotic freedom that they described and their multiple use of biological functions, sexual functions, rape, and even incest.[122] On the other hand, these qualifications have no meaning in a Western context and must be read in the Ṛg Vedic context. We may remember at this point that the sensorium, as used in the hymns, functions in relation to the insights and the viewpoint it might create in those partaking in the Sacrifice and ruled by its criteria. Sacrifice, in the Ṛg Veda, is not a renunciation of action, but rather, a renunciation of the limits of perspectives which interpretations accrue to the structured subject–object sensorium–, from the *Asat* and the *Sat*.

6

The Language of Images and Sacrifice (Yajña)

This One becomes the All.
R.V. 8.58.2

Agni, show your face, since it is Varuṇa's.
R.V. 4.1.2

The Sun is the face of the gods,
Of Mitra, of Varuṇa, of Agni.
R.V. 1.115.1

It is by their words that the poets
Pronounced to be manifold what is
Only One.
R.V. 10.114.5
1.164.46

We stated in Chapter Three that it is through the Sacrifice that the chant becomes human flesh. The purpose of this chapter is to develop this theme further. However, since this project rests on language for its description, i.e., the language in which we are writing this chapter, we must again remind ourselves that the *criteria* by which we read this language, are the criteria implied in the Ṛg Veda: the criteria of sound. As in the previous chapter, we will follow these three main clues to guide us in our investigation:

1) A unitary and indivisible originating power (*māyā*) moves in accordance with the movement of the Norm (*ṛta*) and appears wherever the chant sounds (*Vāc*);

2) This coincidence of power, Norm and chant occurs at any sound–point, any pitch being a possible tonal center for any kind of tonal structure.

3) Gods, heroes, Dragons, etc., are only the prototype (*pratirūpa*) and the embodiment of a multiplicity of perspectives (*pururūpa*) generated from a common origin (*sayoniḥ*), the musical octave, conceived as a field admitting many alternative structures (i.e., "tuning systems").

Through these clues, and by their criteria, we intend to focus on the Ṛg Vedic language of images and sacrifice. However, it might help us to reorient ourselves in view of what we said in the previous chapter.

The language of *Sat* made us aware of a particular cultural body reaching out for its own fulfillment and understanding. This reaching out, however, produced inevitable consequences:

a) The original unity and power became fragmented into a multiplicity of autonomous images, living gods and living dragons: autonomous bodies, human, divine, or animal.

b) Each and every one of these autonomous bodies becomes, in the Ṛg Veda, the space for multiple human *embodiments*, where the human body shares its dimensions with these autonomous spaces. Therefore, it is not the case that the *idea* of the body is previous to any form of embodiment; on the contrary, the embodied song–god and singer are the preconditions for any theory of embodiment. In every case, it is the movement of the chant and its duration that fixes the embodiment and its duration. In no case is it a *theory* of embodiment that determines the body of the Ṛg Vedic singer.

c) The reconciliation between an original source, which is one and indivisible, and the plurality and discontinuity of the autonomous images and spaces of the language of *Sat*, which are multiple, is brought about through the larger, all-controlling, image and language of the Sacrifice. In this sense, the language of the Sacrifice appears as the Fundamental Myth of the Ṛg Veda, regathering the multiple and secondary myth–images which appear in the text.

I will try to clarify the above points by making the following strategic moves: In Part I, I will show how the images of the Ṛg Veda exchange positions and personalities as the chant moves on. Their theoretical atomicity and spaces are created and obliterated by the chant. In this process of creating and erasing boundaries, the Language of the Sacrifice follows a reverse course in relation to the Language of *Sat*; i.e., the *Sat* follows a path of dispersion or exteriority, while the Language of the Sacrifice integrates that dispersion by falling inwards towards the originating and final efficient–moment (*ṛtu*) of the Sacrifice. In Part II, I will show how, on the one hand, the Image of the Sacrifice regathers all the images of the Ṛg Veda within itself, and on the other hand, how this regathering is an integration of the dismembered sensorium into an embodied moment–centered (*ṛtu*) embodied–vision (*ṛta*).

However, I need to add a word of caution to the Western reader. The only models we have that even distantly resemble the Ṛg Vedic Sacrifice are found in psychology, and particularly, in pathology; but to acknowledge the multiple personalities of the psyche in the terms of psychology, is to clinically condemn ourselves to schizoid fragmentation, and to implicate ourselves in a revolt against monotheistic psychology, in favor of a polytheistic phyche. Pathologically, things fall apart when the one becomes the many: breakdown and regression follow; a center cannot hold, and it splinters into multiple fragmentations. But if polycentricity is only a disease, and not also a cultural style, a condition, and an interpretation of experience found in culture, in the past and in our present situation, then all the freedom of contemporary man is reduced to behaviour control and genetic manipulation. Neither monocentricity nor polycentricity are the property of any method; rather, they are each styles the human body can choose for self–expression. Fundamentally, neither form of personality is radical to man, though man may choose to express himself through either, or both, or none. Both, as *ideas* of the body, are condemned to breakdown and regression; no idea of the body is prior to man and therefore prior to his embodiment.

However, from a cultural perspective, polycentricity gives us a clue to our present condition: pervasive nominalism; disorientation of the center; plural meanings; plural personalities; contradictory double–talk; the refusal to give definitions; ambisexuality; the cult of the anti–hero; the anti–establishment; a psyche detached, dismembered into separate body parts. Above all, polycentricity points out the sickness of the heart, which has radically lost its sense of direction. As my compatriot, Miguel de Unamuno, wrote:

> *In order to love everything, in order to pity everything, human and extra-human, living and non–living, you must feel everything within yourself, you must personalize everything. For everything that it loves, everything that it pities, love personalizes . . . we only love—that which is like ourselves . . . it is love itself . . . that reveals these resemblances to us . . . Love personalizes all that it loves. Only by personalizing it can we fall in love with an idea.*[1]

But psychic polycentricity in contemporary man is not a model by which to judge other cultures or other men. Polycentricity in contemporary society is only a symptom of a heart that has lost love for itself, and for the *idea* that held it together as monocentric; the idea that gave the heart its sense of direction. For contemporary society, polycentricity is the path of no return. As Montaigne remarked:

> *Whoever will look narrowly into his own bosom, will hardly find himself twice in the same condition. I give to my soul sometimes one face and sometimes another . . . all the contradictions are there to be found in one corner or another . . . I have nothing to say of myself entirely, simply, and solidly without mixture and confusion.*[2]

On the other hand, in the Ṛg Veda, polycentricity is neither the original nor the final condition of the human body–perspective; nor is it the result of the heart of man gone dry. In the Ṛg Vedic case, it is precisely the exuberance of the heart that creates multiple embodiments, canceling them out and re–creating them again in innovation and continuity. And if the path looks like a wandering course, an endless repetition, it is because the heart of the singer in the Ṛg Veda knows, like Plotinus would repeat later, that his path is the way of the circle. But these points, we hope, will become clearer as we proceed with our meditations.

I

Contrary to the Language of *Sat* (Existence), where we were dealing with names and forms, the Language of Images and Sacrifice (*Yajña*) forces us to focus on the activity (*kriyā*) implied in the movement of the chanted song. In its wake the movement groups and subgroups sensations under the general image of a god, a dragon, or a hero. The gods and dragons, together with the bundle of perceptions and actions for which they stand as prototype, succeed one another in discontinuous continuity; yet the chant moves on with stubborn repetition. Discontinuity in perception, the multiplicity of images, the polycentricity of voices demanding to be heard, sets the stage for the reconciliation of the language of images under the Language of the Sacrifice.

In a society made up of multiple tuning systems, plural perspectives, and a plurality of gods and dragons which the images embody, there is always the temptation to amputate the plural differences so that only one voice be heard. On the other hand, there would be those opposed to the dictatorship of one voice sounding singly, who would propose some form of compromise: let all the voices be heard as long as they all sing, more or less, the same song in a linguistic uniformity, on the model of the harmonically unified polyphony of Palestrina, Bach, and Mozart. Contemporary Western music has achieved something similar with its compromise of equal temperament.

But the Ṛg Vedic way and the Ṛg Vedic Sacrifice point in a different direction. Its philosophical grounding appears to be very solid; no compromise with the human body is possible unless the body is first reduced to an idea of itself. Yet this reduction can also be an alienation of the body from its source of perception, of life: For its innovation and continuity, the human body needs, not only to sing itself constantly through multiple perspectives, but it must also be aware that no perspective cuts the path of the song from going all the way of the circle to its radical, originating power. In the Ṛg Veda, the image of the sacrifice stands for this activity of eternal return; and this is the path the Ṛg Vedic seers chose for themselves, their society, their total cultural body.

We have already pointed out how the activity of *Vṛtra* and his associates is none other than to cover the possibilities of human action. His strategy, and the strategy of those sharing the *Vṛtra*–ideology, is to fortify themselves, through rational explanation and dogmatic action, into spaces of discourse which shut themselves out of the rest of human experience, i.e., the rest of the sensorium and its encompassing synthesis. The mortal enemy and champion of such strongholds is Indra. Indra's activity is none other than the destruction of *Vṛtra* (*vṛtrahan*),[3] and the destruction of the strongholds constructed by the *Vṛtra*–followers. In this sense, an aspect of the Indra activity goes under the epithet *pūrbhiḥ*–, i.e., destroyer of strongholds.[4]

As we saw in the previous chapter, the death of *Vṛtra* was not accomplished in one act forever, but had to be repeated constantly. R.V. 8.89.3 describes this idea as "*vṛtram hanati vṛtrahā*," (let the one who has killed *Vṛtra* once keep doing it again). The same idea is repeated by the constant fights of Indra against the allies of *Vṛtra*.[5] Indra represents all the powers within man to break through the chaos (*asat*), with *kratu*–,[6] *ojas*,[7] *māyā*,[8] vigor *vīrya*–, and *vāja*–(creative power).[9]

There is another sense of the power of Indra worth considering—*maghavan*–, all encompassing, in the sense that it is always available every time man is in crisis;[10] Indra is willing to bestow his own inspiring power, to use his mighty weapon (*vajra*), to save men and gods, by preparing for all of them the path of immortality.[11] In the Ṛg Veda, this activity of Indra–power is never put in action by itself, through sheer will power. On the contrary, the activity of the destruction (*śavas*) of Indra is always in association with his *kratu–* (intentional efficacy) and the whole embodied movement. See, for example, Indra's association with *Soma*[12] (taste, inspiration, vigor), and *vāja–*[13] generative power of plants, food, etc).

Indra's activity is prolonged in time through the maintained effort of his vigorous power—i.e., the times of the destruction of *Vṛtra*, but it turns back upon itself, with the full vigor added to his original power, through *Soma* and his intentionality (*kratu–*) to attain the 'moment of truth,' the 'critical moment,' the instant moment of efficacy, the instant moment of duration and immortality when the Sun, the Sky, and the Dawn are created (1.32.2–4) and Indra lifts the Sun from the ground of *Vṛtra* to the Sky, (1.51.4). Indra's activity becomes efficacious, because, through his action, he not only identifies himself with the intentionality of the *Ṛṣis* (10.29.6), but also, "he made firm a shaky Earth (men),[14] and "endowed the gods with his intentional powers (*sukratu–*)."[15]

A very distinctive characteristic of the Language of Images, viewed from the aspect of power and creative action, is that originally none of the names and forms of the Language of *Sat* can be differentiated; that is, both *devas* and *asuras*—the two opposing camps of the *Sat*—are the same thing, power. We saw earlier in the Ṛg Vedic texts how the gods are called both *devas* and *asuras*; what differentiates them is the movement of their intentionality—those restraining power: *vṛ–*, *dā*, and those operating for freedom of action *aditi*, from *diti–* (bind), and the privative *a*. In this manner, the *Sat* differentiates the two camps of *Vṛtra* from those with creative power, able to create according to *Ṛta*, the embodied order of the *Ṛṣis*, society, Cosmos. The many names given to those creative powers are seen to be essentially the variations of manifestation and differentiation created by the Language of *Sat*. Originally, of course, the power is only the same one, the original heat (*tapus*) out of which all creation emerged and was differentiated.

The Language of Images is an important step forward in establishing this original and final unity. The outward manifestation of the word becomes the internal regathering when the images themselves are considered in the functional character of what they are meant to do: return to the origin.

The main clue to this inner regathering in images of the outward movement of the *Sat* is given through *Vṛtra* himself. *Vṛtra*, as non–existence, comes from the root *vṛ–*, to cover up. However, when the action of creating takes place in the Ṛg Veda, it is from *Vṛtra*'s silence that this creation takes place. In this sense, *Vṛtra* derives from the root

Vṛt–, to "twirl, to turn around," and the same applies to the root *math–*, used in similar instances. This is important for the following reason: the complementary dialogue of the Ṛg Vedic way would be misunderstood if the *Asat* was taken to mean either, *a*) something negative in human experience, or *b*) something isolated—a lower disconnected space—from the human experience. It is not *a*), in the following sense: While the West has been too eager in its search for clear and distinct ideas, discarding whatever is not clear and distinct as unintelligible or as negative to human knowledge, the *Asat* affirms that 'undifferentiated' perception, that is, *obscure* (not clear and distinct) perception, is a positive fact of human experience. Neither is it *b*), for, the *Asat*, as the ground of perception, is human experience; *Vṛtra* is the possibilities of man. *Vṛtra in potentia* is Indra and the rest. Indra, the Sun, etc., *actu* are *Vṛtra*. With this clarification in mind, one can see that, in the *Ṛṣis*' mind, action and energy (or power) combine to make us aware of two ideas: An original space or ground—in logical terms, the absolute affirmation of all negation—and, different created 'spaces' which correspond to the 'phenomenal' world, the world of appearances; in logical terms, both affirmation and negation. The Language of Images will again negate the affirmation and negation of the Language of *Sat*, turning those involved in such an activity back to the original unity, the source of naming, etc. This turning is not, of course, a "return to the womb," but rather, a *turning–in*, a renewal full of insight and new perspectives. Light enters into darkness, noise into silence, heat into cold, etc. In any case, the activity of discovery and of return is the key to '*dhīḥ*,' the efficient vision–action.

Numerous texts in the Ṛg Veda will exemplify the above insights. I will try to select the most appropriate for further research.

The activity of "turning around" and/or "twirling"—what in Western terms we might call a conversion from one way of seeing into another, or a renewal of sensation—may be seen, for example, in relation to 1) the generation of *Agni* by *Mātariśvān* (i.e., *Vāyu*, the Wind) and 2) the rape of *Soma* by the Hawk (*Śyena* = *Agni*).[16]

The nature of the activity involved in both cases is the same, i.e., extracting from; turning around; twirling; churning, as applied to a liquid, the ocean, the original waters. *Agni* is produced, created, by twirling; *Mātariśvān* "twirls him from his ground (*budhnāt*), from the Buffalo's ground (*varpasaḥ*) where he lay hidden (*guhā santam*)" (1.141.3). R.V. 3.55.7 repeats the same idea: "although he became the first, still he stays always within his ground," and is "thus brought to us from the great procreator (*pituḥ paramāt*)."[17] In R.V. 3.9.5, *Mātariśvān* lifts "Agni here from below, who had been hidden (*tirohitam*) from us, brings from the gods him that had been twirled (*mathitam*). In R.V. 6.16.13, it is *Atharvan* who "twirled (*nir amanthat*) *Agni*, from the lotus (*puṣkarāt* which equals *budhnāt* as above),[18] from the head of *Viśva* (*–rūpa*), the seer (*mūrdhno viśvasya vāghataḥ*)."

Soma is also produced by twirling; the "Hawk twirls (grinds, *–amathnāt*) *Soma* from the Rock (*pari śyeno adreḥ*)," (1.93.6); *Soma* "is twirled from Heaven by the Hawk (*yaṃ divas pari śyeno mathāyat*)" (9.77.2); cfr. also 5.30.8 in relation to Indra–Namuci, "Indra . . . churned Namuci's head (*śiro dāsasya namucer mathāyat*)."

The Dragon *Makha* who is *Vṛtra* is "lifted up" by Indra in R.V. 10.171.2 "from his cavern he lifted raging *Makha*'s head (*makhasya dodhataḥ śiro 'va tvaco bharaḥ*)," the same head which in 8.6.6 becomes *Vṛtra*'s "*vi cid vṛtasya dodhato vajreṇa śiro bibheda* (bisected, decapitated)." In 10.171.2, there is a further hint of the same as, "the Sun, *Vaśa*, which had been hidden from the gods is produced as depicted in the previous stanza 2. In this way, we have that *Vaśa*, aided by the *Aśvins*, becomes the Sun (1.112.10; 8.46.33); that the cave, black skin, or hide, equates the darkness Indra hates (*indradviṣtām . . . tvacam asknīm*) (9.73.5); or the Serpent's old skin, as in 9.86.44, where it is said that *Soma* as "*Ahi*—the Serpent—creeps forward from the old skin (*ahir na jūrṇñam ati sarpati*)." Echoes of the same ideas are found in the Brāhmana versions where the serpents become the Sun, and *Makha*'s head; that is, *Vṛtra*, becomes the head of the Sacrifice.[19]

Makha as the head of the Sacrifice equates *Soma* as the same (*mūrdhan vajñasva*) (9.17.6), while in 9.5–6, *Soma* is assimilated to Indra, and *Prajāpati* explicitly and implicitly into *Agni* (1.13). In fact, *Makha* becomes the Sacrifice in 1.134.1; 8.7.27 and in 8.46.25. *Vāyu*, by himself, and the *devas* collectively, are invited to partake of "Makha's sacrifice (*makhasya davane*, being lavish)." *Makha* is also used of *Puṣan*, *Savitṛ*, *Maruts*, etc., in relation to "wrath," or that passionate action (which is what *Makha* really means).

The important point in relation to *Makha* is that, not only is he the Sacrifice, (or identified with it), but also, the Sacrifice is a willing action on his part: "Thou, *Soma*, go willingly (*krīluḥ*, which implies the same as *līlāvatārana*; that is, a willing sacrifice) as *Makha* pregnant with treasures (*makho na maṇhayuḥ*), lending the recitation its efficacious power (*suvīryam*)" (9.20.7).

Soma's identification with both the Sacrifice and *Vṛtra* is given in R.V. 5.43.4 "*bāhū . . . somasya ye śamitārā* (the root *śam* indicating the sacrifice, and 'these arms that give Soma its rest,' meaning the ground, *Vṛtra*)." The grinding of *Soma* is connected with the roots *vṛt–* and *math–*, and the descriptions of the obtaining of *Soma* as a rape or a theft indicate the fact that *Soma* was in the lap of *Vṛtra* (as in 10.97), long before the birth of the gods. *Soma* and *Puruṣa* are identified as the Sacrifice,[20] yet it is as "*Ahi*—the Serpent—that *Soma* comes forth from the old skin . . . and runs and plays," (9.86.44). *Soma* is also the Boar (*varāha*), as may be seen in 9.97.7.

The above notes may already suggest a clear direction in the Language of Images; that the 'ground' of all images is in the *Asat*, and that the return to the ground is through the Sacrifice. When the Language of Images looks for self–identity, it has to turn in towards the ground, but this understanding cannot be accomplished without the Sacrifice. R.V. 1.32 contrasts both aspects more fully than anywhere else: Indra dismembers *Vyaṃsa*. "*Vṛtra*, the first born of the Serpents, as a tree is cut up into logs,[21] and there he lies, emasculated (i.e., inactive, *vṛṣno vadhiriḥ*), divided into many parts (*purutrā . . . vyastaḥ*)" In R.V. 1.61.10, Indra cuts *Vṛtra* to pieces; "severs him joint by joint," (8.6.3); "using his bolt (*vajra*) like a carving knife (on the Serpent)" (1.130.4). In 8.7.23, the *Maruts*, perform the same operation (*vi vṛtraṃ parvaśo vayuḥ*).

Decapitation, dismemberment, and Sacrifice are also identified in R.V. 1.52. 10; 2.11.2; 2.20.6; 4.19.3. *Varuṇa* and *Ahi* are identified in 10.97.16 as is *Yama*, death. That the Serpents are of the same origin as the *Ādityas*, the Sun, is supported by R.V. 9.86.44; 4.13.4; 7.63.1; 10.49.7; 8.41.10; 8.19.23 and 10.63.4. What appears in the Language of *Sat* is no more than the impartite, whole, ophidian (*aparvan*) ground, the *Asat*. A unity described in terms of *tad ekam* in 10.129.2, or Integral Multiplicity (*viśvam ekam*) in 3.54.8, or the unity of the *Puruṣa* (person) and the *Vāc* (word), as in 10.114.5; 1.164.46; "uttered in unison," as in 10.71.3, or "separated distributively," as in 10.125.3. The First Sacrifice, the Sacrifice of the *Puruṣa*, the dismemberment of *Vṛtra*, *Agni*, as the head of the Sacrifice are in the Language of Images the same, and the narration would not change were we to exchange names. In fact, what the Language of Images is pointing out is that the stories made around dragons, gods, persons, events, etc., were stories of self–deception, for, originally and finally, there is no story at all; and this is the background of any story. This last point will become clearer when examining the meaning of the Image of the Sacrifice.[22]

II

The Image of the Sacrifice gathers within itself all the lesser image–myths of the Ṛg Veda; and this gathering within the fundamental *myth–image* of the Sacrifice is the integration of the dismembered sensorium information into an embodied moment–centered activity of maximized efficacy.

The Fundamental Myth of any civilization was defined earlier as "a large controlling Image that gives philosophical meaning to the facts of ordinary life; that is, which has organizing value for experience." The preceding pages of this book have all been moving towards the direction of the Image of Sacrifice in the Ṛg Veda as it performs such a function. The whole Ṛg Vedic life is centered in and around the Image of the Sacrifice.

The previous section of this chapter pointed out how, in philosophical terms, Ṛg Vedic intentionality was centered around the sensorium, perception, and the explanatory myth–images needed for an explanation of the same. The Image of the Sacrifice gathers within itself the whole sense–imagery to give it its own peculiar meaning and its own peculiar movement.

The Sacrifice (*yajña*), as itself or in the form of *Agni*—which is the same, is described in 10.5.6 as being stationed at the "parting of the ways, *panthām visarge*;" that is, between the two opposite forces of action or inaction, *Vṛtra* and Indra, the center "of the gods, great and small, young and old."[23] It is in the "midst of the (three) homes of Agni (that) the breathing swift–moving, living, restless enduring One"[24] is found, and that the "mortal has a common origin with the immortal."[25] It is the Sacrifice which is "the center of the Earth,"[26] for through the Sacrifice "the gods performed it . . . and through it all these powers reach the center (*nāka*) of heaven where the first performers (*sādhyāḥ*), the gods, are."[27] The different images of perception, either as confused or non-differentiated in *Vṛtra*, or differentiated as *Puruṣa*, *Prajāpati*, Indra, *Soma*, etc., all end up in the Sacrifice— through decapitation, dismemberment, interaction, or as the sensorium synthesis. The Sacrifice is *Yajña–Tantu* (the Sacrificial thread), on which all perception is centered,[28] or from which all perception flows, "where those seven rays sprung forth (*ātatāḥ*), there is my navel (*nābhih, amṛtasya*)."[29] *Agni*'s designation as thread–spinner (Spider, *aurṇavābha* and *ūrṇanābhi*) qualifies *Vṛtra*;[30] *Agni*, as in 6.15.16, "*ūrṇāvantaṃ yoniṃ kulāyinaṃ ghṛtavantam*;" *Agni*'s birth place, the altar, as "a creating, soft web"; the Sun, the seers "who spun the web with seven threads;"[31] and *Agni* and the Sun as the *Ādityas* "impelling all things,"[32] and *Viśvarūpa*, as in 3.38.4.

The spider's web image relating to the Sacrifice is repeated again and again in the Ṛg Veda as the "breath of the gods (*ātmā devānām*)."[33] In this connection, it is interesting to note the relation to the terms *abudhyam*, *suṣupāṇam*, and *āśayānam*, which occur in 4.19.3; all these terms have the same connotation of 'turning in,' as when the sun 'goes to bed at night,' 'couching' in the night, or hidden. *Abudhya* means primarily 'un-awakened,' *suṣpāṇam* and *āśayānam* mean both 'sleeping or inactive' and 'lying down.' In this sense, it is interesting to notice, in relation to the Sacrificial image, how in 1.103.7 "Indra . . . awakens the sleeping Serpent with his bolt (*sasantam vajrena abodhayo 'him*)." This characteristic activity of awakening is proper of the gods or *Agni*, the one that is "awakened at Dawn," the *uṣarbudh*, as fire in 5.1.1, or as sound "piercing the deaf ears of Life awakening him," as in 4.23.7–8, or of the Dawn awakening all the worlds, as in 1.113.4. The action of the Sacrifice of awakening the Serpent is an incitement to extroversion (*pravṛt*), while through the Sacrifice that same extroversion is converted (*samvṛt*), literally turning the darkness into (*udvṛt*) Light.

The Sacrifice, in the form of Agni, is made to appear as a discerning activity of knowing its meaning,[34] and also of knowing what it is that has to be sacrificed.[35] The meaning of the Sacrifice is obviously to enter the efficient center of all creative action, *Ṛta*;[36] for it is only through this gained center of efficacy of insights or viewpoints that gods are born,[37] or that these gods increase in efficacy.[38] Thus, the Sacrifice, in the form of Agni, becomes the central image of the Ṛg Veda.

The Sacrifice could be performed only with the help of Agni, and, therefore, the gods become dependent on him (*agnijivhāḥ*)[39] R.V. 1.94.3 and 2.1.13 clearly state that the gods approach the sacrifice through Agni (*tve devā havidaranti āhutam*); in 5.1.11, 6.50.9 and 7.11.5 the gods receive their share of the profits of the Sacrifice through Him. However, in order to counterbalance the possibilities of conceiving Agni as superior to or different from the other gods, or of separating him from his functional characteristic as the center of action and sacrifice, it is said that the "gods fashioned Agni for the sake of the Sacrifice,"[40] because "the gods realized the advantage of Agni's position and his ability,"[41] and that no sacrificial performance could be realized without him (*adhvarīyasi*).[42]

Agni is considered, for the sake of the Sacrifice, to be the first among the gods (*devaḥ prathamo yajñiyo bhuvaḥ*),[43] even though he is only the 'representative' of the gods (*viśve hi tva sajoṣasaḥ devāso dūtam akrata*),[44] the leader of the sacrifice (*yajñasya netā*);[45] and in general, since no sacrifice could be efficiently performed without Agni, he was named *hotā viśveṣām yajñānām*.[46] This going out to the gods and the gods turning in to Agni is emphasized in 10.20.6 (*sa hi kṣemo havir yajñaḥ śruṣṭīdasya gātur eti agnim devā vāśīmantaṃ*).

The Sacrifice, represented by Agni, is also the center of social life of the Ṛg Veda, and essential for the prosperity of the society,[47] and for the good of all (*asmai bahūnām avamāya yajñaiḥ vidhema*). Agni is the center of the creative classes of Ṛg Vedic society, poets, patrons, and priestly families;[48] but above all, Agni, and in Agni the other images of the sensorium, are Sacrificed.

Indra and the Sacrifice go hand in hand. Indra helps the Sacrifice (3.10.15; 3.40.3), and at the same time it is said that the Sacrifice has helped the growth of Indra (*yajño hi te Indra vardhano bhūt*), [49] or has helped his weapon (*vajra*).[50] It is precisely because Indra knows the meaning of the Sacrifice (*adhavarasya pracetaḥ*, 10.104.6) that Indra's energy flows in the right direction growing with the Sacrifice (*yajñavṛddhaḥ*), [51] and above all accepting the Sacrifice (*hotuḥ yajñaṃ juṣāṇaḥ*, 4.23.1).

Soma's strength and efficacy is entirely dependent on the Sacrifice, while the Sacrifice needs Soma for its own efficacy. It is interesting to note, especially for a Western culture which has just made a fad of drugs, that Soma in the Ṛg Vedic context is efficacious only in relation to the benefits of the Sacrifice. Soma is efficacious only when pressed, that is in the Sacrifice, not when bartered, pushed, or enjoyed as a means of escape. In fact, the Ṛg Veda would not accept the pushers of Soma within the fold of sacrificers, nor would it let anyone buy Soma and use it unless they had a supply for three years with them.[52] The Sacrificial function of Soma is stressed with epithets meaning the action of pressing the stones, as *adridugdhaḥ*,[53] *adriṣutaḥ*,[54] *adrisaṃhataḥ*,[55] *adrau duduhānaḥ*,[56] *grāvṇā tunnaḥ*,[57] *sutaḥ grāvabhiḥ*,[58] etc.

Soma, in relation to the Sacrifice, gathers in its image all the offerings of the sense of taste, though in itself it symbolizes "the offering among the offerings, *havir haviṣ ṣu vandhyaḥ*,"[59] "the center itself of the Sacrifice, *Ṛtasya tantuḥ*,"[60] and *ṛtaśya garbhaḥ*."[61]

Soma appears in certain texts to have been offered at the Sacrifice by itself, i.e., unmixed, strong and intoxicating (*tīvraṃ somaṃ*),[62] or mixed with other ingredients, like milk,[63] ghee,[64] and curds.[65]

Under the Soma Sacrifice, other words are used denoting the whole range of things to be sacrificed in relation to the sense of taste. These words relate to food; that is, food with a sacrificial function. In this sense, we have words like *iṣ*, *iḍ*, *iḍā*, *irā*, referring to sacrificial food in association with the Aśvins,[66] the pressing of the stones,[67] Agni;[68] and vice versa, the sacrificed food *converted* into an efficacious meal distributed by the gods, (*iṣaḥ*).[69]

Soma brings to the Sacrifice all the other sense references, like the Aśvins (*aṅgirassvantā*),[70] who also know the meaning of the Sacrifice and take its responsibility.[71] The *Maruts* associated with Indra and the Soma–pressing[72] are also brought to the Sacrifice;[73] as are *Rudra*,[74] *Pūṣan*,[75] and, in general, all the gods (*viśvadevas*), described as "*agnijivhāḥ*, the tongue of the Sacrifice,"[76] "eager for the Sacrifice,"[77] and "knowing the meaning of the Sacrifice,"[78]

The Sacrifice is the meeting place of the Dawn and the Sun; the Sky and the Earth, of *Vāc* (as Word, *gāyatrī*, rhythmic foot, *triṣṭubh*, unit of recitation, *akṣarena*, inspired syllable, and *vāṇīḥ*, seven tones of the musical scale)[79] and, in general, of all the gods. There is no better hymn to summarize the all inclusive aspect of the Image of the Sacrifice than R.V. 10.65. Stanza 7 condenses what we have tried to repeat with different texts:

The gods, whose tongue is Agni, with seats above in
Heaven sit with clear intention of mind in the center
Of the sanctuary.
They powerfully supported the heavens, they poured down
The waters. They, having created (invented, lit. begotten)
The sacrifice, they offered it of themselves.[80]

Agni, as the Image of the Sacrifice, is offered in the Ṛg Veda as the synthetic integration of the dismembered sensorium in an inward moment–centered activity, which alone can account for both efficacy in the cosmic body and immortality.

Agni is the great sacrificer (*hotṛ*), gifted with the right intention (*sukratu*), the right intentionality (*pracetas*, *pravidvas*, etc.), capable of piercing the mysteries (*cikitvas*), through his measuring power (*māyā*), through his concentrated thought (*budh–*), and through his wisdom (*viśvavid*). All this is possible because he gathers in himself the efficacy of the sacrificial science (*satyatara*).[81] Agni shares in the embodiment of the intentions of the great poet (*kavi*, *dakṣa kavik–ratu*)[82] because he knows (*vidvas*), and this knowledge makes his sacrificial act incapable of error (*amūra*). Agni is the embodiment of the efficient intentionality of the gods,[83] and his sacrifice is the only one which can confer continuous life (*viśvāyus*) or make mortals capable of living (*jīvase* = grant us that we may live), or grant immortality.[84]

Agni, as the Image of the Sacrifice, is the efficient center of the discontinuities of spaces of perception and time. He is the seer capable of realizing through his own performing power (*manasā . . . agrabhīt*), without obscurity of confusion (*apradṛpita*), the exact way of acting (*satya*) involved in the sacrifice.[85] It is the Sacrifice, properly understood, which in Agni becomes the connection, the link (*bandhu*) between efficient acts and discontinuous acts, between time and space, and between time and immortality.[86]

The significance of Agni as the Image of the Sacrifice is that all the previous atomic entities, names, and forms given by the Language of *Sat* are erased, and Agni regathers them into an activity (*ṛtu*) that is inward centered, i.e., a convergence of efficient, eternal acts or successions of acts. *Ṛtu*, like *Ṛta*, from the root *ṛ–*, to move, go, make, act, has the added suffix *tu–*, indicating an intention of making all that is dispersed converge in one efficient act, or in a succession of acts.[87] What is dispersed we know as the Language of *Sat*, names and forms; what becomes efficient, regathered, is the convergence, the turning–in of the dispersed activity of the sensorium. Agni is the maker of such efficient moments (*ṛtūn kalpayāti*);[88] these efficient moments, in turn, make the body of right acting (*satya* and *ṛta*), the *ṛtāvān* of 3.20.4. Agni, or the Sacrifice, is in command of the *ṛtu* on account of his organizing intentionality of the past and the future (*prapaśyamāna*),[89] his regathering the sacrificial acts in the moment–centered activity which the *ṛta* establishes.

Ṛg Veda 9.4–5 expressed the above in the following manner:

All the gods, with the same thing in mind,
With the same intention (keta) converge from
Different points (vi) into the unique kratu
(the efficient energy regathered in the
Sacrifice, that is Agni).[90]

Ṛg Veda 10.2 repeats in a most direct manner what is scattered in many texts:

1. *Fulfill the gods, replenish their desires, youthful*
Agni, you knowing the sacrificial moments (ṛtu),
Master of the moment! With the ministers of the
Moments (ṛtvij), Agni, you are the efficiency of
the sacrificers.

3. *We have also entered the path of the gods (sacrificing)*
To prolong our lives as long as we are capable.
Let Agni, who knows, show us the way to offer the
Sacrifice. He is the Sacrificer; the doer of sacrifices,
The builder of the sacrificial moments.

4. *If we stray from your path, since we are ignorant*
Oh gods, let Agni complete the undone, for he
Knows through which acts and their convergence
The path of the gods converge (in the sacrifice).

The above description of the Language of Images shows how the images and spaces created through the Language of *Sat* (the dispersion of the sensorium) regather themselves into a unique force–energy; an efficient centered–moment known as the Image of the Sacrifice. According to the

Ṛg Veda, this efficient instant of concentration and synthesis of dispersed energies is the key for conquering death and prolonging life; or simply for achieving immortality (*amṛta*). However, the Language of Images indicates a further philosophical dimension: The discontinuity of names and forms (time) becomes continuous when the instant moment is captured (when all the activities of the sensorium are regathered in the one center and origin of all energy, the original space, the *Asat*). Time, somehow, by turning on the infinity of the originating space (*Asat*), becomes immortal; from the immobility of the *Asat*, from the non–born (*aja*), immortality is gained. The gaining of this immortality is nothing else than the building of the *ṛtu*, the efficient moments and the *ṛta*, the common body of the Norm:

1. *Agni, the sacrifice on earth and in the Sun,*
The first born of Ṛta, received on this account
The name of dhaṣhyu (who knows his place).[91]

This space, this constructed place, is no longer the chaotic and inactive *Asat*, but the stable foundation (*dhāma*) of *Ṛta*, the true *yoni* (source): "I have covered all the world to regather the extended web of my creation. There, where the gods have attained immortality, all have started back on their path towards their common origin (*yoni*)."[92] This returning to the original infinite space of the *Asat* is no longer the return to inaction, but rather the result of action, an action leading to that illumined instant–moment of light (*dhīḥ*) where the "Father and the Mother meet,"[93] where "*Varuṇa*, *Aditi*, Heaven and Earth unite in a common nest,"[94] since, after all, "the mortal and the immortal have a common origin."[95]

The Language of Images depicts this moment (*ṛtu*) of Agni as "footless and headless, hiding both his ends" (*apād aśirsā guhamāno antā*)[96] i.e., immortal, as opposed to his personified presence in the Language of *Sat* as "footed," (*padavīḥ*).[97] This is the end of a journey where no one is there to ask the traveler from where he came or where he goes; yet the journey goes on. In sum, what the Language of *Sat* identified in terms of stories and persons, the Language of Image negates, for originally and finally, there is no story at all. There is only man's act of creation, becoming flesh *through* the stories of other men.

The Language of Images, however, presents some very interesting philosophical problems. On the one hand, the light–filled–moment of *ṛtu* is already created in accordance with a Norm, *Ṛta*. On the other hand, it is the *Ṛta* as a common body and Norm which is being built by the *ṛtu*, the perfect (*satya*) act of the Sacrifice. This apparent impasse is solved in the Ṛg Veda with its peculiar use and understanding of man's right to innovation and continuity; but for this to occur rationality might also have to take on many faces. It appears Ṛg Vedic rationality is not based on the narrow logic of appeal to premises and conclusion, but rather, on an appeal to a "community of listeners capable of understanding and of changing, or re–directing the movement of their song." This understanding of rationality leads to further interesting philosophical consequences. *Ṛta* becomes an objective Norm, not as the result of an imposed, i.e., dogmatic, law restricting or curtailing action, but rather as the embodiment of the *Norm* as discovered in a community of plural activities. *Ṛta* is the affirmation of plural bodies in a community ambiguous in a plurality of sensations, a plurality of decisions, and a plurality of explanations and descriptions.

7
The Language of Embodied (Ṛta) Vision (Dhīḥ)

Firm-seated are the foundations of Ṛta
In its beautiful form are
Many splendid beauties (contained).

R.V. 4 23.9

Let those possessed by Ṛta
Let down the Norm for universal ruling.
Let those who flow with the Ṛta, who uphold the
Norm, the leaders, overcome all opposing force.

R.V. 8.25.8

Reverence to the ancient Ṛsis,
Who first designed the Way.

R.V. 10.14.15

"There are those," Buddha proclaimed, "who say there is no *Way*. Yet all they have to do is cross the threshold." We have been following the movement of the Ṛg Veda unawares that by following this movement we were following a collision path. The movement of the Ṛg Veda, the trajectory of its path, is pointing straight at the heart of the stillness we never dared to move: the human body. By the *power* of our own meditations through the Ṛg Veda we come face to face with our present most radical problem: the fact that while we have moved heaven and earth, the creatures of the deep and the ghosts of the mind, and while we have traversed the paths to the moon, we have never dared to set into motion our own beliefs about the human body. The movement of the Ṛg Veda is aiming straight at the heart of this stillness; for the path of the Ṛg Veda, as we have seen earlier, is none other than the power to still what moves and set in movement what is still.

It would indeed be a radical failure of the way of these meditations if, at the end of our journey, the human body—this body I carry with me while writing these meditations—remained still, unchanged, undivided, and as silent with its memories and imaginations as when we started this journey. Nor is it arbitrary that the movement of these meditations has landed us straight into the blocking rock of the body. Our path would be no path if we could not traverse through this stumbling block. For while we are experiencing these meditations, what we take to be the human body is watching itself drying up in complete insensitivity, at the mercy of a mind and a heart which have lost their sense of direction; a human body deprived of memories and imaginations, deprived of history, and controlled by a theoretical mind capable only of marking theoretical ways as theoretical fingers keep pointing in every direction. It is time to still the mind, historically moving for so long; time to set the body in motion, which has been historically resting for so long. Let this body, for so long historically silent, break open, release the earth, the sky, the gods; let it become music again.

What we call the language of Embodied (*Ṛta*) Vision (*Dhībhiḥ*) will open for us the context of the Ṛg Vedic *way*. Our strategy consists in describing the following:

1. The relation between insights (*manaḥ*), viewpoints (*dhībhiḥ*), and power: the power to create (structure) or the power to manifest or communicate (language).

2. The embodiment of effective viewpoints (*dhīḥ*) in a common body or Norm (*Ṛta*) in such a way as to establish universal laws for practical action (*satya*).

3. A description of the *Way* as flowing from these meditations.

I

In order to avoid misunderstandings, we must remember once more that we are guided in our speech by the criteria of sound. We need remember also that we are primarily focusing on what we are doing, rather than on theory and communication. When we talk, therefore, of "seeing," "light," or "viewpoints," in relation to the Ṛg Vedic *dhīḥ*, we must immediately remember that sight, in the Ṛg Vedic text, is ruled by the same criteria as sound; that sight, like sound, is not only an efficient power, but it is also time in the same sense that sound is time.

Therefore, *dhīḥ*, as vision, is the power of the movement of light as time. It opens up spaces, lends things and gods their glance, their vision; the sight of things dependent on the movement of light as time. The singer's word makes manifest this movement. Thus, it is capable of making present the space–time–movement context which gives sight to things, shine to appearances. It is the power to bring light into things, move them with the breath of life and filter light into the darkness. This is the *Way* of Vision (*Dhīḥ*): It does not define things, but rather, the manner by which things unveil a whole world–context. Those who know the *Way* are wise, the *ṛṣis*, because in every point they may see the world at a glance; and every point conceals the possibilities of opening up new visions of new world dimensions of space, time and movement.

With his voice, the singer announces the *Way* of a movement of time which opens and closes spaces and distances and lends things their glance as it moves. Sound in motion is the very illumination and institution of this vision; for it is not the case that the sounds the singer makes move; rather, the *singer* moves, and the listener with him, as one tone succeeds another.

The *dhīḥ*, the vision, which the *Ṛṣis* offered to their society and its members, is not only a goal for the mind, but it is also an integration of the whole human sensorium into an activity which is not content with knowing; it is intent, rather, on *becoming* that which it knows: the creator, the means of creation, and the creation.

With these clarifications in mind, we may now resume where we left off in the last chapter: the description of the activity of the sacrifice as *ṛtu*. We translate this word here as instant–moment, in order to clarify the movement of *dhīḥ* and how it leads to the embodiment of a Norm, the *Ṛta*.

Ṛtu, and other words used in the Ṛg Veda indicating time, like *kāla*, *kāra*, *abhīka*, etc.,[1] stand for the same kind of thing: an instant–moment of efficient creativity. As we saw in the previous chapter, *Ṛtu* comes from the root *ṛ*–, to move, go; and the added suffix *tu*–, indicates the intentionality of that movement, or the duration of its completion. In translating *ṛtu* into English, the words instant–moment have been chosen for the following reason: *Ṛ*–, as instant, will stand for the convergence of all the powers (*ayus*) which make that creation possible; while the suffix *tu*–, moment, will stand for the actual new creation emerging from the act of *ṛ*–, (*viśvāyuḥ*). As we saw in Chapter Six, what converges to the *ṛtu* is exactly what makes the *ṛtu* efficient, that is: the whole world, the whole sensorium and its capacity for new creations and new expressions. The concentration of energy brought to the Sacrifice is made necessary by the activity of measuring (*māna*), or of structuring experience in the limited way that any conceptual structure can. The structure does not reach its own fringes and new structures are needed for explanation; yet, the intentionality of man (*ketu*, *pracetas*) makes it possible for this capacity of measuring experience to converge upon itself and see its own limitations, as well as its relations with other measured experiences. It tries to transcend itself through an effort at total presence—the *dhīḥ*, which emerges from sacrificing the experience as structured, or turning the structure into human flesh. This total act of presence is what the *ṛ*– stands for in the act of the Sacrifice.

However, a curious thing happens as soon as presence, (its totality) is manifested: presence is only a flash, an instant of communion, and it is also communication, that is, a new creation. As such, it is no longer an instant, but a moment which takes form and manifests itself in a new form—name, a partial statement. However, the whole activity involved in the *ṛtu*, and *a fortiori*, the epistemology and ontology of the Ṛg Veda, is conveyed in both the *ṛ*–, or the instant flash of enlightenment; is so joined to the *tu*–, or the moment created, that the *Ṛṣis* did not even think of separating viewpoint–action–media–senses–objects. The subjective (?) *ṛtu* is as much a part of the subject as of the media, as of the objects; and the subjective energy is equal to the life *energy* (*ayus* = *viśvāyuḥ*).[2] Interiors and exteriors disappear. Instead, there is an activity which becomes embodied in a universal Norm, *Ṛta*; that is, successive, efficient acts—*ṛtu*—which become the practical body of acting for a community.

I would like to add a few remarks on the kind of activity in the Ṛg Veda which appears as the condition *sine qua non* of its own social preservation. This kind of activity, when viewed in its functional aspects of individual and social integration, leads to the conclusion that it is the same kind of activity which philosophy claims for itself. In other words, Ṛg Vedic philosophical activity is a perfect model for philosophical activity at any time, by any individual or society.

The clue to understanding Ṛg Vedic philosophical activity lies in the words connected with 'power,' or with the concentration of 'energy.'

The Ṛg Veda, as we saw earlier, is full of expressions denoting power. In fact, all creation is the result of powers and the clash of powers. However, a closer examination of such phrases as '*sunuḥ sahasaḥ*,' son of power, or *sahas*, *dakṣa*, *saci*, *ojas*, *kratu*, *tejas*, etc., will reveal the kind of activity the *ṛṣis* foresaw as the practical scope of their philosophy.

One of the characteristics of power is that because of it, all the 'individual entities' of the Ṛg Veda unite, or are gathered: they all are "representatives of power," or "sons of the gods," (*devaputrāḥ*),[3] or just its manifestation (*devas putrāsaḥ*).[4] In this way, the *ṛṣis*,[5] the priests,[6] the sacrificers,[7] immortality,[8] and Agni, hidden in the wood, are united and discovered.[9] It is with a view to "power" (*sahase*, in the dative), that Indra is born,[10] and that he is associated with Soma in "order to show his conquering power;"[11] and it is through his power "that Indra manifests all his *indriyāni*," that is, Indra becomes Indra.[12]

It is in relation to power that manifestation takes place, of Agni (*sahantamaḥ* = most powerful of all),[13] *Bṛhaspati*,[14] *Maruts*,[15] the Sun,[16] etc. It is through power that such manifestations are what they are. In other words, what in the original ground of perception, the *Asat*, is *amitaujaḥ* "of unmeasured creative force,"[17] in its manifestation becomes Indra, "pulling away the wheel of the Sun born with *ojas*,"[18] yet capable of forming 'unions' (*ekibhava*–); that is, a new unity to continue the power of creation.[19]

We could continue the list of comparative texts to greater lengths, yet the few examples given are sufficient to indicate the direction of the Ṛg Vedic mind.[20] We could summarize this whole section by relating the meaning of such a phrase in the Ṛg Veda as *sūnuḥ sahasaḥ* which is applied to Agni,[21] as son of power,[22] to Indra,[23] to the gods,[24] to Soma,[25] etc. It is true that the origin of the gods is the original force of the ground, the father or the father–mother combination; yet when the activity of the son, be they gods, *ṛṣis*, the Sun or Soma, returns through its own power to the ground by the Sacrifice, then the son "becomes his father's father."[26] In this activity of the power to create and the search through intentional structures for new creations, (which of course implies a return to the ground), the *Ṛṣis* understood the kind of philosophical activity which would keep their worlds going eternally.

The summary of the Ṛg Vedic intentional life was already anticipated in the Introduction to Chapter Three. The significant point to make now is as follows: every vision (*dhīḥ*) carries concomittantly an act of creation which can only be effective if that vision coincides with the original viewpoint that created the original world. In other words, no efficient creation is possible unless it shares in the original *dhīḥ*, the original viewpoint of the first Sacrifice. By creating structures of knowledge to see the world in such a manner, the doer of this activity becomes the efficient vision and its concommittant creation. The vision–sharer embodies—becomes—the world of his creation. This philosophical activity of integration is not only a formal understanding, but integrates the formal in a body of practical Law, the *Ṛta*, which establishes the Norm for the exact way of acting (*satya*).

II

The whole movement of interpreting the Ṛg Veda rests in capturing the movement of *Ṛta*: the *Way*. In fact, the most significant reason for many of the misreadings of the Ṛg Veda, is that *Ṛta* has escaped understanding, or has been identified with some form of *subjective* (?) effort. That is, subsequent Indian philosophy, has found and developed individual kinds of activities similar to the one we have described as the *ṛtu*, in such words as *nirvāṇa*, *mokṣa*, meditation, etc., where the individual is taken for granted as being equal to our Western idea of individuality. We have not really found the criteria of individuality, nor the sound model on which the *Ṛta* of the Ṛg Veda stands for its movement; the truth of the matter is that *Ṛta* disappears with the Ṛg Veda, though it is always presupposed in Indian life and philosophy.

However, *Ṛta* is perhaps the most significant contribution both to practical reason and to social acting which Indian Tradition has to offer.

Ṛta comes from the root *ṛ*–, to move, to go, meaning that which is already in movement, going or gone. It is the world created by *Varuṇa*,[27] and in general, it is the result of the sacrificers.[28] It is also a given world, already made; and in this sense, already a tradition and a gift (*rādha*) resulting from the first sacrifice which separated the heavens and the earth and opened the free spaces (*varivas*),[29] thus redeeming man from the anguish of the darkness which surrounds him from everywhere (*vīdvaṃhas*).[30] It is in *Ṛta*, as the embodied tradition of man, that Ṛg Vedic man finds the source of his faith (*śraddhā*), his guiding light, his guarantee that the Norm works and is effective. Examples of this insight may be seen in R.V. 9.113.3; 9.1.6; and in 10.151:

1. *By faith is Agni kindled, by Faith his oblation*
   Offered.
   Full of happiness we rejoice in Faith.

3. *Just as the gods had faith even in the powerful*
   Asuras, make this wish of mind come true for
   Those who are generous in the Sacrifice.

4. *Protected by Vāyu (wind), both men and gods increase in*
   Faith by sacrificing.
   Men gain Faith through the instilled desires of
   The heart and become richer through Faith.

5. *Faith in the early morning, Faith at noon we*
   Implore, Faith at the setting of the Sun.
   Faith, increase our Faith.

Ṛta offers Ṛg Vedic man two most important aspects from which to guide his life: a) it is the store of all that has been rightly formed,[31] (*sukṛta*), and b) it is the guide for action of all that can be formed and integrated within its cosmic form.[32] As *a*, it becomes a common body of Law, a Norm; as *b*, it is a guidance for exact action (*satya*).

Ṛta unifies the whole activity of all the characters of the Ṛg Veda according to its Norm: Agni extends the Earth and Heaven according to *Ṛta*,[33] he sacrifices according to *Ṛta*,[34] he guides his chariot according to *Ṛta*;[35] he is the guide to all those searching for *Ṛta*;[36] in fact, Agni is the first born of *Ṛta*,[37] the creator of *Ṛta*;[38] for he knows *Ṛta*'s meaning,[39] is able to open its path to me,[40] and holds the paths of *Ṛta* opened through the Sacrifice.[41]

Mitra–Varuṇa make man aware of the *Ṛta*[42] and show man how to cross over to the *Ṛta* from darkness.[43]

The path of *Uṣa*, (the Dawn) is the path of *Ṛta*,[44] its horses are yoked to *Ṛta*,[45] since the Dawn was born of *Ṛta*[46] and the Dawn and Night show man the path of *Ṛta*.[47]

Indra's activity is to lead man to *Ṛta*, for only through *Ṛta* can he liberate what was hidden in the Cave. Even his intoxication with Soma, the increase in his own vigor, is only the sign of his approaching the path of *Ṛta*.[48]

Aditi holds *Ṛta*, and thus gives birth to all the gods. The Rivers rush to *Ṛta*,[49] the waters flow from *Ṛta*, *Vena* shines in *Ṛta*.[50] *Ṛta* flows from *Dhenu*, the milch–cows,[51] where the sacrificer finds *Ṛta*,[52] and so does *Ilā* (light).[53]

Bṛhaspaṭi finds *Ṛta* by voicing *Ṛta*.[54] The *Aṅgirasas* destroy the mountain (*Vṛtra*) through *Ṛta*,[55] for they learned to voice their songs from the bow–string of *Ṛta*,[56] and so they destroy the Cavern through *Ṛta*[57] and allow the Sun to ascend to heaven through *Ṛta*.[58] All the gods (*Viśvadevas*) know the path of *Ṛta*;[59] they drink in the streams of *Ṛta*,[60] and in general, there is no effective thought which is not born of *Ṛta*,[61]—the only way for the "Cows"—light—to enter *Ṛta* is through *Ṛta*.[62]

Soma is also born from *Ṛta* and returns to *Ṛta* roaring.[63] It is in *Ṛta* that men may profit from Soma,[64] while Soma's use is made right through the intentionality of *Ṛta*,[65] and so Soma engenders *Ṛta*[66] and his boat goes straight to *Ṛta*.[68]

The Ṛg Vedic seers were very profuse in making clear that the *Ṛta* is both a Norm established from old (*ṛtaṃ pūrvyam*),[69] and also an inspired way of acting leading to the same kind of efficacy (*ṛtasya tantuḥ* or *ṛtasay dhārā*),[70] as a thread to be woven or a stream to be followed.

The first seven stanzas of R.V. 1.164 give us the vision of the first Sacrifice and of the continuation in the Tradition within which the poet finds himself immersed. Numberless epithets repeat the same idea: the *Ṛta* is the store of *dhīḥ* (*ṛtasya dhītiḥ*),[71] the home of *Ṛta*, of the Norm (*ṛtasya dhāman*);[72] it is also the *yoni*, the origin,[73] the seat (*pade*),[74] the navel (*nābhih*),[75] the womb (*garbhaḥ*).[76] Numberless other epithets give the idea of an action in accordance with that Norm: *Ṛtayate* (desire of *Ṛta*),[77] *ṛtayini* (in search of *Ṛta*),[78] *ṛtuthāḥ* (in accordance with *Ṛta*),[79] for those who know *Ṛta* (*ṛtajñāḥ*),[80] or possess *Ṛta* (*ṛtāvān*),[81] or are full of *Ṛta* (*ṛtāvarī*),[82] or go on increasing in *Ṛta* (*ṛtavṛidhau*).[83]

While *Ṛta* appears in the Ṛg Veda as a Norm and path for action, *satya* is practically reduced to mean precisely the exact way of acting which the *Ṛta* demands; that is, acting according to the Norm. In no way may *satya* be translated as any kind of formal agreement between the mind and the objective world. In the Ṛg Vedic context, its meaning can only be deduced from the Norm, which the *Ṛta* offers for an effective way of practical action.

Examples of the use of *satya*, which mostly appears accompanied by *Ṛta* in the same hymns, suggests this interpretation we are just offering. See, for example, 1.20.4, where it is said that the *Ṛbhus* (the spokesmen of *Ṛta*, the fashioners of the gods) act according to the Norm in their mantras, where they are called *ṛtūyavaḥ*, or moving according to the Norm (*Ṛta*). Other examples may be seen from 1.105.12: "the Oceans have impelled *Ṛta*, the Sun has extended *satyam*," that is, acted as ruled by the Norm. In 6.49.6, it is stated that "the poets are those with an ear for the Norm and by expressing it (*satya*) maintain the world and create new ones." R.V. 7.49.3 repeats the same idea in regards to *Varuṇa*: "King *Varuṇa* moves among the waters looking down on those who act according to the truth (*satya*) or falsehood." The same may be found repeated in 9.113.4 in relation to Soma: "Shining with the light of *Ṛta*, and doing the exact action (*satya*) Soma flows for the sake of Indra."[84] The relation between *Ṛta* and *satya* is also indicated in 4.51.7, where the Dawn is said to have released its movement from the *Ṛta* (*ṛtajātasatyāḥ*); or in 1.145.5, where Agni is called wise (*vidvān*) because he knows the path of *Ṛta* (*ṛtacit*), and is therefore truthful (*satyaḥ*); or in 7.76.4, where the Fathers (*pitaraḥ*) who know the path of *Ṛta* (*ṛtavānaḥ*) speak words that sound true, are effective (*satyamantrāḥ*), because through these words they set the hidden light in movement and give birth to the Dawn. The same is said of *Mitrāvāruṇa* in 1.152.1–3, for they too with their thunderous voices bring from the darkness the Dawn, for all beings and as a herald to the sun.

The exact (*satya*) action the *Ṛṣis* had in mind is none other than the action flowing from the Norm (*Ṛta*), which itself was born from the Sacrifice (*yajña*) of structured worlds (the *Sat*) which were made manifest through the power (*māyā*) to make possibilities appear hidden in an undifferentiated sensorium (*Asat*) organized by the criteria of sound, and on which the Ṛg Vedic society rested. But this interpretation of *Ṛta* opens up interesting suggestions and possible corrections of misleading paths for both Eastern and Western interpretations of philosophy.

Indian Philosophical Tradition has been explicitly presented by both East and West on a model of individuality exclusively Western, as an individual effort to gain liberation. This isolation of the individual from the community has been overemphasized in certain aspects of both Indian philosophy and Indian life. Buddhism, for example, insisted on finding liberation away from the world in monasteries; yoga emphasized the individual effort to reach *mokṣa*; Vedanta emphasized the unification with Brahman through the *jivan*, the individual self, etc. In many ways, the criticisms and labels given to the East by the West—such as escapism and some sort of mystic experience reserved for a privileged few—appear, at first, correct. The social–embodied dimension of Indian philosophy has never been fully formalized or insisted upon, despite the implicit acceptance by all Indian Traditions in philosophy of tolerance for each other's views and for mutual discourse and dialogue. In fact, this tacit dimension of mutual dependence of one philosophical system on another, and of the individual on the society as a common reservoir and body of experience, has mostly remained implicit and taken for granted by the followers of the various philosophies of India. In the Ṛg Vedic instance, the case is different and it is here, perhaps, that the statement for tolerance and mutual dependence is first made and made so strongly that no posterior philosophical system felt the need to overemphasize it again. The *Ṛta*, as the common body of Law handed down from earlier generations, accounts for both the continuity of vision (*dhīḥ*) and of action in the community. The *Ṛta* also accounts for the laws of practical reason of their community, and for their understanding of rationality and rational argumentation.

Ṛta, as presented earlier, stands as the body of the Norm, the accumulations of practices, customs, goals, and rules of survival for a community within which individuals are born and foreigners accepted. In this sense, the *Ṛta* is the moving body of the social group, of the embodied community. As such a body, it presents two distinct characteristics: it is a continuous body—i.e., it presents continuity; and it is a body which can be changed and transformed—discontinuity—through the action of that same community. Yet, what no member of the community may ever do is completely rid himself of such a body. In this sense, we see in the Ṛg Veda that, though the continuity of the intentionality of the *Ṛta* exists, there are also changes and mutations in that same body through the particular activity which the *Ṛta* demands or encourages its members to perform, i.e., the *ṛtu*. At times, we see one family's god as more prominent, at other times other gods predominate; at times, one of the members of the sensorium is more prominent, at other times, another member.

To account for both, the continuity and the discontinuity of the *Ṛta*, the embodied Norm, one needs to understand the Ṛg Veda's handling of rationality and rational argument; that is, of formal and of practical reason.

We have interpreted the Language of *Sat* as the dispersion of the sensorium, and we have seen how this dispersion regathers itself in the Sacrifice. The *Ṛṣis* received from their *Ṛta* the belief that experience, and the resulting viewpoints, are the result of constructions. In their tradition, they also received the kind of meaningful experience that they had to construct in order to act efficiently in a community beset by a multiplicity of sensations and experiences. In principle, no experience is possible if, philosophically, the constructions leading to such kinds of experience are not possible; such a condition would result in the partial, and perhaps total, negation of philosophical activity itself. Therefore, since all experience, and *a fortiori* philosophical experience, is the result of an activity construed on certain conceptual structures (formal aspect), and since, in turn, these structures are the result of a way of viewing the world (practical decisions), it will follow that all experience is both practical and reasonable; that is, it is the result of practical reason. The formal aspect of experience is always subsumed by a decision of practical life, or practical reason.

I will try to exemplify the above with Kant's formulation of practical reason and its understanding and use in the Ṛg Veda.

> *Practical principles are propositions which contain a general determination of the will, having under it several practical rules. They are subjective, or maxims, when the condition is regarded by the subject as valid only for his own will, but are objective, or practical laws, when the condition is recognized as objective, that is valid for the will of every rational being.*[85]

A few pages later Kant rounds up his understanding of pure practical reason with the following formulation of the categorical imperative:

> *Act so that the maxim of your will can always at the same time hold good as a principle of universal legislation.*[86]

It is obvious from his distinctions of subjectivity and objectivity, and from his use of 'maxims' and, 'laws,' that Kant gravitates under the understanding of the categorical imperative that is imposed on him by the model of Classical Physics and its narrow viewpoint of selection on formalizable experience according to that model. The subjective is a maxim; the objective becomes a law. The first is valid for the individual will; the latter for the will of *all rational men.* This inner division within man and his isolation from the community we know, from experience, is arbitrary and contradicts experience itself. Any member of any community knows that there is hardly any purely subjective rule, and also that there is no human way for him to know when he is dealing with an objective and universally valid rule. The communal behavior out of which the individual's behavior is initiated, accounts for the lack of arbitrariness in his own will and for the principle of action of the community or at least of some part of the community. It could account for the whole of the communal principle of action if its members decided to accept it as such.

Kant's understanding of rationality in his categorical imperative, opens a more delicate philosophical problem; rationality involving decision and action. Kant, in the grips of classical rationalism, took the sciences as a model for human acting, thus leaving little room for elaborating any human idea of rational decision; practical reason is the result of a formal truth, either certain or probable. Truth, however, is furnished arbitrarily on a 'model' which already conceives of one's ideas as different from, and, therefore, conformable to, an objective reality. To be reasonable, in this perspective, is no more nor less than to assert one kind of conformity or to present another kind with such clarity and distinctiveness as to compel us to admit and to submit to the evidence; an evidence that takes for granted the existence of criteria, values and norms already accepted by those listening to the arguments, and who are thus able to judge the soundness of the argumentation.

However, this understanding of rationality does not fully answer the factual situation in which the philosopher is involved when arguing for or against his case. If the philosopher, addressing his audience, bases his arguments on principles already accepted by his audience, then he commits a *petitio principii.* If he is questioning or going beyond the principles of his audience, then the philosopher has changed the earlier meaning of rationality. Rationality in this latter sense has taken a different perspective. Though it still appeals to reason, it no longer rests on the restrictive understanding of reason as the discoverer of formal truth, but rather, it has become the discoverer of reasonable principles of action for the group of listeners or all mankind; that is, for a present concrete audience, and for a hypothetical universal reasonable audience. If reason is understood in this latter sense, then reason takes on some form of dialectics. It is involved in dialogue and in context dependencies. Practical reason, thus understood, would then be a *proposition* of Norms of action such as can be understood by any rational being, yet it would never constrain human acting by becoming an *imposition* of any one particular way of understanding rationality.[87]

The practical reason of philosophic discourse is not just that it is discourse *about* discourse, but also and principally, that it is the *activity* itself of discoursing. When one focuses on philosophic discourse as the activity it is—this being a practical action—it also shifts the understanding of the 'rational.' Action is involved in decision making; but if rationality is concerned only with the truth, then practical reason has no room for decision making, and must always yield to the truth. As it is in practice, practical reason goes beyond the truth of any formal context insofar as it *has* to justify itself, i.e., to justify a decision on the best reasons available to the philosopher. The best reasons, however, are always linked to the philosopher's world view, which, when decoded, will give us his philosophy of the world. Since we have a considerable amount of irreducible philosophies, it would appear that not one single practical decision could be labeled rational unless a pluralism of philosophies becomes an integral part and condition of rational discourse. And once we accept philosophical pluralism, we have to accept pluralism of sensations, the necessity of dialogue and communication among the different philosophical systems, and the possibility of certain integration. We also have to accept the resulting viewpoints emerging from such dialogues and, therefore, the possibility of viewpoint shifting through the philosophical activity of *dialogue–ing*. We would also have to accept the fact that rationality of practical life integrates the formal aspects of experience and that it is always dangerous for man's safety to reduce his practical life to only that life which is formalizable according to the model of formal reason. Finally, we would have to accept that in practical life and action, a unity is regained which the sciences tried in their formalizations to separate; that is, in philosophic discourse there is a union—inseparable—of speaker, his viewpoint, his means of communication, his world and his reason. Audience, speaker, and means of reaching each other become united in discourse, as they are in practice, because they are inseparable in each instance. In contrast, a formal system does not tolerate outside change or interference, for all its elements are constituted at once and accepted without discussion. Philosophic discourse, in action, establishes a unity and a union which, though unbreakable, may undergo changes according to the reasons of both the speaker and the audience. Philosophic activity must be opened to the rationality of its audience, which in many ways negates the philosopher's own rationality, but becomes, through that activity, a complementary increase of his own experience and reason, leading to increased insights and viewpoints, more comprehensive philosophies, and more efficacy in philosophic and human communication.

If we read the Ṛg Veda in retrospect as a model of philosophic activity, we can see how some of the propositions made above are confirmed.

The *Ṛta* accounts both for the continuity and discontinuity of the text itself, if understood as the *active* Body of a Norm, and not only as a formal search for truth.

The activity which generates such an effective *Ṛta* starts as an open possibility of the power of manifestation in the *Asat*—as *māyā*, *tapus*, etc. This activity (*Ṛta*) may reduce itself to in–activity (*nirṛti*) by constraining itself to only the possibilities of one framework, or it may turn into a dynamic activity (*satya*) which generates insights and integration by contrasting opposing and complementary frameworks and therefore acts efficiently in them. This possibility of acting according to *satya* is what the multiplicity of the *Sat* offers. Yet the *ṛṣis* were able to point out a further dimension of philosophic activity by bringing out the fact that man's action is guided by his internal images. These internal images must be regathered in a concentrated effort of total sacrifice (*yajña*) through the act of *Ṛtu*. Theory must turn to song; it must be performed. This perfect act of *ṛtu* generates the original vision (*dhīḥ*) which generates efficient creation (*Ṛta*) and guarantees man's and society's continuity or immortality (*amṛta*) and innovation.

We have stated many times that what philosophers *do* is as constitutive of philosophy as theory and communication. It is entirely up to the philosopher to decide upon which one of these three aspects of philosophy he is going to direct his attention and focus upon. But by this decision alone, the philosopher commits himself to one way of doing philosophy as opposed to another. Furthermore, by this same commitment he also demands from others what they ought to do when they do philosophy. In practice, communication, theory, and action, are philosophically distinguishable but inseparable. The problems of contemporary philosophy are as old and contemporary as the Ṛg Veda. There are those obssessed with reducing language and communication to a ritualistic per–formance: the recitation of other peoples' sayings. For these the Ṛg Veda has the satyrical hymn of the frogs, R.V. 7.103:

1. *Hibernating throughout the year*
   Like brāhmins keeping a vow,
   The frogs raise their voices,
   The same voice Parjanya sound.

2. *When the rains from heaven fall,*
   As on shriveled skins lying in a pond,
   The music of the frogs sound in unison,
   Just as cows with their calves low.

3. *When yearning and thirsty, yet soaked*
   With water at the start of the rainy season,
   They seek one another, like a son his father,
   And with rapture in the voice they greet all.

5. *One repeats the word of another*
   Like students echoing the voice of the master;
   Together they form a chorus
   When at rain–fall loudly they croak.

There are those, on the other hand, who advocate philosophical pluralism, yet they are committed to a monotheistic form of reason. They, either claim impotence in understanding any discourse about polytheistic reason, or subsume polytheistic reason under the dialectical movement of monotheistic reason. Philosophers should be aware of the fact that giving reasons does not constitute philosophy; but rather that reasons are given because a philosophy is already presupposed. Reasons are ultimately given to preserve one god while rejecting others. On the other hand, the Ṛg Veda shows the way of polytheistic reason through the path of prayer; through prayer one god is now alive, and now another god. For it is only through this polytheistic rationality made chant and prayer, that the regions between the Earth and the Sky are filled with the whole flesh of man without amputations and dogmatisms, with directions for the heart, and memories for the imagination. The gods are not destroyed, they only give mobility to the moving body of man as it lights up with reason the empty spaces between Earth and Sky which surround it at every new step of its path. The reasons—prayers—offered by the *Ṛṣis* to travel from *Nirṛti* to *ṛtu*, from possibility to the perfect Sacrifice, are propositions for reminding the community to keep doing the kind of action which keeps the community moving. The *Ṛṣis* were interested in a program of action which would, of itself, be efficient. This activity is, of course, not formalizable, but the spaces of discourse within which it appears may be formalized (as will be done in Appendix I). In this sense, we may say that the rationality of the *Ṛṣis* is implicitly formal and explicitly practical. It becomes the audience it faces and sounds its voice; and in so doing, it also uncovers the power by which it is a discoverable reason: It breaks open the multiple contexts through which it moves between the Earth and the Sky. But discovering the Ṛg Vedic rationality involves the practical decision of watching out for one's own rationality. Philosophers may take up the challenge and be reasonable—follow the paths of reason—or they may impose their own formal and linear path of rationality and thus destroy all human communion. In any case, the philosopher has to be immediately aware, when faced by another, that the movement of his way of doing philosophy must of necessity be on a collision course with the way of the other. And this is precisely what the context of the *Way* in the Ṛg Veda is trying to point out: all philosophic movement, if it is authentically philosophical, is a movement within the context of the *Way*.

III

THE WAY: BREAKING THROUGH THE EPISTEMOLOGICAL INVARIANCE

There is always the danger of talking about philosophy and to philosophers as if they were the only humans capable of acting according to reason. The fact of the matter is that all human action, sublime or stupid, lyric or prosaic, is done according to some reasonable plan. Man is radically and universally the interpreter of his own life. The context of the *Way* is a universal problem man faces at every step of his human way. And man's human way is always a whole context of silence, mute presuppositions, beliefs, and hidden criteria, of which the words he utters, or those he reads, are only the *consciousness of* which he is aware, but which also unveils a whole other consciousness he *counts on* in order to speak or read the word.

Every verbal gesture one makes, every word that one speaks is a movement within movement: a sound within a context. The verbal gesture, the word, moves; and through this movement, something other than itself is signified: the context. We may focus on the verbal gesture, on the word, and build a metaphysics of reality grounded on it and its relations to other words, (see Chapter Two of this book). Or we may focus on the movement from which the verbal gesture or the word draws its significance: the context. In brief, it might appear that man or philosophers may have a choice: language prescribes meaning to the world, or language draws its meaning from the context of a world. But this choice is only an appearance, or an imposition. And the reason for this lack of choice is very simple: man's body, including his memory and imagination, is an historical product. The silent context becomes human structure; ideas and beliefs become human flesh. Man's emancipation lies precisely in his ability to break the barriers imposed on his memory and imagination by any abstractions which serve to reduce the human body to only the movements of a theory, and deprive man from the whole historical movement of which his historical body is the visible path.

The historical background of which the body of man, his memories and imagination and even his human flesh is made, is the invisible field (context) which lends visibility or voice to any movement or sound of visible–audial historical man. The historical background is not *in* space and time because the silent field is neither temporal nor spatial. Only with the appearance of historical man do space and time arise as a field of action within which things are oriented or related. Human activity opens up this silent field and becomes historical only insofar as something happens, and something happens only insofar as it becomes historical. But the fact that the body of man is radically historical condemns man to a historical path from which no theory can save him. Man's dependence on history, his dependence on the *other* for his own emancipation, is the dependence of man on his own body and his ability to make flesh of his meanderings through the earth.

The reason for man's dependence on history is simple. History is the silent background of all of man's memories and imaginings. The silence is not empty: it is the totality of interpretations by which man at one time or another oriented and orients his life. But by introducing interpretation into life, man made interpretation reality, too. But reality, in human terms, means that the body of man made interpretation his own flesh, and whether man remembers or not, whether he wants to remember or not, man's body stretches as far as man's history. But man's history is as immediate to man as this text of the Ṛg Veda, this page, this line, this word, or this other man or woman confronting him. History is the immediate *other*.

The *other* is a whole world–dimension of space, time and movement. He is also all my present possibilities. I may accept the whole movement of his path, or I may reduce his movement, and therefore, my own possibilities, by falling on my knees and bowing my head to the still ritual of the monotheistic word.

The slice of history which the *other* makes present to me is only one of the historical possibilities of which my human body is already made up. It is only one possible field of signification. The reason for this is that the other may be so close to my own flesh that there is no possibility of any *transposition* of fields of experience. We both might be sharing the same theoretical umbrella, and in a way, the same body. A document like the Ṛg Veda, on the other hand, makes us aware that audial, visual and tactile experience may be synthesized in terms of one of the others. A particular gesture inscribes in its movement a particular structure in the world. It makes visible a particular space–time context within which things appear in significant relationships. This particular space–time structure becomes the context in terms of which all the fields of experience in the human body are synthesized, and interpreted. From a cultural perspective, this means that underlying all the fields of experience, there are various possibilities of space–time and movement structures: different ways of historically turning interpretation into human flesh. The body becomes as many different interpretations of itself as there are space–time–movement structures, and the plurality of these is what makes human embodiment, not only problematic, but a source of constant human crisis. The human crisis indicates the time for a new move, while the problem lies in knowing the direction that the movement should take.

It is an historical fact that man lives by theory; but it is also an historical fact that the absolute identification of man with any theory is a radical sickness of man. From an historical perspective, the human body has been many structures, a plurality of interpretations of itself. Each one of these structures of the human body has lasted as long as the theory held. But while the theory died, the human body could never reject the flesh that once was and forever is. What we call human crisis is the result of an effort to absolutize a theory of the body of man on the body of man, demanding thus that the body cancel out all its historical memories and imaginings. For any theory imposed on the body of man, any image of man imposed on the historical body of man, has itself as the *limit* for the memories and imaginings of man. The body of man is reduced to theory, and his vital way is cut off from reaching its historical origins. Theoretical man has, of necessity, to be sick—radically sick, and precariously alive.

From an historical perspective, it is of crucial importance that we do not presuppose that all fields of experience *have to* be synthesized in visual terms. It is equally important that we assume the possibility that a particular space–time–movement structure may be made present by any field of experience. Above all, we must remember that, from an historical perspective, whatever particular space–time–movement structure we decide to interpret our bodies by, that particular structure becomes human flesh. For example, it is not the case that the human body *is* an organism; but by identifying the human body with the idea of the organism as the particular structure of the human body, that is what the human body *has become*, with all its victories and crises. But historically, the idea of the organism as a context–structure for the human body was later than other contextual structural interpretations of the human body: the human body shared a musical context–structure before it identified itself with the idea of the organism, and the body does not forget these memories without sickness of self–amputation.

The tension between the historical memories of the human body and the demands that the human body be identified with one particular body–structure is further aggravated by a methodological requirement of all human theory and communication; the simple need to have to keep one variable constant—historically resting, while the other variable may be moving—historically moving. In the case of the human body, we decided to keep the body constant, while allowing the mind to move or change. Thus, we have the present proliferation of mind and consciousness expansion, with its need to presuppose that the idea of the body remains constant. But by doing this, all we have done is to reduce the body to an idea, an abstraction which cannot change without simultaneously bringing down the whole mind–body structure. From a scientific viewpoint, it is not sufficient that the current interpretation of the body is *verifiable* in clinics and laboratories, but further, this interpretation must not be *falsifiable*. Yet, the present human condition, the super abundance of the mentally ill, of the psychosomatic sick, etc., points precisely to the absolute falsification, not so much of the method, as of the decision to reduce man to the theoretical body–structure now in vogue: to keep the method constantly invariable. The theoretical way is a way of no return, and so is the immovable method. The memory and imagination of man is sick within its own theoretical confines. The body is clamoring—through the voice of its own sickness—for a way to return to itself; and it is precisely this faint and cracked voice of our own present sick body that unveils for us other silent dimensions we already are, only that we have momentarily forgotten.

Here, once again, we must return to the *Way* of the Ṛg Veda. The separation of the Earth and the Sky, like the separation of the mind and the body, arise on the basis of a common signification which silently allows the separation. This undifferentiated silence, a cluster of mute presuppositions, makes possible the possibility of this separation, either by the criteria of sound or the criteria of sight. To the knowing eye, or ear, the silence reveals itself pregnant with shining possibilities. This silence is the sounding silence of a world, and its wondrous voice is music.

When a *ṛṣi* sings, a god dances, or Indra kills the Dragon, the silence is not only made audible but also visible. The Ṛg Vedic singer lends audibility by way of sound, or visibility by way of a gesture or an image, to a context or field which is constantly tensed with possibilities and broken up by silence, tone and rhythm. What the Ṛg Vedic singer is opening up for us, as much as for himself, is a *Way* which separates and unites and repeats itself through continuous unions and separations. Ultimately, the singer and seer of the Ṛg Veda opens up a *Way* which allows us to see the context within which the whole Ṛg Veda moves. Following this way, the Ṛg Vedic word follows a movement which has the power to make its own way. Once in motion, the word marks a way which by the very movement of its sound opens a region between earth and sky, thus disclosing the background which lets the earth and sky be separated. It is the journey from the Non–Existent (*Asat*) to the Existent (*Sat*) and back, through the Sacrifice (*yajña*). The word can lead directly to its target like an arrow, or open the way between earth and sky like a prayer; it can also fall to the ground because it does not know the way. But the word that knows its path, like an arrow, or like a pair of yoked horses, whether in song or prayer, is understandable because it shares the same movement and freedom which opened the way between the sky and the earth, or killed *Vṛtra* a thousand times. The word is wind, fire, breath, and blowing; it is not an abstraction, but it is the very breath of the poet, the singer, the god and the dragon. The context of the *Way* is the breathing of the word within a movement which is one with the movement of the sounding ways of the Ṛg Vedic world. It is the moving of the breath of the world, of the wind that blows the fire, which spreads light and inspires the singer to move in the ways opened by the path of the song. However, the context of the *Way* cannot be understood without sharing in the original activity, in terms of which the original text of the Ṛg Veda was chanted: the criteria of sound.

It is not my intention at this time to involve myself and the reader in a formal discussion on music. There are others better equipped to do so.[88] My only concern here is to make some significant points to help us follow the *Way* of a language ruled by the criteria of sound. My remarks are primarily directed to an apparent contradiction implied in the very notion of the *Way*. This contradiction may be formulated in this simple form: If any form of life has, as a radical element of its reality, a human interpretation, then the movement of the so–called *Way* cannot transcend its own theoretical barriers. The *Way*, any way, is a non–exit human situation. Existentialism would be right, and man would be condemned to despair, insensibility, sickness unto death, or to a blind leap into a blind faith. In this view, the journeys to the East are only desperate leaps of faith into the unknown. For the East, by these same criteria, is made to appear as the therapeutic kingdom where the impotent of this world find solace in numbers. It is the instinct of the herd, rubbing wool against wool, proclaiming a gospel of happiness containable only within a bag of skin in complete alienation of the world. Philosophically, these people have never moved, regardless of their geographical travellings.

To understand the *Way*, in a general Eastern sense, and in the particular sense of the Ṛg Veda, we must again emphasize the criteria of sound by which the *Way* was understood by these people. The East, like the West, acknowledged, as we have seen earlier, that in order to have any form of human experimental observation, in a primitive or a contemporary form, one variable must remain constant while varying another. Thus, an object, nature, the human body, had to be conceived as historically resting, while the observer, the subject, the mind, or consciousness, as historically moving. The resting invariant is a presupposition for any theory, communication, prediction and control of behavior. Without this precondition, science, the arts, even human communication is impossible. As we shall soon see, the problem arises, not so much from the method, as from the decision to reduce to the method the decision–makers: man. In order to submit man to absolute control, he is required not to see the criteria by which he is controlled; he is required to follow only the way of the demands of any theory and its language, and only as far as the theory allows him to go.

But the fact that theory demands of man to do something, even if it is only submission, the fact that man can do even that much, also opens the possibility that man may transcend theory altogether. But then we are forced to place theory within a different historical context: the context of sound.

By focusing on sound as historically derived from different cultures, and particularly the Ṛg Veda, we can hear it beginning, progressing, and ending. Sound is thus, primarily, movement in time. By extension, the singer is time made chant or music: the singer is history. But sound has a spatial aspect to it. As such, it is a theory, and thus linked to human memory and imagination. Sound as space, as theory, may be transformed, imagined, remembered, as time sequences of sound within a visual space of theoretical patterns; or *vice versa*, the theoretical patterns may be deduced from actual embodied gestures of the human flesh of sounds culturally forgotten. Human memory may thus project pictorially a musical composition on an imaginative plane, and even write it down on paper. Melodies may become horizontal lines; harmonies may become vertical groups. Or they may become Tantric Yantras, or Ṛg Vedic

Yantras, as a clear example of this metamorphosis of musical time into pictorial, theoretical and visual space. However, and this is the important point, musical memory, musical theory, musical space, can only find expression and become human time within its sonorous medium of a temporal order, if the spatial image, the spatial theory is to become music again. In order to actually transform the image into music, in order to transcend theory without forgetting it, we must perform the music again, and thus re–establish the temporality of sound by turning theory into music, memory into human flesh.

The *Way* of the singer, by the criteria of sound, becomes an experienced order of continuous recurrence: musical rhythm within the womb of the musical scale. Rhythm in sound emerges as a grouping of durations wherever groups and patterns succeed each other in a continuum of time. This continuous recurrence, the eternal return, is simultaneously interpreted by the eye, the ear, the touch, the heartbeat, respiration, and the course of the seasons. It is the breath of life itself which knows its own way. It is the dawn lending sound to the light in its path across the sky. It is the path of the sun following the wing of eagles across the sky. It is the singer's voice which gives audibility to the movement of this world. It is the strength of Soma quickening Indra's pulse to kill the Dragon again and again. It is the power of the world's path which the power of the singer's song makes present by releasing again with his song the power of creation.

In music, rhythm is understood as a structural grouping in time. But rhythm must not be reduced to meter. Meter is an imposition on music of concepts of order. Metric order may be part of the composition from its outset, or may be added in performance, or may be imposed by the ear of the listener accustomed to certain expectations; but the metric order of a musical composition is not necessarily self–generated. In vocal works, it may be determined by the text; and in every case, it will have to be discovered historically.

A typical example appears with the music of ancient Greece and Rome: In today's music, the various motifs conform to an *unchanging* meter and its *regular* beats; in the music of ancient Greece and Rome, each motif had its own particular *beat pattern*, and thus, *determined* the meter. In any case, no theory of harmonics may substitute for the historical discovery of the criteria by which music became one form of music as opposed to another; for it was by these criteria of music, that the body of man became now one flesh, now another. Furthermore, without the historical mediation of the criteria of sound, by which man both imagined and lived his worlds, there is no eternal return, and therefore, no emancipation for man's memory and imagination.

Alas, we reach the end of these meditations painfully aware that the themes we have just initiated need, not only to be further developed, but need, above all, to be executed, if all the talk about human emancipation or human freedom is not to remain a wasted human breath. Musicologists and psychologists may contribute to this human task, but even they will fail if the *Way* of emancipation is not included as the most radical, immediate, and urgent discipline in any program of education. Education may perform many tasks for man, but unless it performs the task of setting man free, education will do the opposite: hitch man to the spinning wheel of ideology, desensitization, ignorance and suffering. This is a trip of no return. One need only look at the body of contemporary man and woman for the verification of this situation. But this verification will lead us into a new project. At this point of our own path, however, we are just content with issuing promisory notes in the hope that someone else, maybe even ourselves, might have the power to cash them in at a future age when these hymns of the Ṛg Veda are chanted again.

In sum, therefore, what is the singer's *Way*, the human *Way*?

In a most radical sense—at the root of all human flesh—the *Way* is the power to sing the world, and to make this song human time, human flesh. The *Way* is the ability and power to see that what in our current vernacular we call the mind is as much a body–perspective (an embodied–vision) as what we call the body. It is the ability and power to see that the ideas we interpret ourselves by become our human flesh, and that what we call the body shares with those ideas their dimensions. The *Way*, therefore, is an on–going journey of body–perspectives within the field of human history. But every historical meeting–point is a confluence of irreducible directions. The *Way* is the ability and power to train the body, to make the body ready, to share the dimensions and directions of every perspective it encounters in its human path. It is the ability and power to body–lift itself up to the perspective of every song, thus turning theory into human flesh. It is the ability and power to turn every song into human time.

Since the movement of the *Way* is always an embodied movement, from its origin to the present day, the *Way* is a constant feast for the memory and imagination of the human body. For in the wake of its song, man may recover all the memories forgotten. For memories and imaginations are also human flesh, and their forgetfulness is a conscious and painful amputation of man. The *Way* is the ability and power to recover in song memories forgotten. It is the power to separate the Earth and the Sky and sing to the Dragon that made the separation possible. It is the ability to make time to build images of man and gods, and it is also the ability and power to cancel them by turning them into new songs.

It is the ability and power to create, to wait for creation to populate the earth, and then to listen to the voice that would set the power of creation in motion again. It is the ability and power to break through any epistemological invariance that confines the memories and imaginations of man. It is the power to create song, invent human life, move any invariance that stops the singer from turning his memories and imaginings into music. It is the power to fix the mind—which has been historically moving for so long, and release the memories and imaginations of the human body—which has been historically resting for so long.

The *Way* is the power and ability to move what stands still, and still what moves. Four-dimensional man is neither this man nor that, this woman nor that; it is the ability and power to enter the *Way* so that this man or that, this woman or that, this world or that, may live in innovation and continuity. For it is thus that the wheel of the *Way* moves on eternally.

APPENDICES

Appendix I

On Reading the Ṛg Veda

THE FORMAL LOGICAL STRUCTURE OF THE LANGUAGES IN THE ṚG VEDA

For the sake of clarity, elegance and simplicity, I will try at this time to bring out the formalized logical structures which the dialectics of the Ṛg Veda imply. It is obvious that this formalization is not made explicit in the Ṛg Veda. It is also obvious that this formalization has nothing to do with *the chant* of the Ṛg Veda, but only with *discourse about* the chant in the Ṛg Veda. The reason for bringing it out in the open now is because of the implications it has for understanding discourse or language about other peoples' discourse or language—in this case discourse about the Ṛg Veda—and in a general sense, on account of the implications it has about philosophical discourse in general.[1]

In order to proceed systematically, however, I will summarize here some notions about language and logic which I have presupposed all through this book.

a) In the Ṛg Veda, we understand Language as embodying a pre–conceptual understanding of an all–embracing, undifferentiated energy and source of human activity, which the activity (*kriyā*) of the later grammatical Sanskrit verb expresses and reflects.

b) The native speaker is thereby equipped with an *intentionality*, a possibility of *conceptual systems* and of *purposive action* which enables him to understand and organize experience in the above sense.

c) Language as speech forms one or many sublinguistic systems of *a* and *b*, in the sense that it *has* to express itself through *atomic subjects*, *atomic objects* and *artificial limits*, which, in a sense, distort the pre–conceptual understanding of Reality of *a* as the One undifferentiated activity "with no name," (R.V. 1.164.46).

d) These linguistic subsystems or languages, may, if taken at face value, determine associated conceptual systems, purposive action and new intentionalities, producing as a result, new realities and new facts about the nature of these realities and of their internal and external relations.

e) Grammar, in the perspective of *c*, is not a function of Reality but only of languages.

f) Logic, in any sense of the word, is not a function of Reality but rather, an arbitrary tool of languages, either to establish internal relations within any one of the languages, or for dialectically combining languages as in *c* with Language as in *a* and *b*.

g) Ṛg Vedic logic is called complementary because it combines sub-linguistic systems among themselves (that is, languages), and these with Language, in such a way that the doer of such activity, and because of the activity, transcends sublinguistic systems into Language and 'vision,' as intended in *a* and *b*.[2]

(Note should be taken that what started in this description as a pre–conceptual anticipation, becomes in the final round, a vision which is no longer conceptual, but the result of experience; and it is itself an experience, in fact, an empirical one.)

With regard to proposition *a*, the following clarification is in order: There is no contradiction in the proposition which states a 'pre–conceptual language,' if Language is understood, as in the Ṛg Vedic context, as simply "the power of manifestation of all that is name and form (*nāma–rūpa*)," and *pre–conceptual* is taken in the sense that it operates in the inquirer or community of inquirers as a vector of inquiry, a heuristic goal, an anticipated horizon, to be arrived at through the activity of experience (as opposed to conceptual knowing) and of mounting viewpoints. The latter activity is the result of contrasting frameworks that interpret experience.

It should be further clarified that in the above understanding of Language, proposition *b*, can only be qualified as indeterminate, in the sense that no one action, intension, or possible concept or sets of the same, may contain or define what Language is, in the sense of *a*. In fact, Language understood as in *a* and *b*, is a heuristic anticipation which can never be closed by any of the languages describing it. Language, in the above sense, is only to be reached as a viewpoint gained through the activity of contrasting perspectives. Its only test is experience; its capacity of manifestation and communication, or acting back in the commonsense world, i.e., its efficacy.

It should, therefore, be a clear fact that Language, in the above sense of *a* and *b*, does not generate of itself any one framework, unique and irreformable. Rather, it is responsible for a self–correcting activity, which formulates, criticizes and changes frameworks, in the wake of its own heuristic goal. When a language, in the above sense, is sufficiently complex, and embraces a large enough slice of human experience, or even in principle at least, the whole human experience, we then have a tradition. The Ṛg Vedic case, which manifests itself through an historical family of conceptual frameworks as formulated in propositions *c* and *d* is such a tradition.

In summary, Language as in proposition *a*, may be described as "a heuristic anticipation of a reachable goal, which establishes structures of systematic inquiry guided by sets of canons and embodied in a pattern of human exploratory behavior." When Language is formulated, we no longer have Language, but rather a complete and closed set of semantically linked descriptive predicates internally related and forming one or several sublinguistic systems, or languages as in *c*.

We may, then, define a Language, L_x, of any sublinguistic system as:

L_x = {*p; p is a meaningful and correctly used sentence in a unified linguistic domain 'x'*}

Language, then, is the lattice sum, i.e., the least upper bound, of all these languages, L_x, L_y, etc., under a partial ordering '$\rightarrow$' which has the interpretation $L_x \rightarrow L_y$ if and only if, (p) $p \in L_x$ implies $p \in L_y$, but not necessarily vice versa.

Consider the following different languages of the Ṛg Vedic text:

Let L_A = *the language of Asat (Non–Existence)*
L_B = *the language of Sat (Existence)*
L_C = *the language of images and Sacrifice (yajña)*
L_{ABC} = *language as the embodied (Ṛta) vision (dhīḥ)*

This is true where A, B, and C represent the specialized Ṛg Vedic contexts appropriate for the correct use of the language L_A, L_B, and L_C, respectively, and ABC represents the wider Ṛg Vedic context. L_{ABC}, then, is the sum of the languages L_A, L_B, and L_C that are appropriate to the subordinate contexts A, B, C; it is itself the Ṛg Vedic Language with the widest context. It is also, of course, a philosophy, in the sense that it is the result of a philosophical activity carried to its efficient limit.

Figure 1 is an imaginative set–theoretic aid to express the relations among the languages of the Ṛg Vedic text. Each point in the diagram represents a sentence in a language. The circles represent the different contexts, A, B, C and ABC. L_A and L_C have sentences in common, and so have L_B and L_C. Thus,

$$L_A \to L_{ABC}$$
$$L_B \to L_{ABC}$$
$$L_C \to L_{ABC}$$

but

$$L_A \nrightarrow L_B$$
$$L_A \nrightarrow L_C, \text{ etc., etc.}$$

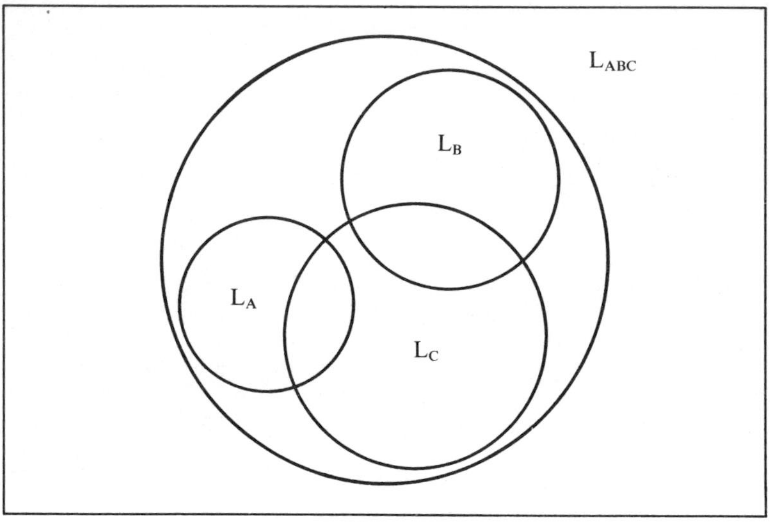

Figure 1
Set-theoretic model of the lattice elements in the Vedic dialogue.

L_A (*Asat*) and L_B (*Sat*) are languages generated by two different Ṛgvedic perspectives. Moreover, we suppose that no statement of L_A is a statement of L_B. L_A and L_B are disjoint.

Let L_C be a third language implying a third linguistic context C, within which L_A and L_B have some ground in common. Let L_A and L_B, then, each have a non–vacuous intersection with L_C. We suppose, moreover, that L_C contains sentences not in L_A and L_B. L_C, in fact, is the Language of images through which L_A and L_B can enter into dialogue. In L_C, the unifying activity is that described in Chapter Six and Seven as the *ṛtu*. The *ṛtu* of itself produces the efficient vision called the *Ṛta*, or L_{ABC}.

L_{ABC} is the new Language resulting from the activity–dialogue among languages L_A, L_B, L_C. These last are now seen as subordinated languages, *complementary* to one another within L_{ABC}, in the sense defined by the lattice below.

Consider the set of complements (L'_A, L'_B, L'_C) which we propose to define in the following way:

$$L'_A = (L_{ABC} - L_A) \cup L_C$$
$$L'_B = (L_{ABC} - L_B) \cup L_C$$
$$L'_C = (L_{ABC} - L_C) \cup L_A \cup L_B$$

The structure of the lattice is represented by figure two. A partial ordering implication ('→') between two languages $L_x L_y$ can be defined in the following way: $L_x \rightarrow L_y$, if and only if every sentence that can be correctly used in context x (either by affirmation or negation) can also be correctly used in context y (although possibly not vice versa), that is, if and only if (p), $p \in L_x$ implies $p \in L_y$, but not necessarily vice versa.

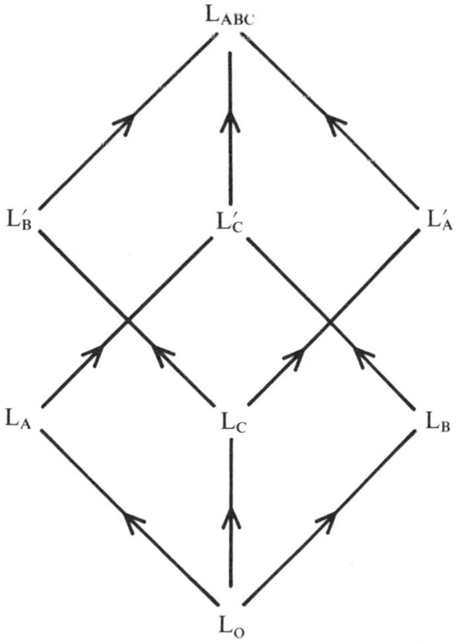

Figure 2
Diagram of Ṛgvedic languages

Then, the following objects constitute a lattice:

> *(L_O, L_A, L_B, L_C. L'_A, L'_B, L'_C, L_{ABC}), where L_O is the set theoretic intersection of L_A, L_B, L_C. The operations of 'Z' 'X' and '→' are schematized in Figure 2 above.*

The lattice is non–distributive as can be seen from the relations:

$$L_A\, X\, (L_B\, Z\, L'_B) = L_A$$
$$(L_A\, X\, L_B)\, Z\, (L_A\, X\, L'_B) = L'_B$$

But since

$$L_A \neq L'_B$$

therefore the distributive law does not hold.

The operation 'Z,' 'X,' '→,' and "·", should be read as "and," "or," "implies," and "not" respectively. For example: for $L_A = L'_B\, Z\, L_A$, read "this is an 'L_A' type situation." For $L'_B = L'_B\, X\, L_A$, read "this is *not* an 'L_B' type situation, *or* it is an 'L_A' type situation." For $L_A\, X\, L_B$, read "this is *either* an 'L_A' type situation *or* an 'L_B' type situation." And so on.

This, then is the model resulting from the dialogue among the different languages of the Ṛg Veda. The sum of the dialogue is the Language L_{ABC}, i.e., the embodied *ṛta* and vision (*dhīḥ*), which plays the role of the largest Language within which all that is rightly said in L_A, L_B, and L_C can be said. More, however, can be said in L_{ABC} than in L_A or L_B or L_C, for L_{ABC} is the Language that regathers the other three making connections between them which cannot be made in any one of them. The embodied Language of *ṛta* and *dhīḥ* performs such function in the Ṛg Veda.

It would be a radical misunderstanding of the Ṛg Veda to read it with the detached objective aloofness with which we in the West are accustomed to view whatever is presented to our speculative reason. This is the precise *error* of knowledge which the Ṛg Veda is trying to correct.

As suggested earlier, the origin of Western man's troubles seems to have been the fact that he detached himself from the objects and powers of the world, his own powers and objects, even his own world. He separated, in the holocaust of objectivity, the observer and the observed, the subject and the object, the agent and the re–agent, life and physiology, mind and body, body and soul. As a result, philosophical activity became, not liberating knowledge, but an alienation of man from man, since he was bent on equating himself with the objects of his knowledge.

The Ṛg Vedic understanding of man centers the activity of creation back in man himself. Man is the center of both time and eternity, each subletting a different language of the lattice, and the passage from one to the other is the passage up or down the lattice from one structure of expression to another within the relationships of action defined by the lattice. Man is at the center of his own activity, creating and recreating himself and his cosmos in relation to how efficiently he climbs or descends the contextual multiplicity within which he constantly operates.

That man, in his expressions and behavior, uses a lattice of languages, was first pointed out by Dr. P. A. Heelan in connection with the peculiar logic of Quantum Mechanics. The logic in question turned out to be, not an ordering of sentences, but a partial ordering (lattice) of complementary descriptive languages. He found this complementarity of languages to be a pervasive phenomenon of human communication:

> *it . . . was merely a historical accident that it took the existence of Quantum Mechanics to bring out the awareness of the structural character and the shift of structures through dialogue of both, our experience and our linguistic performance.*

No *embodied–vision* is possible without the sacrifice of the totalitarian tendencies of partial viewpoints; this totalitarianism is primarily due to the fact that partial viewpoints demand that man be reduced to the theoretical only. The sacrifice the Ṛg Veda offers points out the way for man to return to his whole body through the mediation of a language of images through which dialogue between opposing viewpoints is not only carried out, but all theoretical totalitarianism is cancelled. From the point of view of logic, this sacrifice involves a partial ordering of languages in a non–Boolean logic, the non–Boolean character of which is the mediation for growth and liberation. According to the Ṛg Veda, if man does not constrain his philosophical activity short of its own capacity for liberation, he may re–create himself and his society through the appropriate sacrifice, eternally, exercising thus his right to innovation and continuity. This sacrifice is the constant watch man must keep over himself for re–directing his own radical interpretative activity, wherever and whenever he does philosophy.

Appendix II

Some Terms, Definitions, Axioms and Formulae

I. By classical logic is meant Boolean algebra of sentences.

A. A Boolean algebra is a set B of at least two distinct elements with two binary operations $\cup$ (cup) $\cap$ (cap) and one unary operation $'$ (prime), such that B is closed with respect to each of these three operations, and for all a, b, and c belong to B, the following axioms are satisfied:

A1 $a \cup b = b \cup a$

A2 $a \cap b = b \cap a$

A3 $a \cup (b \cup c) = (a \cup b) \cup c$

A4 $a \cap (b \cap c) = (a \cap b) \cap c$

A5 There is an element $\emptyset$ belonging to B such that $a \cup \emptyset = a$

A6 There is an element I belonging to B such that $a \cap I = a$

A7 $a \cup a' = I$

A8 $a \cap a' = \emptyset$

A9 $a \cup (b \cap c) = (a \cup b) \cap (a \cup c)$

A10 $a \cap (b \cup c) = (a \cap b) \cup (a \cap c)$

A9 and A10 are the distributive laws.

Def.: $a \subseteq b$ if and only if $a \cup b = b$

B. A Boolean algebra of sentences is obtained by adding the following interpretation to the formal syntax A:

a, b, c	stand for sentences
$\emptyset$	stands for the absurd sentence (always false)
I	stands for the trivial sentence (always true)
$a \cup b$	stands for a and/or b (the logical sum)
$a \cap b$	stands for a and b (the logical product)
a'	stands for not–a
$a \subseteq b$	stands for a implies b

II. By a quantum logic is meant an orthocomplemented non–distributive lattice of sentences.

A. An orthocomplemented non–distributive lattice is obtained (rather than an algebra) if the axioms A9 and A10 are dropped in IA. Using

'Z,' 'X,' and '→' instead of cup, cap, and '⊆' to distinguish the non-distributive lattice operations from the Boolean operations, we use the following terminology for a lattice:

a Z b is called the 'least upper bound' or 'l.u.b. of a,b'
a X b is called the 'greatest lower bound' or 'g.l.b. of a;b'
$a \rightarrow b$ stands for a implies b

B. A quantum logic is obtained by adding to the axioms of IIA, the following interpretations:

a Z b stands for a and/or b
a X b stands for a and b
a' stands for not–a
$a \rightarrow b$ stands for a implies b

where a, b, c, $\emptyset$, I are sentences, $\emptyset$ is the absurd sentence and I is the trivial sentence.

One of the most misleading misconceptions, and at the same time the largest presupposition, of language–users and language analysts, is the existence of one universal language. This radical presupposition about language has been explicitly stated by some, either in the form of meta-language, a universal deep grammar, or implied even by those who denied the above possibilities in the name of nominalism, positivism, dialectics, or even realistic knowledge or ignorance. The problem becomes more crucial when within a culture everything that is said is necessarily reduced to what can be said by only *certain criteria* of one particular language. The problem becomes even more dramatic when what other people say, or other cultures say, can only be made understandable if certain criteria of a particular language are used, regardless of the fact that other people or other cultures might have never used the criteria by which they are identified. The problem for language, therefore, is to say whatever it says by those criteria by which it recognizes itself, regardless of what sense it makes by the criteria we decide it makes sense to us to understand them. In short, there is no historical mediation in language if, when speaking about others, we are unable to speak their own language and use the same criteria the others used.

Let me clarify these points with an example from Western philosophy, easily recognizable by all: Plato's Cave.

The problem of Plato's Cave, from a linguistic perspective, is the following one: What does the prisoner of the cave really see when, from the shadows of the cave, he passes to the bright light of the sun? In the world of shadows in the cave, whatever the prisoner saw, whatever the prisoner said he saw, was ruled, not only by the shadows and the flickering light behind his back, but mainly by the criteria of a world organized for the eye and reinforced by the language used to describe it. If the prisoner of the cave arrives to the surface and faces the sun with the same organization of the world and language he used in the cave, and with which he described the shadows; the new world, even with the sun hitting the prisoner straight in the eye, will not be radically different than the world of the cave. If anything, the cave has become larger, the shadows sharper and longer, and the light brighter; but the prisoner is still in the cave, regardless of what he says. Interpreters of Plato have tried to avoid this difficulty by speaking of the cave as an allegory, which is, of course, a way of saying something without actually meaning anything. Language is ruled by the same criteria of sight, which ruled the prisoner in the cave. If the shift in perspective from the shadows to the sun does not bring with it a shift in language—theory and communication—there is actually no shift in perspective, regardless of how emphatic, or obscure with exaggerations, language becomes about it. Needless to say, why the prisoner should want to go back to the cave, or needs to go back to the cave, cannot be explained with the same language of the cave. Nor does the "divided line" have any meaning by the same criteria of the prisoner's language, nor does this language in any way help us understand the criteria of the language Plato was using, or presupposing, in describing the cave, the prisoner, the "divided line," and the sun.

The problem of language, therefore, lies not so much in the ability to clearly define the terms used, but rather in that, with the definition of each term, the whole language from which the term gains meaning needs also to be brought out. Every term has meaning only in relation to a language, and languages gain meaning only in relation to other languages. Thus, Plato's Cave can only be understood by the language and criteria of sound in which its meaning was born. Where language analysis has failed, is not in its ability to reduce all languages to a logic or to a well–defined list of terms, so well defined because of the criteria agreed upon, but which are not part of the language to which all terms are reduced; but in its inability to discover with the terms analyzed, the plurality of languages to which they may belong. Language stands for language, and each language demands from the language–user different activities, theories and communication. Each language, furthermore, is ruled by different criteria, as in the case of sight and sound; and by these criteria they not only become different languages but are also irreducible to one another. Our visions, as philosophers, are bound to be very poor if we deprive those visions of their own language; unless, of course, our play with language is only a fog to cover our lack of visions. Philosophy, as Julián Marías has pointed out, is no philosophy if it is not a responsible (able to communicate) vision.

But vision, again, to mention but one example, means as many different things as the criteria of the language in which it is found allow it to mean. Thus, in a language ruled by the criteria of sight, vision may mean the sum of perspectives from which a *fixed* object can be seen, plus the theoretical perspective of the relationships holding amongst different perspectives of the object, plus the mental acts by which those perspectives, relationships and visions are performed. In any event, the *invariant object* is the condition for the variations in the meaning of vision. The invariant object is, therefore, not a reality, but a theoretical precondition (phenomenal or noumenal) for a whole system or method for establishing facts. Therefore, it is no wonder that when people speak of transcendence, within this framework, they are mostly forced to speak in mystical terms of things unseen or unseeable, either in terms of religious experiences, or in terms of modern physics. In a literal sense, in the latter two cases, speech is about no–things by the same criteria of the speech used to designate things.

In a language ruled by the criteria of sound, perspectives, the change of perspectives and vision, stand for what musicologists call "modulation." Modulation in music is the ability to change keys within a composition. To focus within this language, and by its criteria, is primarily the activity of being able to run the scale backwards and forwards, up and down, with these sudden shifts in perspectives. Through this ability, the singer, the body, the song and the perspective become an inseparable whole. In this language, transcendence is precisely the ability to perform the song, without any theoretical construct impeding its movement *a priori*, or determining the result of following such movement *a priori*. Nor can any theoretical compromise substitute for the discovery of the movement of "modulation" itself in history. The human body would then be asked to lose the memory of its origins; a task the human body refuses to do by its constant return to crisis.

It is up to the philosophers to discover the language ruled by the criteria of sound, rather than presuppose *a priori* that the only language universally human is the one ruled by the criteria of sight. Needless to say, the difficulty of such a task is great, as Plato's Seventh Letter indicates. But difficulty is the bread and butter of the philosopher, and the sight of corpses is a constant reminder of life.

Appendix III

Selected Chants from the Ṛg Veda[1]

ṚG VEDA 1.1

HYMN TO AGNI

1. I sing to Agni, The Priest and God,
 The Chanter, The Source of Wealth.

2. Sung by ancient Ṛṣis, Agni
 Is sung by new ones too; he will bring us the gods here.

3. Agni gives man prosperity and growth
 From day to day, He gives glory and heroes for sons too.

4. Agni fills with his presence the sacrifice;
 Its only way is to the gods.

5. May Agni, Wise Priest, True,
 Radiant God, bring us all the gods.

6. Whatever blessings, Agni, you give, those,
 Aṅgiras (Agni), are your truth.

7. To you, Agni, eraser of night, we come
 With prayer and song day by day.

8. King of the Sacrifice, Radiant Protector of Ṛta,
 You grow wider in your own home.

9. Agni, like a father to his children, be easily
 Accessible to us. Be with us, Agni, for our good.

ṚG VEDA 1.11

HYMN TO INDRA

1. Indra, boundless as the ocean,
 Charioteer born on chariots,
 God of strength, a true god,
 Has been praised by hymns.

2. Indra, assured of your friendship,
O Lord of Might, we have no fear.
We glorify You with praises,
Invincible Lord of Victories.

3. Many are from old the gifts of Indra,
His saving aid never exhausted,
He showers the singers of his praises
With gifts of wealth and cattle.

4. He was born the destroyer of forts,
Young, wise, with unlimited strength.
Indra sustains every sacrifice,
He is acclaimed for his weapon.

5. Lord of Vajra (thunder–bolt), you burst
The cave of Vala (Vṛtra) open and released the cows.
The gods came pressing to your side,
And free from terror aided you in the attack.

6. I, Hero, came by your gifts to the waters,
Singing your praise.
Here the singers stand, O Song-lover,
Witnesses of your deeds.

7. Indra, you destroyed with your power
The artful Śuṣṇa (dragon of drought).
The sages who witnessed this,
Now see beyond their songs.

8. Our songs have praised Indra
Who rules by his might.
His gifts flow a thousandfold
And even more abundantly.

ṚG VEDA 1.26

HYMN TO AGNI

1. Put on your robes, Lord of Sacrifice,
And offer for us this our sacrifice.

2. By our songs, by our chants, Agni,
Young god, favorite priest, ready yourself.

3. For here father and son, noble and commoner,
   Friend and friend choose each other through the Sacrifice.

4. Let Varuṇa, Mitra, Aryaman, sit here
   Like Manu, upon the spread grass.

5. Ancient Chanter, be pleased with our ritual and
   Friendship. Hear our songs.

6. When we offer sacrifices to this god or that god,
   To You alone we offer them. Accept them for all the gods.

7. Lord of tribes, joy–giving Priest,
   May we please You with our fires.

8. The gods have granted us gifts with red fires.
   With the same fires we pray to you.

9. Immortal One, may the praises of mortal men
   Belong as much to You as to us.

10. Agni, Son of Strength, find pleasure, with all your fires,
    In this our sacrifice, and in this our song.

ṚG VEDA 1.32

HYMN TO INDRA

1. Let me sing what Indra did,
   The first deed the thunder–wielder performed.
   He killed the Dragon, released the Waters,
   He split open the side of the Mountain.

2. He killed the Dragon hiding in the Mountain;
   His thunder–bolt Tvaṣṭar made for him;
   Like cattle lowing for their calves,
   The Waters rushed, roaring and tumbling to the sea.

3. With the strength of a bull he took Soma,
   As it lay pressed in three full vats;
   Powerful, he took thunder for his weapon
   And killed the first–born of the dragons.

4. Indra, when you killed the first–born of the dragons,
   You uncovered all that lay hidden;
   You created the Sun, the Dawn and Heaven,
   And you did not find anyone who could stand against you.

5. Indra with his powerful and deadly thunder,
Dismembered Vṛtra, most powerful dragon.
Like the trunk of a tree fell by the axe,
The Dragon lies limp on that spot of the earth.

6. A mad and weak warrior, the Dragon challenged Indra,
The Soma–drinking Hero, destroyer of many;
He could not stand the rush of Indra's weapon,
And crushed, he brought down the forts when falling.

7. He fought Indra without hands and feet;
The thunder–bolt pierced him between the shoulders;
Castrated ox, yet claiming to be a bull,
Vṛtra lay dismembered, his limbs scattered.

8. As he laid there, an overflowing pool,
The Waters were released, and flowed over him.
Vṛtra, with his power, had encircled them
And at the feet of torrents he always stayed.

9. Vṛtra's mother was weakened in power:
Indra had hurt her with his weapon.
The mother was above, the son was under,
Like a cow with her calf, the she–dragon lay.

10. Swept by the currents of the water,
Vṛtra's body found no place to rest.
Back and forth flows Vṛtra's body,
Indra's enemy sunk into deep darkness.

11. Ahi, and the host of dragons, girded the Waters,
Like cattle held by thieves.
But He killed Vṛtra, striking open the cave
Where the Waters were held in jail.

12. Indra, powerful god, a horse's tail you were
When you smote down the Dragon.
You won back the cattle, won Soma,
And released the flow of the Seven Rivers.

13. Of no use was thunder, nor fog, nor lightning,
Nor weapons thrown around him:
When Indra and the Dragon fought together,
The powerful god gained victory over him.

14. Whom did you fear to avenge the Dragon, Indra,
When after defeating him you were so frightened
That you ran through ninety–nine rivers,
And like a hawk, you flew through the sky's regions?

15. Indra is king of all that moves and stands still,
Of tame creatures and horned things.
Over all the people he is the ruler,
Encircling all, like a rim the spokes.

ṚG VEDA 1.48

HYMN TO UṢAS (DAWN)

1. O Dawn, daughter of the Sky,
Shower on us prosperity,
O generous, rich, shining goddess,
Bless us with your gifts forever.

2. Rich in horses, cattle and things,
You have brought light in the past.
Utter now in my behalf good words,
And move the generous to give.

3. Uṣas has dawned in the past,
Let her rise now and speed our chariots,
Held on their course by her coming,
Like (ships) seeking wealth on the seas.

4. Here Kaṇva, the best of the Kaṇvas,
Sings loud the glories of your name.
The princesses, as you approach,
Bend their thoughts to liberal giving.

5. With joy, like a young woman, the Dawn
Rises swiftly stirring all.
Rousing life, she awakens two–footed creatures,
And makes the birds of the air fly.

6. She sets the pursuits of men in motion,
As she speeds after the course of the Sun;
As the beautiful goddess rises at dawn,
No bird can rest that has flown.

7. She rides from distant regions,
From the sources of the sun, and yoking
A hundred chariots she speeds
This long distance to come to us.

8. The world bows at her brightness,
Beautiful as she creates light.
Let Dawn, the shining daughter of the Sky,
Dispell by her light the shadows of our way.

9. O Dawn, Heaven's daughter,
Shine on us with your brilliant light;
Bring us endless happiness,
And shine on our daily Sacrifice.

10. The life breath of all things is in you,
Beautiful woman that wards off darkness.
Come to us on your shining chariot,
Listen to our prayer and shower on us light.

11. O Dawn, grant us the light,
That shines forth among men.
From them bring to the Sacrifice
The strong that offer you praise.

12. O Dawn, lower from the skies all the gods,
That they may drink the juices of Soma.
Rich woman, give us cows and horses,
Grant us gifts of power and praise.

13. May Dawn, whose shining light
Is all around us,
Surround us with the wealth
We need for our life's journey.

14. O great Dawn, though the wise of old
Already implored from you protection,
Accept now graciously our songs
And pour on them your brilliant light.

15. O Dawn, as you today have, with your light,
Open the doors of the Sky,
Grant us an equally wide and secure home;
Full of nourishment and cattle.

16. O Dawn, shower on us wealth of all kinds;
Grant us food and conquering splendor.
Bountiful woman,
Fill us with endless nourishment.

ṚG VEDA 1.50

HYMN TO SŪRYA (THE SUN)

1. Propped up by his own white rays,
Sūrya, the god, lends his glance
Upon all that lives,
So that all things may behold him.

2. The constellations of the sky
Steadily retreat with their light,
Like thieves,
Before the all–beholding Sun.

3. His blazing rays are now apparent,
Shining over the world of men.
Like flames of fire
He warms and burns.

4. Swift and beautiful are you,
O Sun, maker of light.
You brighten with your rays
The whole, wide space.

5. You face the congregation
Of the gods,
And face also the world of men,
So facing all for all to see.

6. With the same eye,
O shining Varuṇa,
You make life quiver
Within the world of men.

7. Crossing the sky
And the mid–air region,
You make the days with your rays,
O Sun, and witness the birth of things.

8. Seven mares draw you,
O God, in your chariot,
All–seeing Sun,
Sūrya, with flames for hair.

9. Sūrya has yoked
The pure, bright Seven,
The daughters of the Sun's chariot;
With this willing team, he moves on.

10. Rising up above the darkness,
We have come to the Sun;
To the God amongst the Gods,
To the light that shines brightest.

11. Rising today, Wealth of friends,
Mounting to the highest heaven,
Remove, Sūrya, my heart's disease,
Take from me my yellow mood.

12. Let my yellow mood
Pass on to sparrows and parakeets;
Let my yellow mood
Pass on to the Haritāla trees.

13. This Āditya has risen
With all his conquering might.
Let me not be my enemy's prey,
Overcome the enemy for my sake.

VISION IN LONG DARKNESS (ṚG VEDA 1.164)

ASYA VĀMASYA HYMN

(*At the time of the morning Sacrifice*)

1. Here, the Lord of tribes I behold,
A benign, greyhaired priest with seven heroes as sons,
Flanked by his two brothers:
Lightning and the oil sprinkled Fire.

2. He rides a one–wheel, seven–yoked chariot;
A horse with seven names draws this triple–naved,
Ageless and uncheckable wheel;
All these worlds rest on her.

3. Seven steeds draw the seven–wheeled chariot,
Sounding with seven sacred notes.
Seven sisters call out to the place
Hiding the seven names of the cows.

4. Who was there to see the structured one
When the unstructured one first bore him?
Where was the Earth's life, her blood, her breath?
Who may seek some light on this from a sage?

5. I, simpleton, asking this in ignorance,
Meditate on the footprints set down by the gods.
Wise singers have spun a seven–stranded tale
Around the Sun, this calf from heaven.

6. I, ignorant, unknowing, seek knowledge
From those seers who may know.
What was the One? Who was the Unborn One
Who propped apart the six regions?

7. Let him now proclaim here, who really knows,
Where that benign bird, the Sun, sat;
From his head seven cows drank milk,
And water with their feet (when in a cloud).

8. The Mother (the Dawn) following the Norm (*Ṛta*),
Yielded to the Father (Sky) his share, as in the beginning with one mind.
A reluctant prude, she got pregnant when pierced,
In reverence the worshippers applaude her fecundity.

9. The Mother was yoked on the right,
The child hidden in the watery cloud,
The calf made a lowing search for the dappled dam
Across the three spaces.

10. Solitary he rises with three fathers and mothers on his shoulders;
The weight does not wear him down.
On top of the distant sky there stands
The Word (*Vāc*), encompassing all,
Yet she does not enter all.

11. Never does the twelve–spoked wheel of *Ṛta* wear out
As it keeps revolving in the heavens.
Agni, look, there stand seven hundred
And twenty sons in pairs.

12. Some call the Father, with five feet and twelve forms,
Affluent, residing in the far side of heaven.
Others say, the white–seeing One
Is moving on the seven–wheeled six–spoked chariot.

13. On the five–spoked wheel, as it rolls, are the worlds supported;
Though heavy–laden, its axle hardly grows hot;
Even from its very start, as it was fitted right
With its navel, it is unbreakable.

14. The undecaying wheel with its felly,
Has been drawn upwards by the ten–yoked ones.
The eye of the Sun, though covered by darkness,
Rolls on; on it are all the worlds kept in motion.

15. Besides the months in pairs, there is a seventh, born singly,
The six set of twins are god–born *ṛṣis*,
Their sacrifices set in harmony with definite rules,
Alterations introduced by arrangement.

16. They are feminine; yet, people tell me they are masculine.
One who sees this, the blind does not understand.
The son who is a seer knows; and thus knowing
He becomes his father's father.

17. Below what's above (sky) and above what's below (earth)
The cow rises carrying her calf by the feet.
What region is she gone to? Where is it she gives birth?
She is not in the herd.

18. Who has ever known the Father,
Who is below what's above, and above what's below?
This mystery, who explains it as a seer?
The knowledge of the gods, where does it begin?

19. They say that future sacrifices are also ancient,
And that the ancient are also present.
Soma, all you and Indra have done
Is carried back and forth as yoked to the chariot pole of the Sky.

20. Two birds with fair wings, inseparable companions,
Have found refuge in the same sheltering tree.
One incessantly eats from the fig tree;
The other, not eating, just looks on.

21. Here, where the birds (priests) sing endlessly,
In wise assembly, their share of immortality,
The mighty herdsman of the whole world, the wise one (Agni),
Has entered me, the simpleton.

22. The sweet berry grows at the top,
On that tree where the honey–sucking birds roost and breed.
No one reaches the top
Who does not know the Father.

23. They alone gain immortality
Who know that the *gāyatrī* foot is based upon the *gāyatrī* hymn;
The *triṣṭubh* foot is shaped from the *triṣṭubh* hymn;
The *jagat* foot is based on the *jagat* hymn.

24. With the *gāyatrī* foot a hymn is fashioned, with the hymn a chant;
With the *triṣṭubh* foot a unit of chant;
With double or quadruple units, a chant.
From the primary unit (*akṣareṇa*) they fashion the seven tones
(*vāṇīḥ*).

25. With the *jagat* the river in the sky is fixed.
One beholds the Sun in the *rathaṃtara* chant.
They say the *gāyatrī* has three kindling sticks;
And so it has excelled by its immense power.

26. I call here, that Cow, easy to milk,
That the dextrous milker may milk her.
May Savitṛ inspire us!
The fire is kindled; let me happily announce.

27. The mistress of wealth (Dawn) has come lowing,
Snuffling at her calf (Sun) with great yearning.
May this cow give milk for the Aśvins;
May she swell for great prosperity.

28. The cow lowed at her blinking calf (Sun);
She licked his head to make him low.
Longingly she pulls his mouth to the warmth of the udder;
Again she lows and swells with milk.

29. This (pot) enclosing the cow (milk) sings.
The cow (milk) spilling over the flame bellows.
With her sound she has fell her enemy.
She has become lightning and knocked over the lid of the pot
(the covering).

30. Breathing and moving fast, life is at rest.
Rushing, yet firm in the (three) homes (of Agni).
The life of the dead wanders at will (the Sun already set);
The immortal has a common origin with the mortal.

31. I saw the Cowherd (Sun) of the world
Move along the pathways around us and beyond.
In his spreading garments he has gathered light,
And moves on among the worlds (now in light, now in shadow).

32. He who made him does not see him;
He has hidden from him who saw him.
Enclosed within his mother's womb he
Has entered *Nirṛti* (non–action), yet full with progeny.

33. The Sky was my progenitor and Father.
The navel, the place of union; my Mother was this great Earth.
The space between these two outstretched regions was my womb.
Here the Father has made his own daughter pregnant (Dawn).

34. I ask you: What is the ultimate limit of the Earth?
I ask you: What is the central point of the Universe?
I ask you: What is the semen of the Cosmic Horse?
I ask you: What is the ultimate dwelling of Language?

35. This altar is the limit of the Earth.
This Sacrifice is the navel of the Universe.
This Soma is the semen of the Cosmic Horse.
This Brāhman (singer) is the center of Language.

36. The seven wombs of the cosmic halves (the Sky and Earth) and the semen,
Rise for their function at Viṣṇu's command.
Shaking with creative power and knowledge, the wise (wombs)
Surround (the semen) moving on all sides.

37. In relation to what I can say, 'This I am,'
I do not know. Lost in thought I wander.
Then came to me *Vāc* (speech), *Ṛta*'s first born;
Of her I got a portion.

38. The immortal has a common origin with the mortal,
And moves up and down by its own power.
The two take different directions.
When people see one, they do not see the other.

39. All the gods in the highest heaven,
Stand on the *akṣara* of the *ṛc* (the hymn and its meter).
What is a hymn (*ṛc*) for him who does not know this?
Only those who know this are assembled here together.

40. Eating good barley, may you be prosperous;
And may we too be prosperous.
O Inviolable Cow (*Vāc*) eat plentiful grass,
And drink pure water as you graze around.

41. The red Cow lowed and the flood waters came.
She sits in the highest heaven with thousand syllables:
Thus she becomes one–footed, then two–footed,
Then four–footed, eight–footed and nine.

42. From her (*Vāc*) flow the oceans,
By her live the four regions.
From her flows the *akṣara*;
On it the entire universe stands.

43. I saw in the distance cowdung smoke,
Covering equally above and below.
The heroes sacrificed the spotted bull (Soma).
These were the first Norms.

44. The three long–haired ones appear at the right time.
One of them consumes all in one year's run,
Another cast his glance of power on things,
And the third lets his trail be seen, but not his form.

45. Speech is divided into four levels,
The wise singers know them all.
Three levels are hidden, and men never attain them.
Men speak only the fourth.

46. They call it Indra, Mitra, Varuṇa,
Agni and Garutmān (Sun), the heavenly bird.
Of the One the singers chant in many ways;
They call it Agni, Yama, Mātariśvan.

47. The yellow birds soar high to heaven,
Along the dark path, clothed in waters.
They have returned here from *Ṛta*'s home,
Thc Earth is soaked in prosperity.

48. Twelve spokes, one wheel, three navels,
Who can comprehend this?
On it three hundred and sixty pegs rest;
They do not wobble in the least.

49. From your inexhaustible breast, Sarasvatī,
You cause the best nourishment to grow with vigor;
You grant wealth and bring treasures;
Give us your breast here that we may suck.

50. With the Sacrifice the gods sacrificed the Sacrifice.
This was the first Norm.
That power (thus generated) reaches the top of heaven,
Where the ancient *sādhyāḥ*, the gods, are.

51. The same amount of water goes up and down with the days.
While the rain clouds (Parjanyāḥ)
Replenish the earth,
The flames (of the Sacrifice) replenish the sky.

52. The great heavenly bird (Sun), of beautiful wings,
The child of the waters, and of the herbs,
Which brings the light with the moisture of rain—
To Him, Sarasvat, I offer this chant for help.

ṚG VEDA 2.6

HYMN TO AGNI

1. Agni, accept this burning fire,
Accept my prayer,
Bestowe grace on this song of praise.

2. Let me Honor you with this song,
Son of Strength, Lover of Horses,
Let me sing to the noble–born.

3. With songs, Lover of Songs,
Wealth–lover, Wealth–giver,
Let us sacrifice you.

4. Be for us a gracious Prince,
Lord and giver of precious things,
Drive those who hate away from us.

5. Being who you are, drop rain from heaven,
Give us unbreakable strength;
Give us the food we need.

6. Youthful god, whoever sings to you,
Asking help, through our song,
Heavenly envoy, come close.

7. Agni, Sage, you know how to pass
From men to gods, back and forth;
You are the friendly envoy of mankind.

8. Sage, All–knowing, be our friend,
Sacrifice the gods,
Sit with us on this spread grass.

ṚG VEDA 2.39

HYMN TO THE AŚVINS

The two horsemen; the twin heralds of the Dawn; duality.

1. Sing, like two press–stones, with a common song;
Move, like two greedy men to a tree with treasure;
Like two chanting Brāhmans to the ritual;
Like two peoples' messengers to many places.

2. Like two chariot heroes racing in the morning;
Like two leaders agreeing on a compromise;
Like two women making their bodies beautiful;
Like a wise married couple among the people.

3. Like two horns, thrust to us here;
Like two hooves, trot with rapid motion;
Like two Cakavās (birds), come to us at dawn;
Like two chariot wheels, come to us in the morning, Powerful Ones!

4. Like two boats, take us across the river;
Like two poles, axles, spokes, fellies, carry us.
Like two dogs, ward off harm to our bodies;
Like two crutches, protect us from falling.

5. Like two undying winds, two confluent rivers,
Two quick–seeing eyes, come towards us with vision.
Like two hands, be helpful to the body;
Like two feet, direct us to treasures.

6. Like two lips that sweeten the mouth with words;
Like two breasts that feed the milk of life;
Like two nostrils that protect our health;
Like two ears that vibrate with sound, so be You to us!

7. Like two hands, give us strength;
Like heaven and earth, contain the mid–air;
Aśvins, sharpen our songs that strive towards you,
Like an axe, sharpen them on the whet–stone.

8. Aśvins, these prayers, exalting you,
The Gṛtsamadas have made into a song of praise.
Accept them, Heroes! And come to us.
May we sing praise with brave men in the ritual.

ṚG VEDA 3.33

HYMN OF A SINGER AND TWO RIVERS

The Singer

1. Rushing down from the side of mountains, eager,
Like two mares set loose,
Vipāś and Śutudrī, the rivers, rush down their waters,
Like two young mother–cows licking their calves.

2. Impelled by Indra, praying that He urge you,
Sea–ward you rush, as if charioteered,
Flowing the two together, swelling with waves,
Each seeking the other, O Crystal Streams!

3. I have come to the most maternal river,
I have reached Vipāś, the broad, the blessed,
Licking the banks as mother–cows their calf.
Both flow together to a common bed.

The Rivers

4. Full are we with waters,
And moving to the home set for us by the gods.
No one may stop our flow when set in motion,
What does the singer want with us?

The Singer

5. Stop at my friendly word of request, Holy Ones,
Rest for a moment in your cosmic course.
With a noble hymn, asking your favor,
I, Kuśika's son, calls on the Rivers.

The Rivers

6. Indra, wielding the thunder, has dug our course,
Destroying Vṛtra, who had held our flow.
Savitṛ, the God, with his beautiful hand led us,
And with his urge we flow expanding.

The Singer

7. Praised forever will be Indra's deed
Of dismembering Ahi (the serpent).
With thunder He leveled all obstructions,
And the waters flowed, yearning for their home.

The Rivers

8. Do not forget, O Singer, these words;
Let future generations hear them from you.
In your songs, O Singer, be loving to us,
Do not let us down amongst men. To you, honor.

The Singer

9. Sisters, listen well to the Singer,
Who with car and chariot has come from far away.

Bow down quite low, be easy to cross,
Stay, Rivers, with your stream below the axles.

The Rivers

10. Yes, Singer, we will listen to your words,
Who with car and chariot has come from far away.
I will bend low like a nursing mother,
I will yield to you like a woman to her lover.

The Singer

11. As soon as the Bharatas, the warriors, have crossed you,
As they are urged and sped by Indra,
Let your streams flow in rapid motion.
Grant me this favor, who deserve my song.

12. The warriors, the Bharatas, have crossed over;
The Singer has won the favor of the Rivers.
Swell with your billows, rush, pour wealth.
Fill full your beds; run swiftly onward.

13. Let your waves be below the pins;
Let them keep the leather dry.
May you, harmless and sinless.
Pair of Bulls, not waste away.

ṚG VEDA 4.26

HYMN TO INDRA

1. I was Manu, I was Sūrya;
I am the *ṛṣi* Kakṣīvat, the singer;
I am greater than Ārjuni's son, Kutsa;
I am the sage Uśanā, behold me!

2. I gave the earth to the Ārya;
Rain to the mortal who sacrifices;
I set free the roaring waters;
The gods followed in my path.

3. In the wild joy of Soma I demolished
Śambara's ninety–nine forts;
I destroyed the hundred house entirely,
When helping Divodāsa Atithigva (a liberal prince).

4. Maruts, may this Bird rank higher
Than all birds; this Eagle higher
Than all swift–flying eagles, for, by his own power,
With no car to bear him, brought to Manu the potion of the gods.

5. When the Bird flew from here, darting away,
He sped forth on a wide path, swift as thought.
Eagerly he flew with the sweet Soma, and thus
The Eagle gained glory.

6. The Eagle, speeding onward, bearing the stem, the Bird
Bringing from afar the sweet drink of inspiration,
A friend of the gods, brought, holding fast,
The Soma, stealing it from the highest heaven.

7. The Eagle, having taken the Soma, bore it
To a thousand and ten thousand pressings;
Then the Bold One left behind the hostile ones,
The Wise One, the foolish, in the wild joy of Soma.

ṚG VEDA 4.27

HYMN TO THE EAGLE (HAWK, FALCON)

1. Being still in the womb, I knew
The births of all the gods in order;
A hundred iron forts confined me, but then I,
And the Eagle, flew forth with speed.

2. Not for pleasure did he bear me;
By power and virility he conquered.
The Bold One left behind the enemies,
And, expanding, he surpassed the wind.

3. When the Eagle screamed down from heaven,
He bore the Bold One as if he were the wind;
Then Kṛśānu, the archer, looking for prey,
Aimed and released the bow–strings toward him.

4. The Eagle carried him from the vault of heaven,
As Indra's friends (*Aśvins*) carried Bhujyu;
But there down fell a flying feather
Of the Bird darting along on his flight.

5. May, now, Maghavan accept the bright juice,
The white beaker, the liquid overflowing with milk;

May Indra drink to his joy, the best part
Of the mead, offered by the singers; may the Hero drink to
rapture!

ṚG VEDA 5.85

HYMN TO VARUṆA

1. Sing a song, solemn, with heart,
To Varuṇa, the Ruler, glorious and sublime.
He spread the earth in front of the sun,
The victims' skin he offered in sacrifice.

2. A mantle of air he extended over the tree–tops;
He put milk in cattle and in horses great speed;
He set wisdom in the heart, fire in the waters,
The Sun in heaven and Soma in the mountains.

3. Varuṇa lets the huge cask, open downward,
Flow through the heavens, the earth, the mid–air region,
For the waters of the universe to fall
In rain and moisten the young grain.

4. When Varuṇa wants milk, he sprinkles the sky,
The land, the earth to her foundations.
The Maruts (rain–gods) enshroud the mountains with rain–clouds,
The Heroes, with their power, then set them loose.

5. Let me sing this great deed of Varuṇa,
The glorious Lord of Immortality:
Standing on high, the Sun and the Earth
He measured in full, as with a rule.

6. No one ever allowed this deed of power,
Nor did prevent the wise god's way.
All rivers cannot a single sea fill,
Regardless of their floods and torrential flows.

7. Varuṇa, if we have wronged those who love us,
Our brother, companion or friend,
If we have slighted a neighbor, a stranger,
Remove, Varuṇa, from us this sin.

8. If ever did we cheat when gambling,
Or done wrong by chance or with full knowledge,
Remove these sins from us, Varuṇa,
Set us loose, that we may be forever your own.

ṚG VEDA 6.40

HYMN TO INDRA

1. Drink, Indra, drink the juice shed to make you happy;
Loose your Horses and give your friends freedom.
Sing, Indra, sing a song in our company,
Give strength to sacrifice to him who sings.

2. Drink, Indra, drink of the juices you drank at birth,
Mighty One, for power and rapture.
Men, the pressing–stones, the cows,
The waters, have made this Soma ready for your drinking.

3. Indra, the fire is kindled, the Soma pressed,
Let your best Horses draw you here.
Indra, with concentrated heart I call on you.
Come, be with us for our prosperity.

4. Indra, come here: Your arrival is always
Heralded by our desire to drink Soma.
Listen, hear the prayers we now offer;
Let this sacrifice increase your power.

5. May you, Indra, on the day of trial, absent
Or present, wherever you are,
With your team, Song–lover, following the Maruts,
Guard our sacrifice for our protection.

ṚG VEDA 6.53

HYMN TO PŪṢAN

1. Pūṣan, god of the path, we have yoked
And bound you to our song,
Like to a car to win a race.

ṚG VEDA 6.54

HYMN TO PŪṢAN

1. Pūṣan, bring us to the man who knows,
Who will set us straight,
And tell us: "It is here."

2. Pūṣan, may we walk with you
While you point out the houses to us
And say: "These are the ones."

3. Pūṣan's chariot–wheel is never harmed;
The box never falls to the ground;
The felly is never loose or shakes.

ṚG VEDA 7.63

HYMN TO SŪRYA (THE SUN)

1. The cosmic eye, auspicious Sūrya,
Mounts upward for the good of all;
The God, the eye of Varuṇa and Mitra,
Has rolled up darkness like a hide.

2. Sūrya's wide sail moves fast,
Restless as the billow, urging men to action.
The well–rounded wheel, onward it moves,
For Eteśa (Sun's horse) harnessed it to the car–pole.

3. From the womb of Uṣas refulgent he rises,
The joy of all the singers.
This god, Savitṛ, my chief joy and pleasure,
Never breaks the universal Norm.

4. Shining, shedding gold, he rises in the sky;
He gazes far and moves on fast.
Inspired by him men speed to their tasks,
And do the works assigned to them.

5. Like a falcon he moves through the heavens,
Through the pathway that mortals made.
When the Sun has risen, O Mitra–Varuṇa,
To you hommage and oblations we will serve.

6. Mitra, Varuṇa, Aryaman, give us freedom
And space, for us and our children.
May we find paths that are fair and good to travel.
Preserve us, O Gods, with blessings forever.

ṚG VEDA 7.77

HYMN TO UṢAS (DAWN)

1. Like a youthful woman, Dawn shined brightly,
Stirring to motion every living creature.
Agni (sacrificial fire) was kindled for the use of man;
Dawn made the light, driving away the dark.

2. In white robes, resplendent, shining,
She rose lighting all, as she sent out her beams:
Golden–colored and glorious,
Mother of plenty and Path of the days she shone.

3. Auspicious woman, bearing the gods' own eye, the Sun,
Leading the white stallion (the Sun), magnificent to behold,
The Dawn reveals herself with her robes of beaming lights,
And with her boundless gift she transforms the world.

4. Come to us, banish the enemy with your light!
Prepare for us wide pastures free from danger!
Remove hatred, bring us your priceless gifts!
Generous woman, shower blessings on the singer!

5. Wrap us up with your most shining beams,
O Dawn, divine goddess, lengthen our lives.
You who own all precious things, grant us nourishment,
Cows, cattle, horses and chariots!

6. O Dawn, daughter of the Sky, of noble birth,
Whom the Vaśiṣṭhas celebrate in songs,
Grant us vast and glorious wealth!
O gods, protect us always with your blessings!

ṚG VEDA 7.86

HYMN TO VARUṆA

1. Wise are the works of Him Who with his power
Rent the Sky and Earth asunder and held them there.
He set the high and mighty Sky in motion,
Moved the Sun, and spread the Earth beneath.

2. Talking to myself, alone, I ask:
How may Varuṇa and I be united?
What gift of mine will He accept in joy, not anger?
When may I calmly look on Him and find Him gracious?

3. Wishing to know my sin, Varuṇa, I ask from others;
I seek the wise to question them.
The sages always give me the same reply:
"Surely, Varuṇa, is angry with you."

4. O Varuṇa, what was my chief transgression
That would destroy a singer of your praise?

Tell me, Invincible One, so that sinless
I May approach you with my song.

5. Free us from the sins of our fathers;
Free us from those we ourselves committed.
O King, set free, like a thief who feeds the cattle,
Or like a calf from the rope, Vasiṣṭha (the singer).

6. It was not my own will, but malice, Varuṇa,
Gambling, drinking, anger, that betrayed me.
The older man leads the younger one astray,
And even sleep does not avoid transgression.

7. Like a slave I will serve the bountiful God,
Without sin, I will serve the angry God.
This gentle God gives wisdom to the simple,
And in his wisdom leads the wise to wealth.

8. Varuṇa, God, let this song of praise
Reach you, close to your heart.
May we find peace in rest and labor.
O Gods, protect us forever with your blessings.

ṚG VEDA 7.104

HYMN TO INDRA-SOMA

Description of the Asat

1. O Indra and Soma, burn the Rākṣasa (demon), subdue it;
Throw down those who prosper in darkness, you two bulls.
Crush down the unthinking (*acitas*), destroy them, slay them;
Push down the Atrins (devourers), weaken them.

2. O Indra and Soma, let the glowing heat—like a kettle near the fire—
Burn the dangerous one who plots evil against (us).
Direct your unyielding hatred against the
Brāhman–hating, flesh–eating, horrible–looking Kimīdin.

3. O Indra and Soma, pierce the evil–doers that they may fall into the cave,
The endless darkness,
So that not even one would come up here again;
Let this angry strength be for the benefit of your power.

4. O Indra and Soma, turn (your) crushing weapon from heaven,
Turn (your) crushing weapon from the earth,
Towards the one intent on wickedness;
Form (your) crushing (weapon) out of the mountains;
With which (weapon) you two burn down the Rākṣasa
Who has been prospering (in the darkness).

5. O Indra and Soma, roll from heaven
With the fire–heated strokes of stone;
Pierce the Atrins with the unaging, glowing weapons,
Till they fall into the abyss. Let them go silently.

6. O Indra and Soma, let this hymn encircle you on all sides,
As the girth (encircles) the two swift steeds;
(This is) the sacrifice which I offer to you by my understanding,
Give speed to these words, like two kings.

7. You two should remember back (when you were) with
Your swift–moving horses;
Slay the hostile, malicious Rākṣasas; who hate us and would
break us to bits.
Indra and Soma, let there be no happiness for the evil–doer,
Who, at any time persecuted us with hate.

8. Whoever works against me with lies
That are counter to the *ṛta* (*anṛta*)
As I follow my path with honest heart,
Let him go to non–existence (*asat*),
Like waters held in the fist,
As he pronounces non–existence, O Indra.

9. Those who tear apart, in the usual way, one with honest intensions,
And who corrupt an excellent man wantonly,
Either let Soma give them over to Ahi
Or let him place them in *Nirṛti*'s lap (inaction).

10. Whoever, O Agni, tries to harm the essence of our drink,
Of our horses, our cows, our bodies,
Let him, our enemy, a thief and a sorcerer, fail;
Let him be put down (in the darkness), his body and his offspring.

11. Let him be far away, bodily and with his descendents,
Let him be below all three worlds;
Let his renown wither, O Gods,
Whoever wishes us harm during the day or at night.

12. It is easy to distinguish, for a man who is wise;
He has contended with the two words 'existence' and
'non–existence';
Of the two, whatever is true, whatever is more just
That, indeed, Soma favors: he destroys non–existence.

13. Soma does not, indeed, further the guileful (man),
Nor the man who gains rule through false practices.
He kills the Rākṣasa, he kills the one who works false doctrines.
Let them both lie in Indra's power.

14. If I have ever been one who made *anṛta* his god (*anṛtadeva*);
Or if I understand the gods wrongly, O Agni,
Why are you angry with us, Jātavedas?
Let those who speak maliciously obtain destruction.

15. May I die today if I am a sorcerer,
Or if I have burned the life of a man;
Then, may *he* be deprived of ten sons
Who wrongly calls me 'sorcerer.'

16. Whoever calls me a sorcerer when I am not a sorcerer,
Or whoever says that I, undefiled, am a Rākṣasa,
Let Indra strike him with his mighty weapon.
Let him fall below all creation.

17. She who raids about at night like an owl,
With craftiness disguising her body,
May she fall into the endless caverns.
Let the soma–pressing stones with their noises
Destroy the Rākṣasas.

18. O Maruts, scatter yourselves among the people.
Search for, seize the Rākṣasas,
Crush them who becoming birds fly about at night
And have deposited droppings on the godly Soma–sacrifice.

19. Throw from the sky, Indra, the stone
Sharpened by Soma; sharpen it, O Maghavan;
From the east, west, south, and north
Strike the Rākṣasas with your boulder.

20. Here fly the dog–sorcerers!
With harmful intent they seek to harm Indra, the unharmable.
Śakra sharpens his weapon for betrayers;
Now may he hurl his thunderbolt at those who practice sorcery.

21. Indra has been a destroyer of sorcerers,
Of those who disturb sacrifices, of those who are hostile;
The mighty one approaches those who are Rākṣasas,
(Shattering them) like earthenware, just like an axe splitting wood.

22. Strike the owl–sorcerer, or the wolf–sorcerer,
The eagle–sorcerer or the vulture–sorcerer,
As if with a mill–stone, smash the Rākṣasa, O Indra.

23. Don't let the sorcery–practicing Rākṣasa reach us,
Drive off with brightness the two Kimīdins who work in couples;
O Earth, protect us from earthly distress;
O Mid–Air, protect us from heavenly (distress).

24. O Indra, strike the male sorcerer and the female
Who triumphs by her magic (māyā).
Let the Mūradevas (false worshippers) with twisted necks dissolve.
Let them not see the rising sun.

25. Watch over and around, O Indra and Soma!
Be wakeful!
Throw your weapons at the Rākṣasas,
Your thunderbolt at the sorcerers.

ṚG VEDA 8.30

HYMN TO THE VIŚVEDEVAS (ALL THE GODS)

1. Not one of you, gods, is small,
Not one a feeble child:
All of you are truly great.

2. Let you, Thirty-three gods,
Destroyers of the enemy, gods of men,
Holy Ones, be thus praised.

3. Speak to us with inspiration; defend and help us;
Do not let us stray from our Fathers' and Manu's path
Into the distance, away.

4. Gods, you who are now ours, and those of all mankind;
Protect us on all sides;
Give shelter to our horses and cattle.

ṚG VEDA 8.68

HYMN TO SOMA

1. This is Soma: impossible to restrain, always moving,
All–powerful, bursting,
Ṛṣi and Sage by knowledge.

2. He covers the naked; cures the sick;
Gives sight to the blind;
Makes the cripple walk.

3. Soma, you give powerful defense
Against the hate of strangers,
The hate that weakens and wastes us.

4. Powerful Soma, through your vision and skill,
You drive the transgressor's guilt
From heaven and earth.

5. May those who thirst quench their thirst,
When with dedication they set themselves to sacrifice;
May they obtain the Giver's grace.

6. And so may he find what was earlier lost,
And quicken the man who sacrifices,
And lengthen the rest of his life.

7. Generous, Love–Lover, Unconquered,
Of gentle thoughts, Soma,
Be sweet to our heart.

8. Soma, King, do not terrify us;
Do not strike us with panic;
Do not wound our heart with confusing flames.

9. King, Generous One, when in your hands,
If I see your enemies raise their heads,
Chase the fear away, dispel the host.

ṚG VEDA 9.3

HYMN TO SOMA

1. This god, here present,
This immortal god, like a bird upon his wings,
He flies, to settle in the vats of wood.

2. This god, made ready with songs,
Swiftly, through winding ways, he flows,
Unchanging in his course.

3. This god, while flowing,
Is beautified, like a steed for war,
By men skilled in songs.

4. This god, like a warrior marching with heroes,
Flows, eager to win
The booty of the war.

5. This god, speeds like a chariot,
As he flows, giving gifts,
And lets his voice be heard by all.

6. This god, praised by the singers,
Dives into the waters,
And treasures he bestows.

7. This god, ready for sacrifice,
Has gone up to heaven, across the regions,
His path unopposed.

8. This god, looking for gods,
In search of the old ways,
Eager he flows to the straining cloth.

9. This god, is the god of many laws,
For he is strength even at birth.
Wide, onwards he flows in streams.

ṚG VEDA 9.60

HYMN TO SOMA PAVAMĀNA

1. Sing, sing a song, a song of praise
To the swiftly flowing Pavamāna,
The crystal Indu with a thousand eyes.

2. It is those with a thousand eyes,
It is those with a thousand weights,
That have filtered through the sieve.

3. Swiftly ran Pavamāna, streaming
Through the sieve, rushing into the jars,
Finding its way to Indra's heart.

4. For Indra's sake, flow
Soma; flow for our own sake.
Give us the seed of children.

ṚG VEDA 9.112

HYMN TO SOMA PAVAMĀNA

1. Our thoughts wander in all directions
And various are the ways of men:
The cartwright looks for accidents,
The physician for the sick,
And the brāhman for a rich patron.
    For the sake of Indra,
    Flow, Indu, flow.

2. With ripe plants and glowing fan,
With bird's feathers and tools of stone,
The blacksmith seeks
The customer with gold.
    For the sake of Indra,
    Flow, Indu, flow.

3. I am a singer, my father a leech (doctor),
My mother grinds corn with a millstone.
Diverse in means, we all strive,
Like cattle, for wealth.
    For the sake of Indra,
    Flow, Indu, flow.

4. The horse draws a swift carriage,
The generous host an easy laugh and play.
The penis seeks a hairy slot
And the frog hankers for a flood.
    For the sake of Indra,
    Flow, Indu, flow.

ṚG VEDA 10.5

HYMN TO AGNI

1. Agni, you are the sea, source of treasures,
Born many times, you see within the heart of man.
You hide in the heavenly couple's bosom;
The heavenly bird's seat (the sun) in mid–fountain hides.

2. Sharing a common stable,
Strong stallions and mares live together.
The singers guard the seat of *Ṛta*,
And high secrets are concealed in them.

3. The Holy Pair (Heaven and Earth) of great power,
Moved by *Ṛta*, have copulated, giving birth to a child.
You are the navel of all that moves and stands still,
Of your movement the sages have spun a thread.

4. *Ṛta*'s overflow and ritual foods
Nurse forever the healthy child.
Wearing him as a mantle, Heaven and Earth
Grow strong by pleasant food and drink.

5. He called the seven red sisters in heat (fire of sacrifice),
To be seen with the sweet of their drink (Soma);
Born long ago, he stood in mid–air,
And looking for cover, he found Pūṣan's robe (the sun).

6. The singers fashioned seven paths,
He was given only one.
He stands in the highest spot,
A pillar, strong in the middle of the ways that part.

7. When *Sat* and *Asat* were in Aditi's bosom,
In Dakṣa's origin, in the vault of heaven,
Agni was for us *Ṛta*'s first–born,
A bull and a cow at the origin of life.

ṚG VEDA 10.71

HYMN TO WISDOM

(*Addressed to Bṛhaspati, Lord of Speech*)

1. When men, Bṛhaspati, by name–giving
Brought forth the first sounds of *Vāc*,
That which was excellent in them, which was pure,
Secrets hidden deep, through love was brought to light.

2. When men created language with wisdom,
As if winnowing cornflour through a sieve,
Friends acknowledged the signs of friendship,
And their speech retained its touch.

3. They followed the path of *Vāc* through sacrifice,
Which they discovered hidden within the seers.
They drew her out, distributing her in every place,
Vāc, which Seven Singers her tones and harmonies sing.

4. Many a man who sees does not see *Vāc*,
Many a man who hears does not hear her.
But to another she reveals her beauty
Like a radiant bride yielding to her husband.

5. They speak of a man too cold in friendship,
Who is never moved to act courageously,
All caught up in his futile imaginings;
The Word he hears never yields fruit or flower.

6. Who forsakes a friend, having known friendship,
He never had a part or a share of *Vāc*.
Even though he hears her, he hears in vain;
For he knows nothing of her right path.

7. Even friends endowed with eyes and ears,
Are not equal in the swiftness of their minds.
Some are like shallow tubs that reach only the mouth and shoulder,
While others are like deep lakes fit for a bath.

8. When brāhmans in harmony offer the sacrifice
Fashioned by the heart and inspired by the mind,
In attainment one is far behind the others,
Though brāhmans in name some wander senselessly.

9. Those who move neither forward nor backward
Nor are brāhmans, nor prepare libations,
They are poor craftsmen, misusing *Vāc*,
Ignorant, they spin out a useless thread for themselves.

10. All the friends rejoice for their triumphant friend
Who has won in contest with other brāhmans (in debate)
For he removes guilt and provides food,
And he is ready for acts of strength.

11. One man recites verses,
Another chants hymn Śakvarī measures.
The brāhman talks of existence, and yet
Another sets the norms for the sacrifice.

ṚG VEDA 10.72

HYMN TO THE GODS

1. Let us with tuneful skill
Proclaim here the origin of the gods,
So that in future generations these origins
May be seen, when these songs are sung.

2. Brahmaṇaspati, like a blacksmith,
Forged them.
In the beginning, Existence (*Sat*)
Was of Non-Existence (*Asat*) born.

3. In the beginning, Existence (*Sat*)
Was of Non-Existence (*Asat*) born.
From the parturient's bosom (*Uttānapadaḥ*),
Did the Directions rise.

4. Earth from the Parturient rose;
From the Earth came the Directions;
From Aditi's bosom was Power born (*Dakṣa*),
But Aditi was Power's child.

5. Aditi came into the world,
Who, then, was your child, *Dakṣa*?
The gods followed in her footsteps,
And with them the seed of immortality.

6. When you gods were in the deep,
Undifferentiated and hidden,
From your feet a cloud of dust arose,
As from the feet of dancers.

7. O Gods, like clever magicians,
You, then, let all beings flow;
You propped up the Sun,
Who lay hidden in the sea.

8. Eight sons of Aditi's own flesh
Were born.
With seven she climbed to the gods,
Mārtāṇḍa (the sun, man) she left behind.

9. With seven sons Aditi climbed
To join the gods of old.
To Earth Mārtāṇḍa she brought,
So that he could live and die.

ṚG VEDA 10.90

THE HYMN OF MAN

(PURUṢA SŪKTA)

1. Thousand headed is Man,
With thousand eyes and feet.
He envelopes the whole earth
And goes beyond it by ten fingers.

2. Man indeed is all that was and is,
And whatever may come in the future,
He is the master of immortality,
Of all that rises through nourishment.

3. Such is his power and greatness,
Yet man is still greater than these:
Of him all the worlds are only one–fourth,
Three–fourths are immortal in Heaven.

4. With three–fourths of Himself, Man rose,
The other fourth was born here.
From here on all sides he moved
Toward the living and the non–living.

5. From him was Virāj born,
And Man from Virāj.
When born he overpassed the earth,
Both in the west and in the east.

6. When with Man as their offering,
The Gods performed the sacrifice,
Spring was the oil they took
Autumn the offering and summer the fuel.

7. That sacrifice, balmed on the straw,
Was Man, born in the beginning;
With him did the gods sacrifice,
And so did the Sādhyas and the Ṛṣis.

8. From that cosmic sacrifice,
Drops of oil were collected,
Beasts of the wing were born,
And animals wild and tame.

9. From that original sacrifice,
The hymns and the chants were born,
The meters were born from it,
And from it prose was born.

10. From that horses were given birth,
And cattle with two rows of teeth.
Cows were born from that,
And from that were born goats and sheep.

11. When they dismembered Man,
Into how many parts did they separate him?
What was his mouth, what his arms,
What did they call his thighs and feet?

12. The Brāhman was his mouth;
The Rājanya (Princes) became his arms;
His thighs produced the Vaiśya (professionals and merchants);
His feet gave birth to the Śūdra (laborer).

13. The moon was born from his mind;
His eyes gave birth to the sun;
Indra and Agni came from his mouth;
And Vāyu (the wind) from his breath was born.

14. From his navel the midair rose;
The sky arose from his head;
From feet, the earth; from ears, the directions.
Thus they formed the worlds.

15. Seven sticks enclosed it like a fence,
Thrice seven were the sticks of firewood,
When the gods bound Man
As the offering of the sacrifice.

16. By sacrifice the gods sacrificed the sacrifice.
Those were the original and earliest acts.
These powers (of the sacrifice) reach heaven,
Where the Sādhyas and the gods are.

ṚG VEDA 10.121

HYMN TO PRAJĀPATI (FATHER OF ALL CREATURES)

1. In the beginning was Hiraṇyagarbha (Golden Womb),
Only–lord of all that was born.
He upheld the heaven and earth together.
What god shall we sacrifice?

2. He is the giver of life's breath, power and vigor;
His command all gods obey.
He is the lord of death, whose shadow is life immortal.
What god shall we sacrifice?

3. Of whatever breathes, moves or is still,
He, through his power, is the ruler.
He is the god of men and cattle.
What god shall we sacrifice?

4. By his power the snow–clad mountains stand,
Men say that the sea and the sky–river (*Rasā*) are his:
These are his arms, these heavenly regions.
What god shall we sacrifice?

5. He made the heavens and the earth strong,
He established the dwelling place of the sky and of the gods;
He measured the regions in mid–air.
What god shall we sacrifice?

6. The two armies, ready for battle,
Look to him for support, trembling in their breath.
Over them the rising sun brightly shines.
What god shall we sacrifice?

7. He saw the waters rushing forth,
Bearing the cosmic seed and delivering Agni.
Then, the gods' breath was born.
What god shall we sacrifice?

8. May the earth's father never harm us,
For he made the heavens and followed the Norm (*Dharma*).
He released the powerful and crystal waters.
What god shall we sacrifice?

9. Prajāpati, you alone embrace all these
Created things and none other beside you.
Grant us the wishes of our prayer;
May we have a store of wealth in our hands.

ṚG VEDA 10.125

HYMN TO VĀC (WORD)

1. I move with the Rudras and the Vasus,
The Ādityas and the Viśve Devāḥ.
I support Varuṇa and Mitra,
I hold Indra, Agni, and the Aśvins.

2. I lift the swelling Soma, and
Tvaṣṭṛ, Pūṣan, and Bhaga.
I shower gifts on the faithful patron of the sacrifices,
Who makes oblation and presses Soma.

3. I am the queen, the gatherer of wealth,
I know knowledge, the first to be sacrificed.
The gods have scattered me to all places;
I have many homes, (for) I have scattered the chants in many places.

4. Through my power, he eats and sees,
Breathes and hears, who hears me as *Vāc*.
Even if they do not know, they dwell in me.
In truth I speak: hear me, famous men.

5. Only I utter the word that brings joy to gods and men.
The man I favor, to him I give my power;
I make him like a god,
The seer, a perfect sacrificer.

6. I stretch the bow for Rudra, so
That his arrow may pierce wisdom's enemy.
I rouse the battle fury for the people.
I have pierced Heaven and Earth.

7. On the brow of the universe I give birth to the Father.
My birthplace is in the waters, in the deep ocean.
From there I spread out over the worlds on all sides.
And with the height of my head I reach the sky above.

8. I breathe like the wind holding all the worlds.
I am so powerful
That I go beyond the heavens
And beyond this broad earth.

ṚG VEDA 10.127

HYMN TO NIGHT

1. Goddess Night, with all her twinkling eyes,
To different points in splendor she comes.

2. Immortal, she broods over the high and low;
The Goddess, with her gaze, lightens the dark.

3. In her trail, her sister Dawn follows,
And with her the darkness vanishes.

4. Favor us, O Night, for we follow your pathways
As birds their nest upon a tree.

5. The villagers, all that flies and walks
Are closed in their homes. Even vultures ignore their prey.

6. O Ūrmyā (Night), fence off the wolf and its mate;
Fence off the thief. Be easy for us to pass.

7. Bright she has come near me, the darkness subdued
With light's promise. Dawn, cancel darkness like a debt.

8. Night, Child of Heaven, I have brought these songs to you
Like cattle. Accept them as for a conqueror.

ṚG VEDA 10.129

THE HYMN OF CREATION

1. Neither Existence nor Non–Existence was as yet,
Neither the world nor the sky that lies beyond it;
What was covered? and where? and who gave it protection?
Was there water, deep and unfathomable?

2. Neither was there death, nor immortality,
Nor any sign of night or day.
The ONE breathed without air by self–impulse;
Other than that was nothing whatsoever.

3. Darkness was concealed by darkness there,
And all this was indiscriminate chaos;
That ONE which had been covered by the void
Through the heat of desire (*tapas*) was manifested.

4. In the beginning there was desire,
Which was the primal germ of the mind;
The sages searching in their own hearts with wisdom
Found in non–existence the kin of existence.

5. Their dividing line extended transversely.
What was below it and what above?
There was the seed–bearer, there were mighty forces!
Who therefore knows from where it did arise.

6. Who really knows? Who can here say
When was it born and from where creation came?
The gods are later than this world's creation;
Therefore, who knows from where it came into existence?

7. That from which creation came into being,
Whether it had held it together or it had not
He who watches in the highest heaven
He alone knows, unless . . . He does not know.

ṚG VEDA 10.130

HYMN OF CREATION

1. The Sacrifice, drawn out with threads on every side,
Stretched by the song of one hundred singers and one.
The Fathers who have here gathered, weave these songs,
They sit beside the warp and chant: "Weave back, weave forth."

2. Man stretches it and man shrinks it;
Even the vault of heaven he has reached with it.
These pegs are fastened to the seat of the Sacrifice,
They made the Sāma–chant their weaving path.

3. What were the measures, the order, the model?
What were the wooden sticks, the butter?
What were the hymn, the chant, the recitation,
When the gods sacrificed the god (*Prajāpati*, *Puruṣa*).

4. Gāyatrī was linked to Agni, and Savitṛ with Uṣṇiḥ;
Soma, brilliant with song, was linked with Anuṣṭup;
Bṛhaspati's voice
To Bṛhatī's was joined. (See R.V. 1.164)

5. Virāj joined Varuṇa and Mitra;
Triṣṭup became Indra's measure, day by day.
Jagatī became the measure of all the gods.
By this knowledge men became Ṛṣis.

6. When the first Sacrifice, Our Fathers, was born,
By this knowledge men became Ṛṣis.
Now I behold those
Who first performed the Sacrifice.

7. Those who knew Sacrifice and meter, songs
And measures, were the Seven Divine Ṛṣis.
Knowing this ancient path, the sages
Have taken up the reins like chariot–drivers.

ṚG VEDA 10.139

HYMN TO SAVIT(A)Ṛ (INSPIRATION)

1. Savitṛ, with golden light for hair,
Has risen from the east, source of eternal light.
Pūṣan (sun–god), led by his energy, marches wise
Surveying the world like a shepherd.

2. He sits amidst the heavens with his eyes on man,
He covers the two worlds from the mid–air region.
He lights up Vāyu (wind) and this sacred fire;
He lights up inspiration back and forth.

3. He, the source of wealth, the store of treasures,
Grants the gaze of his power to all name and form.
Savitṛ, a god according to *Ṛta*, the Norm,
Like Indra, he stands in battle awaiting the spoils.

4. O Soma, when they saw Him, the Waters rushed
From the Sacrifice to the Gandharva Viśvāvasu (Soma's guardian).
Indra, in close pursuit, marked their path
And released them from the containers of the Sun.

5. Viśvāvasu, heavenly Gandharva, mid–air's
Celestial meter, sung for us this song,
So that we may learn what we ignore:
Inspiration of our song and help of our praise.

6. In the footsteps of the flood he found Indra,
Gatherer of wealth, destroyer of the caves:
The Gandharva disclosed they flowed with *Amṛta* (drink of the gods).
Indra knew well the power of the Dragon.

ṚG VEDA 10.146

HYMN TO ARAṆYĀNĪ (THE FOREST)

1. Goddess of the wild and the forest,
Who remains always unseen.
How is it that you do not seek the village?
Are you not afraid?

2. Every time the grasshopper sings,
Or the cicada's voice shrills,
As if tinkling bells would sound,
The goddess of the forest fills with joy.

3. Cattle seem to graze in the distance,
Near what seems a dwelling place:
It would appear as if the goddess of the forest
Would set the wagons free.

4. Here a voice calls a cow, there a man
Felled a tree: When the evening falls,
The dweller in the forest imagines
Someone else's scream.

5. The goddess never kills, even if
A murderous enemy approached.
Man eats of her sweet fruit, and then,
At will rests in her womb.

6. This is my song to the goddess of the forest:
The sweet–smelling, fragrant mother
Of a world of green. She does not till,
Yet, stores the food for us all.

ṚG VEDA 10.151

HYMN TO FAITH

1. By Faith is Agni kindled,
By Faith is the Sacrifice offered.
Full of joy, we sing to Faith.

2. Faith, favor the man that gives,
Favor he who gives not; favor those
Who sacrifice; favor this song I sing.

3. As the gods had faith to defeat
The powerful dragons, make this prayer
Strong for those who are generous in the Sacrifice.

4. Protected by Vāyu, men and gods increase
In Faith by Sacrificing.
Men gain Faith through the desires of the heart,
And become rich through Faith.

5. Faith in the early morning, Faith at noon,
Faith at the setting of the Sun we implore.
Faith increase our Faith.

ṚG VEDA 10.168

HYMN TO VĀYU (WIND)

1. O the Wind's chariot! What power, what glory!
Crashing it goes with the voice of thunder.
It touches heaven and turns its faces red;
As it moves it gathers all the dust of the earth.

2. Along the footsteps of the Wind the whole world rushes,
   They come to Him like women to a party.
   Borne on his moving car, with the breezes as his attendents,
   The god speeds forth, powerful like a king.

3. Rushing through the mid–air pathway, he whirls fast,
   With no time to rest or sleep.
   The first–born of the Waters and a friend, yet
   Where was he born, in which region?

4. He is the breath of the gods, the seed of the world,
   He moves by the will of his own voice.
   His roar is heard, his form is never seen.
   To the powerful Wind, let us offer this song.

ṚG VEDA 10.191

HYMN TO AGNI

1. You take possession, Powerful Agni,
   Of all that is precious for your friend.
   As you are kindled at the Sacrifice,
   Bring us all wealth.

2. Come together! Speak together!
   Let your minds be in harmony.
   As the gods of old together
   Sat in harmony for their share of the Sacrifice.

3. Common is the counsel, common the assembly,
   Common the mind; let your thoughts be common too.
   I lay before you a common purpose,
   With united minds we offer the Sacrifice.

4. Let your aim be one and single;
   Let your hearts be joined in one;
   Let your mind too be united,
   Let all, about these, willingly agree.

Footnotes

CHAPTER ONE

1. In practical terms our claim would read as follows:

Any statement in the Ṛg Veda can be traced to an original language source, either *Asat*, *Sat*, *Yajña* and *Ṛta*, where the meaning of that statement is grounded. Each one of these languages is also the ground of action through a particular intentionality. Thus *nirṛti* (non-action) is the modality of being in the world of *Asat*, either in consideration of possibilities to be discovered, or of stagnant dogmatic attitudes. *Satya* is the modality of acting in the world of *Sat*, as the truth to be built, formed or established. *Ṛtu* is the modality of acting in the world of *yajña*, as the activity of regathering the dismembered sensorium and the multiplicity of the worlds of *Sat* by sacrificing their multiple and diverse ontologies. *Ṛtadhīḥ* (embodied–vision) is the modality of having gone through and being in a world which remains continuously moving because it comprehends the totality of the cultural move on which it is grounded. Simultaneous with the languages as origins of the meaning and the activities through which these meanings are originated, there is also a multiplicity of images, dragons, heroes, birds and gods, etc., which synthesize, and embody both the languages and the activities of a whole cultural orientation. Thus we have Vṛtra, the dragon, and his cohort of ophidians as the prototypes (*pratirūpa*) of the *Asat* covering up the possibilities of cultural man, either through inaction or dogmatism. Heroes like Indra and a multitude of gods are the prototype of the multiple ontologies of the *Sat*. Agni, Varuṇa, Prajāpati, etc., are the prototypes of the sacrifice. While *ṛta* is seen as embodying the totality of languages, activities, images, and in general the total cultural movement that needs its own continuous sacrifice of particular perspectives so that the whole cultural body may remain totally alive without partial amputations.

2. Philosophical experience is, to say the least, a strange notion. Nothing is ever experienced unless it is experienced *as* something. But to experience something is not only to develop conceptual categories which serve to articulate the experience, but also to share in a 'way of knowing' which makes us 'see' the experience as such. Even if the conceptual categories may bring us closer to the experience, it is only in the 'sharing' of a theory of knowledge, a 'vision,' that makes the experience possible and discourse about it effective. The contrary is also true.

3. The Vedic meter is nearer to music than to poetry as encountered today. Variations of sound, accent and rhythm convey a stronger impression on the listener than readings of modern poetry. Syllables grouped into verse–division (*pāda*) constitute the metrical base. Three eight–syllabic *pādas* make a Gāyatrī meter (8–8–8); four, the Anuṣṭup (8–8–8–8); five, the Paṇkti (8–8–8–8–8). Four eleven–syllabic *pādas* make the Triṣṭup (11–11–11–11); four twelve–syllabic *pādas* the Jagatī (12–12–12–12). There are also mixed *pādas*; the Uṣṇiḥ (8–8–12); the Bṛhatī (8–8–12–8) and the Satobṛhatī (12–8–12–8). The combines the last two. There are other less common, like the following four–*pāda* meters: Virāj (10–10–10–10); Sakvarī (14–14–14–14); Aṣṭi (16–16–16–16) and Atyaṣṭi (17–17–17–17). In reading the Vedas one has to pay attention to the different accents. The Sāmaveda (which is sung) has three accents: *udātta* (high), *svarita* (middle) and *anudātta* (low). In the other three Vedas, only the last two hold. A verticle stroke is used in place, and above, the *svarita* accent, and a horizontal line below the *anudātta* accent. The accent is most important in Vedic language since a change of accent changes also the meaning of the word.

For a detailed study of the Veda recitation in old times and today, also for further bibliography, see: J.F. Staal, *Nambudiri Veda Recitation* (s-Gravenhage: Mouton & Co., 1961).

4. *Ṛgarthādīpikā on Ṛgvedasaṃhitā by Mādhava*, ed. L. Sarup, Lahore, 1939, V. S. Bhandari. "*Yāska and Vedapauruṣeyatva*," Summary of paper of the *20th All Indian Oriental Conference*, (Bhubaneshwar, 1959), pp. 28–29.

Yudhisthira, *Vararucikṛta Nirukta–Samuccaya*, Prācya–Vidyā–Pratiṣṭhāna, New Delhi.

5. (Died, 1387). See his *Ṛgveda Saṃhitā and Pada Text* (ed. Max Müller, Sec. ed. 1890–2, 6 Vol., London. First ed. 1849–74).

6. Aurobindo, Sri, *Hymns to the Mystic Fire* (Pondicherry: Sri Aurobindo Ashram, 1952).

The Life Divine, 3rd ed. (Calcutta: Arya Publishing House, 1947) 2 Vol.

7. V. S. Agrawala, *Vision in Long Darkness*, (Agrawala, Varanasi, 1963). *Sparks from the Vedic Fire*, (Agrawala, Varanasi, 1962).

8. Max Müller, *The Vedas*, (Calcutta: Susil Gupta Ltd. 1956).

A. Berriedale Keith, *A History of Sanskrit Literature* (Oxford University Press, 1920).

Arthur A. Macdonnell, *A History of Sanskrit Literature* (London: 1905).

9. Edwin Gerow, "Renou's Place in Vedic Exegetical Tradition," (*JAOS*, Vol. 88, n. 2, April–June 1968), pp. 310–333.

10. See as an example Renou's *Les Maitres de la Philologie Vedique* (Paris: 1928). H. Oldenberg, *Die Religion des Veda* (Stuttgart und Berlin: 1917) 2nd ed. *Vedic Hymns in Sacred Books of the East*, Vol. 46 (Oxford: 1897). *Textkritische und exegetische Noten* (Berlin: 1909–1912).

11. See Louis Renou, *Les Maitres . . . op. cit.*

12. *Ibid.*, also Renou's EVP 7, pp. 9.14.46, etc.

13. H. Zimmer, *Indische Spharen*. Verlag R. Oldenbourg (Schriften der Corona 12, Zurich, 1935). Also: *Maya: Der Indische Mythos*, (Deutche Verlags–Anstalt, Stuttgart: 1936).

14. A. Hildebrandt, *Aus Brāhmanas und Upaniṣaden* (Jena: 1943).

15. H. Oldenberg, *Vedaforschung*, (Stuttgart: 1960).
Die Religion des Veda (Stuttgart und Berlin: 1917), 2nd edition.
Vedic Hymns, Sacred Books of the East, Vol. 46 (Oxford: 1897).
Textkritische und exegetische Noten (Berlin: 1909–1912).

16. J. Gonda, *Die Religionen Indiens* (Stuttgart: 1960)
The Vision of the Vedic Poets (Mouton & Co., s–Gravenhage, The Hague: 1963).
Four Studies in the Language of the Vedas, (The Hague, 1959).
Epithets in the Ṛgveda, (The Hague: 1959).
Change and Continuity in Indian Tradition, (The Hague: 1965).

17. Abel Bergaigne, *La Religion Vedique*, 4 Vol. (Paris: Librarie Honore Champion, 1963), 2nd ed.

18. On the 'romantic' or 'lyrical' Veda of von Roth, see Oldenberg *Vedaforschung*, (*op. cit.*,) p. 6.

19. Karl Friedrich Geldner, *Der Rig–Veda* (Harvard Oriental Series, Vols. 33–36).

20. H. Grassman, *Worterbuch zum Rig–Veda* (Wiesbaden: Otto Harrassowitz, 1964), 4th ed.

21. See Renou's commentaries on Ludwig in *Maitres . . . op. cit.*, p. 18.

22. Louis Renou, *Études Védiques et Pāṇinéennes* (EVP) (Paris: Publications de l'Institut de Civilisation Indienne, 1961–66). Tomes 9–10, 12–15.

23. Louis Renou, *Vedic India*, (Calcutta: Susil Gupta Ltd. 1957).

24. One of the gravest temptations of those approaching the Ṛg Veda is to read in it later developments in the Indian Tradition. In concrete the temptation is to read in the Ṛg Veda the ritualism of the Brāhmanas and therefore interpret the 'sacrificial language' of Ṛg Veda as one instance of Brāhmanical ritual. See further examples in Macdonnell, Keith, Griswold and Bloomfield. See also the criticism on these authors by Potdar, K. R., in his *Sacrifice in the Ṛgveda*, (Bharatiya Vidya Bhavan, 1953).

Something similar occurs in the case of philosophical frameworks. Rakhakrishnan, for example, uses only those hymns of the Ṛg Veda which explicitly mention being or non–being (equating being and existence in two different connotations), or some familiar philosophical theme. See for example his selection of hymns in *Sourcebook of Indian Philosophy*, (Princeton University Press, 1957). He uncritically takes for granted the unity of philosophical perspective of both the Brāhmanas and the Ṛg Veda. The same may be said of practically all those who have mentioned philosophical themes or statements of the Ṛg Veda.

25. Paul Ricoeur, *The Symbolism of Evil*, trans. Emerson Buchanan (New York: Harper and Row), pp. 23–24.

CHAPTER TWO

1. F. Nietzsche, *La Volonté de puissance*; Fr. tr. G. Bianeuis, 2 Vols., (Paris: Gallimard, 1947), Vol. I, p. 65. The above is a fragment of 1886.

2. M. Heidegger, "Letter on Humanism" in *Philosophy in the Twentieth Century*; English tr. by William Barrett and Henry D. Aiken, (New York, 1962), p. 271.

3. *Ibid.*, p. 280.

4. Man, understood as primarily active, i.e., ethical, religious, searching for himself in his own unity of presence, was, for Kant, primarily hypothetical, i.e., neither an *established* truth nor an *establishable* truth. In fact, man so understood, was no part of any proper philosophical doctrine. On the other hand, it is also true that Kant, as part of his rational faith, believed it to be so. This part of Kant was the one latched onto most firmly by the crop of philosophers and poets who arose in his wake. And justly so, for it was really the underlying notion of the ultimate nature of things which would have made all the rest of the philosophy of Kant not just 'critically' true, but also 'ontologically' so. But Kant was already committed to a reduction of knowledge to only the *categorical*, to Being and not to Existence, to the thoughts of man rather than the actions of man. For clarity's sake I reproduce Kant's Transcendental Hypothesis:

> "*Human procreation is entirely contingent, taking place as occasion offers opportunity in the same manner as that of other, irrational creatures. But human procreation depends, in addition, upon some further coincidental factors, such as the standard of living, the vagaries of governmental interventions—and even vice! It is indeed difficult to believe, therefore, that a creature whose life has its beginnings under circumstances so trivial and so utterly dependent upon arbitrary human action should have an existence extending to all eternity. Were the question only that of the continued existence on earth of the human race, the difficulty would be negligible, because the coincidental character of individual cases could be seen to fall under some general rule, at least. But to expect such a marvelous result as the eternal life of each individual from such insignificant cases strikes us as very strange indeed. However, in order to meet such objections as*

these, we can propound the transcendental hypothesis that all life is really noumenal only, not subject at all to temporal changes—neither beginning in birth, nor ending in death; that the life of change and birth and death is phenomenal only—a mere representation, through the senses, of a purely spiritual life—that the whole world of sense is only a picture hovering before us, formed by our present mode of knowledge—a dream lacking any objective reality in itself. Indeed, we may say that, if we could see ourselves as spiritual beings whose connections with the spiritual world of noumena did not begin with our birth and will not end with our death—both birth and death being mere appearances."

Immanuel Kant, from the end of Part 3 "The Discipline of Pure Reason" in *Sammtliche Werke*, Vol. III, ed. G. Hartenstein. Leipzig: Leopold Voss: 1867, p. 516. Trans. Harry Proch in *The Genesis of Twentieth Century Philosophy* (New York: Doubleday, 1964), p. 294.

5. Wilfred Sellars has clearly pointed out the seeming paradox that one cannot have a concept without having a conceptual system; or rather that in order to have a concept one must in a sense have them all. See: *Science, Perception and Reality*, (Routledge & Kegan Paul, New York: Humanities Press, 1963), p. 148.

6. See Williard Van Orman Quine, *From a Logical Point of View* (New York: Harper Torchbooks, 1953), p. 19.

"In earlier pages I undertook to show that some common arguments in favor of certain ontologies are fallacious. Further, I advanced an explicit standard whereby to decide what the ontological commitments of a theory are. But the question *what ontology actually to actually adopt*, still stands open, and the obvious counsel is tolerance and an experimental spirit." (Underlining, mine.)

7. "What is evident (*pratyakṣam*) to men is concealed (*parokṣam*) to the gods, and what is concealed to men is evident to the gods," (*yad vai manuṣyānām pratyakṣam tad devānām parokṣam atha yan manuṣyānām parokṣam tad devānām pratyakṣam. Taṇdyamahā–brāhmaṇa* 22.10.3)

8. I do not restrict the term 'thing' to Wittgenstein's use of the term. See *Tractatus Logico–Philosophicus*, (Routledge & Kegan Paul, New York, 1961. 1st German edition published in 1921.) In 1.1, the "world is the totality of facts, not of things," a distinction is made between a thing (object) and a fact. A thing, however, is an irreducible entity, substance, not to be identified with objects like tables, stones, animals and plants.

I take the term in Sellars' sense: "not only 'cabbages and kings,' but numbers and duties, possibilities and finger snaps, aesthetic experience and death." See: *Science, Perception and Reality*, *op. cit.*, p. 1.

9. See the analysis of this theme in Herbert Marcuse's *One–dimensional Man*, (Beacon Press: Boston, 1964).

10. See Quine, *From a Logical Point of View*, *op. cit.*, pp. 44–45.

11. *Ibid.* The reader will at once appreciate that, in this view, 'mythology' gains a new perspective and importance that it never had before when viewed

as the poetic imagination of primitives. The functional relationship of an atom or an electron to sensation is the same as that of the Sun, Uṣas, Agni, Vṛtra, etc., to sensation. Man has changed myths, not problems.

12. For a detailed comparative study between the negative value of Language in East and West (Buddhism sp. and Hegel) see Th. Stcherbatsky, *Buddhist Logic*, 2 Vol. Dover Publications, 1962. First published in 1930 USSR Leningrad, passim. Vol. I, pp. 482–505.

13. See Th. Stcherbatsky, *Buddhist Logic*, *op. cit*., Vol. I., pp. 62–78.

14. 'Conceptual empiricism' reduces all meaningful ideas or concepts to the status of language about the particulars of sense experience (Hume) or their immediately observable common characteristics, (Ayer, etc.) The particulars of sense experience whether said to be 'sense date,' 'appearings,' 'impressions,' or 'objects,' are construed as immediately given or noninferentially cognizable. Ideas are names or systems of names for those particulars and their observable characteristics. Thus, the concept 'red in general' (redness) is analyzed either as a generalized use of a general 'red impression' (Hume) or as a concept whose empirical 'object' is the "straightforward resemblance between the things whose color we call red." (A. J. Ayer, *The Problem of Knowledge*, Penguin Books, Middlesex, 1956, p. 11). In any case the result is that that which can be *signified* is that which is *given* ('the myth of the given') in sense experience.
On behaviorism see: *One–dimensional Man*, *op. cit*., pp. 172–194.

15. For a phenomenologist criticism of language theories by other phenomenologists and linguist analysts, see: Paul Ricoeur, "Husserl and Wittgenstein on Language," in *Phenomenology and Existentialism*, eds. E. N. Lee and M. Mandelbaum, The Johns Hopkins Press, 1967. "Structure, Work, Event" trans. Robert D. Sweeny, *Philosophy Today*, Vol. XII, N. 2/4, Summer, 1968. (Originally "La Structure—le mot 'Levenement" in *Esprit*, *Mai*, 1967) "New Developments in Phenomenology in France: The Phenomenology of Language," translated by P. G. Goodman, *Social Research*, Vol. 34, No. 1, Spring, 1967.

"Existence et Hermeneutique," *Dialogue* Vol. IV, No. 11965. As for Ricoeur himself, one must be aware that he is still in 'process' and his theories of language are not yet fully formulated. It is also apparent that his theories of language are changing in the 'process' as it is obvious by comparing these later articles with his earlier books. However, even in these later articles, Ricoeur seems to find that for man there is only "eschatological hope." "We are forever separated from life by the very function of the sign; we no longer live life but simply designate it. We signify life and are thus definitely withdrawn from it, in the process of *interpreting* it in a multitude of ways . . . We are no longer engaged in a practical activity, but in a theoretical inquiry . . . philosophy itself is made possible by the act of reduction, which is also the birth of language." ('Husserl and Wittgenstein' . . . *op. cit*., p. 2.7.)

16. Suzanne Langer, *Philosophy in a New Key* (Cambridge, Mass.: Harvard University Press, 1957).

17. Sir James Jeans, *The New Background of Science* (Ann Arbor, Michigan: University of Michigan Press, 1959), p. 113.

18. Max Born, *The Restless Universe* (New York: Dover Publications, 1951), p. 1.

19. James Jeans, *The New . . . op. cit.*, p. 1. Further readings in this subject: Henry Margenau, "Einstein's Conception of Reality," in P. A. Schilpp, *Albert Einstein: Philosopher–Scientist* (New York: Harper & Row, 1959). Also: Max Planck, *Where is Science Going*? (London: George Allen & Unwin, 1933). Also: J. R. Oppenheimer, *Science and the Common Understanding* (New York: Simon & Schuster, 1966).

20. Though many 'quantum logics' have been proposed, we follow the one proposed by G. Birkhoff and von Neumann, "The Logic of Quantum Mechanics," *Ann. of Mathematics*, 37 (1936), pp. 823–843.

21. See Patrick A. Heelan, *Quantum Mechanics and Objectivity* (The Hague: Nijhoff, 1965).

——"Horizon, Objectivity and Reality in Physical Sciences," *International Philosophical Quarterly*, 7, 1967, pp. 376–412. SEE especially two papers by the same author, on which my own formulation is based:

1. "Quantum Logic and Classical Logic: Their Respective Roles."
2. "Complementarity, Context–Dependence and Quantum Logic."

The first paper was read at the *Boston Colloquium for the Philosophy of Science*, in January 1969 under the title "Quantum Logic Does Not Have to Be Non–Classical." This paper appeared as "Quantum and Classical Logic: Their Respective Roles," in *Synthese*, 21 (1970), pp. 2–33. I am very much indebted to Dr. Heelan for his personal assistance in my own formulation of the contextlanguage dependence of the languages of the Ṛg Veda. He saw my field of application as a concrete example of his own thesis as formulated in the above mentioned papers, even though at first glance it would appear that our fields are miles apart. This is, again, a further example of the unity of the human experience and of the dialectical nature of our own context–language interdependence.

For a survey of the different forms of Quantum Logics see "The Labyrinth of Quantum Logics," by Bas C. van Fraasen, a paper read at the *Biennial Meeting of the Philosophy of Science Assoc.*, Pittsburgh, October 1968.

22. See Bohr's "Discussion with Einstein," In *Albert Einstein: Philo . . . op. cit.* Also Bohr's *Atomic Theory and the Description of* (Cambridge University Press, 1961), and his *Atomic Physics and Human Knowledge*, Science ed., New York, 1961. See in particular the essays: "Biology and Atomic Physics," and "Natural Philosophy and Human Culture." See also, W. Heisenberg, *The Physical Principles of the Quantum Theory*, Dover ed.

23. Bohr's "Discussions with Einstein" . . . *op. cit.*, p. 209, and W. Heisenberg, *The Physical Principles . . . op. cit.*, pp. 15–19.

24. Bohr's "Discussions with Einstein" . . . *op. cit passim* and W. Heisenberg, *The Physical Principles . . . op. cit.*, pp. 13–14 and 20–36.

25. P. A. Heelan, "Quantum Logic and Classical Logic" . . . *op. cit.*

26. Nietzsche, Friedrich, *The Will to Power*, edited by Walter Kaufmann and trans. by Walter Kaufmann and R. J. Hollingdale, (New York: Random House, Vintage Books, 1968), pp. 268–269. This is fragment 485, 1887.

For a more complete analysis of the themes touched here, I direct the reader to my book: *Avatāra: The Humanization of Philosophy Through the Bhagavad Gītā*, (New York: Nicolas Hays, Ltd., 1976).

CHAPTER THREE

1. The honorable exceptions I have in mind are principally these two people:

Ernest McClain, "Plato's Musical Cosmology," *Main Currents in Modern Thought* 30, 1 (Sept.–Oct. 1973), pp. 34–42; *The Myth of Invariance: The Origin of the Gods, Mathematics and Music from the Ṛg Veda to Plato*, (New York: Nicolas Hays, Ltd., 1976). and

Robert S. Brumbaugh, *Plato's Mathematical Imagination*, (Bloomington: Indiana University Publications, 1954, and New York: Kraus Reprint Corporation, 1968).

2. The "return to Greece" started in Greece itself by the Greeks with their superior way of handling the barbarians. (See: Walter J. Ong, *The Barbarian Within*, New York: The MacMillan Company, 1954.) Greece was culturally selfpossessed, while the barbarian was an "outsider." But as Oedipus already points out: "I was evil from birth;" a remark which has escaped those who have found absolute *integrity* in Greece to be the worthwhile reason to return to it again and again. Rome, the Fathers of the Church, the Italian Renaissance, Romanticism, all turned to Greece for a justification of their present glory; but in doing so, they established Greece as the exclusive "origin" of our own culture. The preponderance of Greek studies, as opposed to the scarcity of other cultural studies, the exuberance of praise over metaphorical Greece, easily clouded the fact that Greece was taking over and submerging all other cultures out of existence. "No other mythology known to us—developed or primitive, ancient or modern—is marked by quite the same complexity and systematic quality as the Greek." (G. S. Kirk, *Myth, Its Meaning and Function in Ancient and Other Cultures*, (Cambridge, Eng. and Berkeley, Calif.: The Univ. Press and Univ. of California Press, 1970), p. 205.) This sounds great, but it is not true; for all other mythologies and cultures have not been measured by their own criteria, but by the metaphorical "Greek" criterion. For the "Greece" we return to is as mythological as its myths. It includes all periods from Minoan to Hellenistic, all localities from Asia Minor to Sicily, and a multitude of other cultures from the Far and Near East. In fact, ". . . until the age of Romanticism, Greece was no more than a museum inhabited by people beyond contempt." (Roberto Weiss, *The Renaissance Discovery of Classical Antiquity*, (Oxford: Blackwell, 1969),

p. 140.) And had it not been that we needed to go somewhere else—the past—in order to patch up the present, we would have left the dead buried.

Augustin went to Greece to rationalize the universal *image* of man he already believed in. St. Thomas Aquinas did the same. Petrarch, who could not read Greek, and did more in the fourteenth century than anyone else to revive the literature of Greece, strived to discover a way of acting which, by being more Greek, would be more human. Winckelmann, who invented the modern worship of Greece in the eighteenth century, never set foot there. Nor did Racine go there, nor Goethe, Hölderline, Hegel, Heine, Keats, or even Nietzsche. Yet for these people, as much as for Stravinsky, Picasso, Heidegger, Joyce, Freud, and Jung, the return to Greece was essential for aesthetic, philosophical and psychological reasons. But this Greece we are told to return to is an "emotion charged image of Greece." (J. M. Osborn, "Travel Literature and the Rise of Neo–Hellenism in England," *Bull.*, N.Y. Public Library 67 (1963): 300.) And by focusing on that metaphorical image, all we do is reinforce the present condition of whose disintegration the need to return to Greece was born in the first place. But by closing ourselves into a pre–established image of our past, we miss the chance of rediscovering the primordial ground of our flesh, and of our culture. Neither memory nor imagination may liberate us from our *present* predicament—from the predicament of the present—but rather, sink us more deeply into it. We need to discover not theories, but the activity by which both theories and communication about theories may be radically falsified. Or we are stuck.

3. William D. Whitney. "On the History of the Vedic Texts," JAOS, Vol. IV, (1854), pp. 247–261.

4. *The History and Culture of the Indian People*, *The Vedic Age*, Vol. i, General Editor R. C. Majumdar, Bharatiya Vidya Bhavan. (Bombay, 1951), p. 143.

5. *Ibid.*, p. 143.

6. *Ibid.*, See Appendix on the "Aryan Problem," pp. 220–221. Also Chapter X in full. See also John B. Chethimattam, *Dialogue in Indian Tradition*, (Bangalore, Dharmaram College, 1969), Chapter Two.

7. 1931 Census, Vol. I, p. 425. *Also the History and Culture. . . . op. cit.*, p. 144. By the time the Aryans arrived in India the following races were already there: (a) *Negritos*, brachycephalic Negroids from South Africa. Earliest people to arrive in India. They now survive in the Andaman Islands, and in Malaya; in India traces of them are found among the Nāgās in Assam, and certain tribes in South India: (b) *Proto–Australoids*, black, dolichocephalic, platyrrhine, appear as an early offshoot of the Mediterranean race (Palestine): (c) *Early Mediterraneans*, leptorrhine dolichocephals. Brought some earlier forms of the Austric speech: (d) *Civilized or Advanced Mediterraneans*, leptorrhine, dolichocephals, who became the "Dravidians" of India: (e) *Armenoids*, from the standard Alpine stock, brachycephalic, probably came with the Civilized Mediterraneans (Dravidians) and spoke their language: (f) *Alpines*, brachycephalic, leptorrhine; found in Gujarāt and Bengal; earlier than Vedic Aryans but probably speaking Aryan dialects: (g) *Vedic Aryans*, or *Nordics*,

leptorrhine dolichocephals who brought the Vedic Aryan (Sanskrit) speech: (h) *Mongoloids*, brachycephals; remained in northern and eastern fringes of India and were not influential in any way to the rest of India.

8. *The History and Culture . . . Vedic Age*, *op. cit*., pp. 160–169; P. T. Srinivasa Aiyangar (Iyengar), *Life in Ancient India in the Age of the Mantras* (Madras, 1912), p. 125; *Dravidic Studies*, (University of Madras) n. III, pp. 61–62; *Dialogues in Indian Tradition*, *op. cit*., Chapter Four, p. 22.

9. See my book, *Avatāra*: *The Humanization of Philosophy Through the Bhagavad Gītā*, *op. cit*., especially Chapters One and Two.

10. R.V. 8.69.1: "*prapa vastriṣṭubham iṣaṃ mandadvīrāy endave dhiyāvo medhasātaye puraṃdhyā vivāsati.*"

11. R.V. 4.20.10: "*mā no mārdhīrā bharā dadhi tan naḥ pra dāśuse dātave bhūri yatte tabye teṣṇe śaṣṭe asminta ukthe pra bravānia vayam indra stuvanta.*"

12. R.V. 10.88.8: "*sūktavākaṃ prathamamādidagnimāddidhavirajanayanta devāḥ sa eṣāṃ yajño abhavat tanūpāḥ.*"

13. R.V. 1.120.1: "*Kā te asti araṃkṛtih sūktaih, Kadā nūnaṃ te maghavan dāśema. Visvā matīrātatane tvāyā adha me indra sṛnavo havemā.*"

14. "*Ka rādhad hotrā asvinā vām . . . kathā vidhāti apracetāḥ.*"

15. "*ā kalasesu dhāvati pavitre pari sicyate ukthairyajñesu vardhate.*" (It hastens to the pitchers, poured upon the sieve, it grows strong, at the Sacrifices through the hymns.)

For further references of the Soma and Hymns to win, for example, the Sun—higher viewpoint—See: 9.20.5; 9.106.11; 9.25.2; 9.64.10; 9.113.5; 9.26.6; 9.40.1; 9.43.2; 9.43.3; 9.86.24; 9.34.6; 9.107.24; 9.25.6; 9.50.4; 9.47.3 (*āt soma . . . vajrah sahasrasā bhuvat uktham yadasya jāyate.*) As soon as the song sound, Soma . . . becomes a thousand–winning thunderbolt.

16. "*subrahmā ya jnah susami vasūnāṃ devaṃ rādho janānāṃ.*" (The sacrifice with good hymns becomes well performed and then brings the gifts) *devaṃ radhah*.

17. "*nābrahmāno maghavānam sutāsah mamaduh.*" (Indra is not delighted in the Sacrifice, Soma offering, without hymns.)

18. "*nābrahmā ya jnah ṛdhag joṣati tve.*" (Indra does not delight in Sacrifice without hymns.)

19. "*matiriyaṃ viprā medhasātaye,*" or in 8.26.16 "*vāhistho vāṃ havānāṃ stomo dūtaḥ.*"

20. "*dustaraṃ yasya sāma cit ṛdhag yajño no mānuṣaḥ.*" (Not man's but god's is the sacrifice whose hymn–song is unassailable.)

21. "*Ukthe ukthe soma Indram mamāda nīthe nīthe maghavānaṃ sutāsaḥ.*" The same is said in stanza 1.

22. R.V. 1.131.6.

23. R.V. 1.135.5.

24. R.V. 6.65.5.

25. R.V. 7.16.2.

26. 1.96.2. The variety of hymns, even those connected with the sacrifice directly, like the Aprī hymns, give us a clear indication of the 'variety of ways' in which the 'idea' of the sacrifice was handled by different authors, but they only offer a very general idea of the practice of the sacrifice and its growth.

27. The notion that ideas are perspectives and not substances, I have developed all through my earlier book, *Avatāra*: *The Humanization of Philosophy Through the Bhagavad Gītā*. In this same book I showed, principally in *The Forest*, how this was one of the familiar themes of Ortega y Gasset, which he himself discovered in the Renaissance. See his *Meditations on Quixote*, translated by Evelyn Rugg and Diego Marín, (W. W. Norton & Company: New York, 1963).

The relationship between perspective in space and polyphony in sound has been pointed out by Lowinsky, who reminds us that many musical expressions are borrowed from space (high, low, ascending, pitch, scale, etc.). (E. E. Lowinsky, "The Concept of Physical and Musical Space in the Renaissance," *Papers of the American Musicological Society*, 1946, pp. 57 ff.) Likewise, many musical problems refer to the relationship between the one and the many, or the relations of multiplicities among themselves—discord, dissonance, harmony, counterpoint, parallel movement, etc. Chapter Seven will clarify further the relationship between time and space by the criteria of sound.

27a. For the sake of clarification, we shall summarize them here:

Total Number	Family	Agni	Indra	Viśvadevāḥ	Other gods
43	Gṛtsamada	10	12	5	Brahmaṇaspati 4;
62	Viśvāmitra	29	23	5	. . . .
58	Vāmadeva	15	17	1	Ṛbhus 5;
87	Atri	28	12	11	Maruts 10; Mitrāvaruṇa 11; Aśvins 6;
75	Bharadvāja	16	30	7	Pūṣan 6;
104	Vasiṣṭha	17	16	17	Mitrāvaruṇā 6; Aśvins 8; Uṣas 7; Indra–Varuṇa 4; Varuṇa 4;
87	Kaṇva	7	34	26	Soma 8; Aśvins 8; Maruts 4;
19	Bhṛgus	1	2	1	Soma 12; Maruts 12;
92	Aṅgiras	11	28	—	Soma 23; Ṛbhus 2; Aśvins 3;

The above classification is almost trivial except for two facts: It reiterates the plurality of perspectives we have been insisting upon, and beyond that, it introduces the most radical element, a justification of the need to recover the Ṛg Vedic text.

28. I don't feel I need to develop some of the points I am making here, since they have already been so brilliantly made by Ernest McClain in *The Myth of Invariance*: *The Origin of the Gods, Mathematics and Music from the Ṛg Veda to Plato*, (New York: Nicolas Hays, Ltd., 1976).

For further readings on the relationship between Platonism and music see: I. Horsley's review of the facsimile edition of G. Zarlino's *Le Institutioni Harmoniche* (1558) in *Music Libr. Assoc. Notes*, Series I, 23 (1966–67): 515–19; G. Zarlino, *The Art of Counterpoint*, trans. by G. Marco and C. Palisca (New Haven: Yale Univ. Press, 1968); P. O. Kristeller, "Music and Learning in the Early Italian Renaissance" in his *Renaissance Thought II*: *Papers on Humanism and the Arts*, (New York: Harper Torchbook, 1965), II, 156–59.

29. R.V. 10.72.1: *ukthesu śasyamnesu yaḥ paśyād uttare yuge.*
R.V. 10.129.4: *sato bhandum asati nir avindan hṛdi pratiṣyā kavayo manīṣa.*

30. R.V. 1.88.1.

31. R.V. 3.61.7: the power by which the Sun divides day and night (R.V. 1.32.13).

32. R.V. 5.6.3–4; 9.83.3.

33. R.V. 3.20.2; 4.30.21; 1.20.6; 10.53.9.

34. R.V. 3.30.15. Much has been made of the magic of words in "primitive" cultures. See, for example: Keith, *The Religion and Philosophy of the Vedas*, *op. cit.*, p. 379; Oldenberb, Macdonell, *Encyclopedia of Religion and Ethics*, *op. cit.*, "Vedic Magic," pp. 311–321, etc.; J. Gonda, *Epithets in the Ṛg Veda*, *op. cit.*, see, for example, pp. 135–138 in connection with *rakṣas* (demons). Note that it expresses the idea of 'evil power, harm' impersonally or collectively, i.e., it refers to a 'state of mind' rather than an atomic individual being.

In this connection it is interesting to note certain words which may sound similar to our Western ears, yet their Vedic meaning is certainly different.

The neuter *enas–*, which appears 29 times in the Ṛg Veda would be a near equivalent to our 'sin,' (Gonda, *op. cit.*, p. 136); yet, its sense in the Ṛg Veda, as in R.V. 1.189.1 would be: "Remove (Agni) from us the sin (mental block) which leads us away from our path (to you). *juhurāṇam.*"

The same care in translation must be exercised when reading similar words denoting manifestations of evil, like: *myṛtu–* (death); *anṛta–* (falsehood, disorder, opposing order); *dhūrti–* (fraud, injury); *duchunā–* (calamity, harm); *abhisasti–* (curse, calumny); *amivā–* (disease); *āgas–* (sin); *kṣudḥ–* (hunger); *jaras–* (decay, old age).

As Gonda mentions in the above citation (p. 131), these names never receive epithets in the Ṛg Veda–which is a peculiar happening since 'powers' and gods and vision receive so many. The answer might be that the *Ṛṣis* were content with establishing an initial original power of opposition to the energy of vision and that the power which overpowered this power, i.e., that of the gods and their vision, is the one that carries the epithets to increase the expressions and carry the idea of how much greater is that power which liberates.

But the real difficulty in understanding the Ṛg Vedic use of *Vāc* (word) as an active power that becomes human flesh while it speaks, lies principally in our own present understanding of language. Linguistically we are *nominalists* to the core. As such we have emptied words from power—activity—and reduced them to simple names. From the eleventh century with Roscellinus, through Descartes, Locke, Berkeley, Hume, Leibniz, Kant, Hegel, Marx, Wittgenstein and his followers, there has been a systematic reduction of large, abstract, plural ideas in favor of small, concrete, particular, single–meaning names. The word has been emptied of power and reduced to a theory to which all word has to conform. We have suffered "a tidal wave of nominalism;" for, "all modern philosophy of every sect has been nominalistic." (C. S. Pierce (1903), quoted from R. J. van Iten, ed., *The Problem of Universals*, (New York: Appleton–Century–Crofts, 1970), pp. 152f.) This tidal wave of nominalism is nowhere more apparent than in the daily battle waging between the man in the streets with his fistful of facts and emasculated human powers, and the nominalistic professions (science, psychology, theology and law) bent on keeping him so. (See: M. Foucault, *Madness and Civilization: A History of Insanity in the Age of Reason*, trans., R. Howard, (New York: Pantheon, 1965). But on this point we shall say more later.

The other problem we shall have to face in understanding the Rg Vedic culture is that our present vocabulary to understand or describe any man is derived mostly from a theory that organizes the human sensorium primarily for a "vision" derived from the sense of sight. Ṛg Vedic man, on the other hand, or Plato for that matter, derives his vocabulary from an organization of the sensorium where "sound" is primary. Even more, sound is the essence of the human body, and on the model of tuning theory we are working on, "plucking" the string at any point will simultaneously give us two perspectives—sound–sight, or body–perspective. But on this, more as we proceed.

35. For a detailed study of words connected with 'vision' etc., see: Gonda's *The Vision of the Vedic Poets . . . op. cit.*

For a detailed study of the word *māyā* in the Ṛg Veda, see: Gonda's *Four Studies in the Language . . . op. cit.*

36. In R.V. 1.61.2 we read about the devotees of Indra: *indrāya hṛdā manasā . . . dhiyo marjayanta* (they polish their visions for Indra with heart, mind and reflection.) Heart and mind constitute the point of revelation and vision. Also R.V. 1.71.2.

37. R.V. 1.44.9; 7.66.10; 1.89.7; 16.1; 5.26.2.

38. R.V. 5.8.6.

39. R.V. 9.13.9; 6.5.11; 9.6.7; *antaḥ paśyan vrajanā.*

40. R.V. 7.32.22.

41. R.V. 1.155.5.

42. 1.35.2: *hiranyayena savitā rathenā devo yāti bhuvanāni paśyan.* R.V. 1.23.3: *indravāyā manojuvā havanta ūtayo sahasrāksā dhiyas patī.*

43. R.V. 1.23.2. To see from the pinnacle of *turiyam brahman* in 5.40.6.

44. R.V. 1.139.2.

45. R.V. 10.130.6.

46. R.V. 8.25.9.

47. R.V. 10.82.1. One criterion that the Ṛg Veda offers with a change of perspective is certain intoxication, happiness. The *ṛṣi* is made violent, agitated, heated, with this vision, as in R.V. 5.52.13–14. Or he trembles with a sweet vibration (*vipra*) of wisdom, as in 3.32.4 and 10.5. But he always remains an enthusiastic seer, as in 7.43.1; 2.11; 8.42.4; 39.9, and he also intoxicates his listeners with the light of heaven, as in 9.105.1; and 2.97.32.

48. R.V. 1.89.8.

49. R.V. 10.17.4.

50. R.V. 1.164.22.

51. R.V. 1.64.18; 7.9.5.

52. R.V. 9.100.3.

53. R.V. 1.164.5; 139.2: *dhībhis cana manasā svebhir akṣabhiḥ*; with our mind, through our own eyes.

54. R.V. 1.164.8.

55. R.V. 1.164.8.

56. R.V. 10.42.

57. R.V. 10.55.1.

58. R.V. 10.61.6.

59. The passage from one way of seeing to another is often described in the Ṛg Veda as a kind of shock, in Pali called *saṃvega.*

See Coomaraswamy, Ananda K., "Saṃvega—Aesthetic Shock" in *Harvard Journal of Asiatic Studies*, 6, p. 358.

It is philosophically interesting to notice the two kinds of phenomena which may 'shock' someone into a new vision. The Ṛg Veda gives us visual images, like in 1.164 and also auditive images of *Vāc*, and sound as in 7.104. Our Western, images are mostly visual, and more so as our civilization moves on.

60. Francis M. Cornford, Trans. by, *Plato's Timaeus*, (New York: The Liberal Arts Press, 1959), 50b and 51a.

"We may fittingly compare the Recipient to a mother, the model to a father, and the nature that arises between them to their offspring." This is Plato's explicit generalization of the function of sexual metaphor, and it is offered in the context of a dialogue in which the "World–Soul" itself is modelled on his Greek Dorian scale.

61. R.V. 1.164.16.

62. R.V. 8.7.7.

63. R.V. 1.7.9.

64. R.V. 7.79.1.

65. The *brahmodya* (or *brahmavadya*) is a discussion held amongst the priests in the form of dialogue. The hymn we are seeing, 1.164, is one of the earliest examples. R.V. 8.29, Atharvaveda 9.9 and 10, are other examples. The practice is carried on in the Brāhmaṇas.

See for further studies: Keith, *The Religion and Philosophy . . . op. cit.*, pp. 344–345, 435. Bloomfield, *Religion of the Veda, op. cit.*, pp. 216ff.

"The Marriage of Saranyu Tvaṣṭar's Daughter," *JAOS*, Vol. 15, pp. 172ff.

66. pṛcchāmi tvā param antam pṛthivyāh
pṛcchāmi yatra bhuvanasya nābhiḥ
pṛcchāmi tvā asvasya retaḥ
pṛcchāmi vācaḥ paramam vyoma

67. Equal–temperament may serve as a kind of warning to all of us on how a creative advance in one age can lead to cultural isolationism and dogmatism in the next. The introduction of equal–temperament was born of a need to make chromatic modulations—of increasing importance during the 16th century and of critical importance by the 18th—practicable on keyed and fretted instruments. Temperament was understood as a lamentable, albeit useful, compromise with the purity of thirds, fourths, and fifths within the rigid matrix of the octave, but its twelve tones required two or three times that many *names* to keep alive the "intentionality" of the composers. (Hence C = B♯= D♭♭ became physically invariant while remaining psychologically differentiated according to tonal context, and all other tones similarly.) By the twentieth century, however, a still newer stylistic development abandoned as totally as it could the "tonal intentionality" kept alive by the naming system, and a search began for a new musical notation whose total intentionality was restricted to exactly twelve elements in the octave. War and commerce intruded, however, to make the World One. The melodic freedom of the East—never incarcerated in a fixed scale, together with its horror of reductionism—now promises to deflect the West from its rigidity, freeing it from the demand that the act of music–making be reduced to conforming to the theory of 12–tone equal temperament.

68. I have sketched the plight of contemporary philosophy and its inability to reach other cultures through analysis in my book, *Avatāra*—especially in Chapter Two. What is most significant to language analysis, however, is its nominalistic ground. As a consequence, words are, on the one hand, very important, but on the other, they are empty of content; they are cut off from things and truth, and exist in a logical world of their own. In contemporary structural linguistics, words have no inherent meaning, for they can be reduced to basic quasi–mathematical units. The search for a basic number of irreducible units out of which all speech can be constituted is an *a priori* demand of the analytic method which demands that Language be reduced to logical atomism: a suicide of the activity of language–making for the security of a theory of language.

The reduction of language to a theory of language has created a political confusion which even the American broad–mindedness finds it difficult to deal with. The following excerpt from the editorial page of *Newsday*, Monday, March 8, 1976, will make my point clear: (Reprinted with permission of Newsday.)

HOW DEMOCRATIC ARE EUROPE'S COMMUNISTS?

The more vigorous the debate in an American political campaign, the healthier our system is deemed to be. That raises an interesting question about the 25th Communist Party Congress that wound up last week.

For the first time in Moscow, Communist Parties from outside the Soviet Union stood up and publicly disagreed with their supposed masters in the Kremlin. Is that a sign of weakness for world communism, or of strength?

Only time can tell, of course. But there's no doubt that communism has moved into a new stage of evolution when delegates from the Italian and French Communist Parties (the largest outside the Soviet Union and China) assert the right to support 'a pluralistic and democratic system' in clear defiance of the teachings of Marx and Lenin, not to mention Stalin and his successors. Italy's party leader, Enrico Berlinguer, went so far as to endorse Italian membership in the Atlantic alliance.

Shocking as this must have seemed to more docile Russian and Eastern European delegates, last week's disputation was in fact only the latest evidence of the western Communists' new desire to work within the democratic system. In Italy, that attitude plus the corruption of parties further to the right has already has already won them control of numerous cities and regions, a large contingent in the national parliament and an excellent chance of participation in the Rome government itself. Somewhat belatedly, French Communists are adopting the same strategy of independence from the Russian-directed "socialist camp."

Whether this is just the latest ploy of the Marxists or a genuine change of attitude, the fact remains that Americans must start thinking seriously about the strong possibility that they'll soon have a NATO ally with Communists in the cabinet.

To all appearances, there's more thought being given this prospect outside the State Department than inside. The United States is still represented in Rome by an ambassador known for right-wing views, and many Italians of all persuasions still bristle over the granting of a U.S. visa to a neo-fascist leader while one was denied to a distinguished member of parliament who happens to be a Communist. French socialists have publicly accused the American ambassador to Paris of interfering in politics by urging them not to cooperate with homegrown Communists.

The drastically changed political climate in Europe has prompted Fortune magazine—hardly a hotbed of leftist sentiment—to publish a series of articles giving sober consideration to the likelihood that Communists may soon, by vote of the people, be helping govern some of America's closest allies.

"When a professed democrat says he belongs to a 'camp' that admits totalitarians, it is natural to wonder about the depth of that commitment to democracy," Fortune's executive editor, Daniel Seligman, wrote in his concluding article. "At the same time, it would be foolish to deny the possibility of democratic communism. There is no inherent reason why Communist Parties must be totalitarian."

> *If that is so, an American foreign policy based on automatic opposition to Communists everywhere (except Moscow and Peking) may soon be a blueprint for political disaster; after all, we can hardly begrudge our allies the right of self-determination. Since the present management of the State Department seems incapable of response to the new circumstances, it would be interesting to hear from America's presidential contenders how they'd handle the change that looms ahead. It may be the biggest foreign policy question of the next four years.*

What do we have here? George Orwell's *Nineteen Eighty-four*'s "Newspeak"? A new language where war is peace, freedom is slavery, ignorance is strength? This is the up-side down world of totalitarian ideology where the act of creation in man has been given over—never fully taken—by the ideological needs of the state. We are not, of course, dealing with a political problem. The problem is radically philosophical. The whole political world of the West, communist and non-communist, shares the same "set of facts" derived from the same shared science. Using this category of facts as fundamental, language games of the types seen in the above quotation appear even logically democratic, except for one thing. They hide the fact that the constituents of democracy, the people, have systematically been deprived—or demanded that they be deprived—from "doing" anything except conform to the ideology of the state or the party, which, by that same activity, lobotomizes the people and cultures it controls. In this activity communists, scientists and the democratic American *Newsday* are all equal conspirators against the people. They all demand from us that we give up the activity—original and authentic—of being men and women which is ours, and surrender to the "theories" about men and women which are theirs. Language is reduced to the names of a theory, according to them. Language is making new flesh through our own speech, according to us and also according to what they demand us to *do*. Let no one amputate our flesh.

Nowhere is this amputation of the human activity, the human flesh, carried out more systematically than by the high priests of the sciences of the human psyche, psychology and religion. Again we find that in order to carry out this human lobotomy with impunity men and women are systematically trained to pay attention to *theories*, rather than the activity of being men and women, of which theories derive. Nominalism, that is, a theory with its names, is practically all one needs to learn and accept in order to join the "therapy" set.

I have already dealt with this problem in my book, *Avatāra*; and I refer the reader to Chapter Four. I already mentioned there how the problem of personal identity has found three main images by which it apparently resolves itself. I also mentioned how easy it is for man and woman to verify any of the images it chooses to embody, for very soon these images have a way of becoming human flesh; and that the human sickness itself, which psychiatry and psychology try to cure, is the radical falsification of any and all theories when applied to man and woman. It was suggested that the radicality of man and woman lies precisely in the activity that falsifies as much as in the activity that verifies theories. The fact that patients are so knowledgeable today about their symptoms and illnesses is because both patients and doctors are both the victims and executioneers of a theory of man which is radically nominalistic and identifies itself by focusing on the theory and the names of the theory. By this theory, the world of the mind, like the world of plants and animals, may be classified into categories, subclasses, genera and species. The eighteenth and nineteenth century institutionalized for psychiatry what Aristotle had started for biology and medicine: to isolate specific disorders by inventing new names. Words so familiar, alcoholism, autism, catatonia, claustrophobia, homosexuality, masochism, schizophrenia, as well as psychiatry, psychopathology and psychotherapy have been with us for only that short a time. The technical terms, which to a saner society would sound as popular insults, become accurate clinical sketches of symptoms, their origin and cause, and their statistically expected outcome. Nothing further about the patient or the symptom itself is necessary for applying one of those psychopathological labels. Abnormal behavior can be precisely described and attributed to a person independent of whatever might be its underlying reasons: genetic, toxic, psychodynamic, biochemical, social, familiar, cultural or semantic. The empirical nominalistic view calls for nothing more, nothing deeper, than mastering a technical vocabulary.

There are those, on the other hand, who want to do away with psychopathology altogether; because classifications, they contend, are only linguistic conventions deriving their authority from a consensus of experts and from tradition and textbooks. These words become power words, political words, words of a psychiatric priesthood. (R. D. Laing's work is the best example of this paradigm.) But by reducing the activity of man and woman to categorizing and naming, this group also agrees with the previous one that man and woman have no activity of their own but to surrender to a theory given by others. The nominalistic game is so closed within its own verification that it forgets to check out if its theories are historically mediated, or if, in fact, people *decide* to adopt certain behaviors which might be described as a form of illness under any cultural or societal conditions. This is, of course, a case for discovery and not for theory.

Meanwhile, psychopathology has become a covert moral philosophy. What is mentally healthy or mentally ill is taking the place of what ideas, behavior, and fantasies are right or wrong. An ideology of compliant humanism is propagated by mental health, is policed by professionals, infiltrates the community, the courts, clinics, welfare centers, schools—and is subsidized by the taxpayer. To refuse mental health, or the mental health approach, confirms only one's sickness. Everybody needs therapy, psychic sessions at the state church, or community mental health conversion center. At these centers the young priests of serious good will, whose community influence begins early with "disturbed" children, counsel whole families about divorce, suicide, orgasms, and madness—in short, about crucial events of human life. These professionals are the guardians of the nation's bodies and souls. But to whom are they accountable for the death of the act of creation in man which they have monopolized by interferring with man in crisis? (See on this point the brilliant work of: James Hillman, *Re–Visioning Psychology*, Harper & Row: New York, 1975, especially pages 58–77.)

69. R.V. 8.70.11: *anyavratam amānuṣam ayajvānam adevayum.* R.V. 10.22.8: *akarmā dasyur abhi no amantur anyavrato amānuṣaḥ.*

70. Since I have mentioned some of the musical and mathematical criteria accompanying and implied in the hymns, the reader might find it interesting to see how Ernest McClain summarizes these languages, as described in the earlier version of my book, *Four–Dimensional Man*, as essential to the foundation of any theory of music in his book, *The Myth of Invariance*.

> *His "language of Non–Existence" (Asat) is exemplified by the pitch continuum within each musical interval as well as by the whole undifferentiated gamut—chaos—from low to high. His "language of Existence" (Sat) is exemplified by every tone, by every distinction of pitch, thus ultimately by every number which defines an interval, a scale, a tuning system, or the associated metric schemes of the poets, which are quite elaborate in the Ṛg Veda. The "language of Images and Sacrifice" (Yajña) is exemplified by the multitude of alternate tone–sets and the conflict of alternate values which always results in some accuracy being "sacrificed" to keep the system within manageable limits. The "language of Embodied (Ṛta) Vision (Dhīḥ)" is required for the all–embracing theories which protect the validity of alternate tuning systems and alternate metric schemes by refusing to grant dominion to any one of them. We are dealing with a primitive science and a mature philosophy.*

PART II: THE ṚG VEDIC INTENTIONAL LIFE

INTRODUCTION

1. E. Husserl, *Erfabrung und Urteil, Untersuchungen zur Genealogie der Logik*, (Praguer: Academia Verlagsbuchhandlung), 1939, pp. 12–14.

2. *Ibid.*, pp. 20–28.

3. *Ibid.*, p. 36.

4. For a more detailed reading on these points I refer the reader to the following works:
E. Husserl, *Ideen zu einer Reinen Phaenomenologie und Phaenomenologischen Philosophie*, (Haag, Martinus Nijhoff) 1952, p. 55ff
E. Fink, *Zur Ontologischen Fruehgeschichte von Ram–Zeit–Bewegung* (*Haag*, Martinus Nijhoff), 1957
U. Claeges, *Edmund Husserls Theorie der Raumkonstitution*, (Haag, Martinus Nijhoff) 1964, p. 309
J. Gebser, *Ursprung und Gegenwart* (Stuttgart, Deutsche Verlags–Anstalt) 1966, p. 309
D. Frey *Grundlegung zu einer Vergleichenden Kunstwissenschaft*, (Darmstadt, Wissens, Buchgesell) 1971, p. 29
H. G. Gadamer, *Wahrheit und Methode* (Tuebingen, J. C. B. Mohr) 1972, p. 97ff.

5. See Gonda, J., *The Vision of the Vedic Poets*, *op. cit.*, pp. 40–51.

6. R.V. 1.89.9 and 10.17.4, respectively.

7. R.V. 10.129.6.

8. Cfr. Gonda, J., *op. cit.*, pp. 51–56.

9. See previous Chapter Three.

10. R.V. 1.164.4 and 10.129.

11. See Lilian Silburn, *Instant et Cause: Le discontinu dans la Pensée Philosophique de L'Inde*. (Paris: 1955), Chapter 1.
Unfortunately the author has in mind only the ritual experience of the Brāhamanas rather than the more comprehensive of the Ṛg Veda.

12. R.V. 6.7.4 and 1.72.9.

CHAPTER FOUR

1. R.V. 10.72.3: *devānām yuge prathama śataḥ sad ajāyata.* The same is repeated in stanza 2 of the same hymn (song–poem). R.V. 7.104 gives a full description of the *Asat*, while echoes of the same are repeated in A.V. 8.4 and 17.1.9, where the *Sat* is said to be established in the *Asat*.

2. A.V. 10.7.10—a repetition of the Directions (*uttānapad*) of R.V. 10.72.3.

3. A.V. 107.25.

4. R.V. 3.49.1; 3.33; 1.32; etc.

5. R.V. 6.7.4.

6. R.V. 1.72.9 and 6.7.4.

7. Piaget, *The Child's Conception of the World and the Child's Conception of Physical Causality* (Littlefield: Adams, 1960).

8. Theodore Roszak, *The Making of a Counter Culture* (New York: Doubleday), p. 208.

9. Douglas A. Roberts, "Science as an Explanatory Mode," in *Main Currents in Modern Thought*, Vol. 26 n. 5.

10. Mark Schorer, "The Necessity of Myth," in *Myth and Myth Making*, Henry A. Murray, (Braziller), 1960, p. 356.

11. Claude Levi–Strauss, *The Savage Mind*, (Chicago: University of Chicago Press, 1966), p. 6.

12. In the translation of these song–poems, I have followed the traditional ones with some changes of my own for better understanding or clearer reading. See *A Philosophy in Song–Poems* by J. B. Chethimattam and Antonio T. de Nicolás (Dharmaram College: Bangalore, 1971). See also, on this same topic: W. Norman Brown, *Man in the Universe*, Univ. of California Press, 1966.—"The Ṛgvedic Equivalent of Hell," *JAOS* 61, 76–80.—"Creation Myth of the Ṛgvedic Equivalent of Hell," *JAOS* 61, 76–80.—"Creation Myth of the Ṛgveda," *JAOS*, 62, 85–98.

13. A.V. 8.4 repeats the same hymn (song–poem) of the Ṛg Veda. Hymn 10.72 gives a description of the *Asat* in relation to the rest of Existence, while Hymn 10.5, especially in stanza 7, points to the ontological unity between the whole imagery of Ṛg Vedic mythology.

14. On the Ṛgvedic conception of the underworld, see:
W. Kirfel, *Die Kosmographie der Inder* (1920) p. 49.
A. A. Macdonell, *Vedic Mythology . . . op. cit.*, p. 169.
M. Falk, "Sat and Asat" Summary of Papers. 14th All India Oriental Conference, Poona, 1948, pp. 117–20.

15. Roth thought that there was extinction for the wicked, see *JAOS* 3, 329–347. In *Vedic Index . . . op. cit.*, Macdonell and Keith (I.176) contradict him.

16. There is no doubt that the most comprehensive description of both dismemberment and creation are found in R.V. 10.90.

17. The above mentioned Ṛg Veda 10.90 would read equally well if instead of *Puruṣa* we substitute *Vṛtra*.

18. R.V. 10.114.5 and 10.129.4–7.

19. This is a clear reference to *Agni* in R.V. 1.164.46.

20. Gabriel Marcel, *Man Against Humanity* (London: The Harvill Press Ltd., 1952), p. 127.
See also: Richard Zaner, "An Approach to Philosophical Anthropology," in *Philosophy and Phenomenological Research*, Vol. XXVII, n. 1. September 1966, pp. 55–68.

21. Heidegger uses also the formula: "being–able–to–be," (Seinkonen) Cfr. *Sein und Zeit*. Max Niemeyer. (Tubingen, 8th Aufl., 1957), pp. 267–333.

22. On *Vṛtra*: see L. Renou and E. Benveniste, *Vṛtra et Vṛdragna* (Paris: 1934). On *Nirṛti*: see L. Renou, "Vedic nirṛti" in *Indian Linguistics* (Chaterji Jubilee Volume), 16, 1955, p. 11f. and 13.

23. R.V. 1.11.7

24. R.V. 10.22.7

25. R.V. 1.101.2; 2.19.6; 4.16.12; 6.20.4; and 6.31.3

26. R.V. 7.19.2

27. R.V. 10.61.13

28. R.V. 1.51.11

29. R.V. 1.101.2

30. J. Gonda, *Epithets in the Rgveda*, *op. cit.*, pp. 130–138.

31. *Ibid.*, p. 134.

32. The most suggestive study on this topic, together with a wide bibliography, is offered by Walter Ong, *The Presence of the Word* (Yale University Press, 1967).

33. See *The Presence of the Word*, *op. cit.*, p. 4.
William M. Ivins, *Art and Geometry: A Study in Space Intuitions* (Cambridge: Harvard University Press, 1946).

34. Ernest McClain, *The Myth of Invariance* (New York: Nicolas Hays, 1976).

35. Several interesting studies are being conducted by modern phenomenologists on the topic of 'space' as here described. In visual space, movement comes from somewhere to go somewhere. The visual space functions as the condition for such a location and relocation. In sounds, the field of their origin is silence and they return to silence. Silence being the field–condition for sound to appear. The same proportion: silence/sound; visual space/movement, holds for the other senses, i.e., cold/heat; death/life, etc.
On the above suggestions see, for example, a modern study by Don Ihde, "Studies in the Phenomenology of Sound," *International Philosophical Quarterly*, Vol. X, n. 2. June, 1970.
Listening and Voice (Ohio University Press, 1976).

CHAPTER FIVE

1. Aristotle, *The Generation of Animals*, Tr. by A. L. Peck (Cambridge, Harvard Univ. Press) 1953, pp. 723a 25–733b 16.
———, *De Anima*, Tr. by X. S. Hett (Cambridge, Harvard (1957, pp. 414; 29–415.
R. Burckhardt, "Das koische tiersystem, eine Vorstufe der zoologischen Systematik des Aristoteles," *Verhandlungen der naturf, Fesellsch, in Basel* 15, 377–413 (1904). Discussion of earlier classification of animals in use by Asclepiad medical school, cited by Peck, *op. cit.*, p. vii. See also A. Castiglione, *A History of Medicine*, Tr. by E. B. Krumbhaar (N.Y., Knopf) 1958, p. 180; D. Ross, *Aristotle* (Lon. Methuen) 1949, p. 1; C. Singer, "Biology" in *The Legacy of Greece*, R. W. Livingstone, ed. (Oxford, Clarendon) 1921, especially comments on the Asclepiad classification, pp. 168–169.

2. R.V. 1.159.1; 7.53.1; 1.185; 6.17.7; 1.106.3; and 4.56.2

3. R.V. 7.192.1

4. R.V. 3.25.1

5. R.V. 2.36.2 and 5.54.10

6. R.V. 10.37.1

7. For the word *Aditi*, see Hildebrandt, *Ueber die Gottin Aditi* (Breslau, 1876), 17 ff.
The Sky is characterized by *Aditi* in R.V. 10.63.3.
For the word *asura* and derivate forms see *Wortenbuch . . . op. cit.*, *asura*, *asurtva*, *asurya*.

8. R.V. 1.64.2.

9. R.V. 5.51.11.

10. R.V. 9.74.7, 9.99.1.

11. R.V. 5.83.6.

12. R.V. 10.124.3.

13. R.V. 10.74.2.

14. R.V. 2.23.2.

15. R.V. 1.131.1, 6.51.8. Cfr. Bloomfield, *Rig–Veda Repetitions*, *op. cit.*, 204.

16. R.V. 6.20.2 and 7.21.7

17. R.V. 2.27.1

18. Indra is not called a son of *Aditi* in the Ṛg Veda, yet his association with the *Ādityas* makes him one of them.

19. *Mārtāṇḍa*, a form of the Sun is father of *Yama*, the first man as in R.V. 10. 14.5 and 10.17.1.

20. R.V. 10.88.11

21. R.V. 8.96.16 and 10.120.6

22. R.V. 10.92.2

23. See Norman W. Brown, "Creation Myth of the Rigveda" (*JAOS* 62) p. 87 note.

24. R.V. 8.25.5

25. R.V. 3.27.9

26. R.V. 10.10

27. See "Two: Its significance in the Ṛgveda" by Stella Kramrish in *Indological Studies in Honor of W. Norman Brown*, (Ernest Bender, American Oriental Series, Vol. 47), pp. 118–123.

28. R.V. 9.5.9

29. R.V. 1.13.10

30. R.V. 3.55.19: *devas tvaṣṭā savitā viśvarūpaḥ pupoṣa prajāḥ jajāna*

31. R.V. 10.110.0; 1.160.2; skillful 1.160; 4.56.3

32. R.V. 3.54.6

33. R.V. 4.56.3

34. R.V. 1.159.4; perhaps also, 1.144.4

35. The terms *pitṛ* or *janitṛ* are applied to many gods: *Dyaus* is called *pitṛ* in 1.71.5; 7.52.3 and *janitṛ* in 4.17.4; 1.164.33; 4.1.10; 1.10.12; 4.17.12. Agni has the same names in 9.90.1. Indra in 3.49.4; 8.36.4–5; may be 8.99.5. *Soma* in 9.86.10; 9.87.2. *Viśvakarman* in 10.83.2 and *Matariśvan* in 1.96.4. In *Tvaṣṭṛ*'s case both names are used to signify the paradoxical fact that he combines in himself male and female qualities. The A.V. 9.4.3–6 echoes this same insight.

36. R.V. 3.55.19 and 10.10.5

37. R.V. 1.164.35

38. R.V. 7.101.3

39. R.V. 8.98.2 and 10.81–83

40. R.V. 10.70

41. R.V. 10.90

42. R.V. 10.71.1; 10.82.3; 10.125

43. R.V. 8.100.3

44. R.V. 1.164.46

45. A.V. 10.7–8

46. A.V. 19.53–54

47. The embryo (*garbha*) is variously called Sun (*sūrya*) or fire (*Agni*). In 3.31.1 and 3 there is also the implication that the impregnation of *Uṣas* (Dawn) with the Sun was accomplished not through a physical incest but through mental operation, since after all the Waters were in the belly of *Vṛtra* and therefore not reachable. The Sun was conceived as the "first seed of the mind," (*manaso retaḥ prathaman*, 10.129.4). The Jains, in fact, did recognize a world in which intercourse between husband and wife was only a mental operation.

48. R.V. 10.124

49. R.V. 2.11.5 and 8.96.16

50. R.V. 3.49.1

51. R.V. 2.12.1

52. R.V. 2.13.5

53. R.V. 4.18.10 and 10.111.2

54. Equal disclaimers to motherhood have epithets like *devī janitri . . . bhadrā janitrī*, as used in 2.30.2; 3.48.2; 10.134.1–6; or the Dawn in 1.124.5, or the Sacrificial Act (*ṛtu*) 2.13.1.

55. R.V. 10.35.7

56. R.V. 1.185.6; 3.31.12

57. R.V. 6.59.2

58. R.V. 3.2.2; 3.11.3; 3.24.1; 3.31.1–2; 4.15.6; 6.49.2; 10.45.8

59. R.V. 4.18.12

60. R.V. 9.96.5; 9.97.38

61. R.V. 3.48.1; 8.79.14; 10.99.10

62. R.V. 8.69.15

63. R.V. 3.32.7

64. R.V. 10.86.11–12

65. *Amuyā* always has evil connotation in the Ṛg Veda; it is used for the place of *Vṛta* 1.32.8; where demons live 10.89.14; where those who practice sorcery by sexual intercourse are to go 1.29.5; 10.85.30; may be 10.135.2 where Indra is to strike down the wicked 5.34.5; and this is the meaning here, of the words *vavrāṃ anantām ava sā padīṣṭa*, 7.104.17.

66. R.V. 1.74.3; 10.4309; 7.8.6

67. R.V. 5.31.3

68. *nir ayā durgahā . . . triaścatā pārśvān nir gamāni*: the same idiom *tirasi durgahā*, which appears in 1.41.3; 6.51.10; 7.60.6; 10.182.1.

69. R.V. 8.45.4.5; 8.77.1.2

70. R.V. 3.48.4; cf. 1.61.7

71. See, David M. Knipe, "The Heroic Theft: Myths from the Ṛgveda IV and the Ancient Near East." (*History of Religions*, 1967), pp. 328–360.

72. R.V. 8.98.2; 10.15.35

73. R.V. 6.30.5; 8.36.4; 10.29.6; 10.54.3; 1.63.406

74. R.V. 1.32.11; 50.30.5; 8.85.18

75. R.V. 8.15.6; 10.43.8

76. R.V. 4.30.9–12; 2.15.6; 10.138.5; 10.73.6

77. R.V. 1.117.5

78. R.V. 1.51.4; 1.52.8

79. R.V. 1.130.9

80. R.V. 3.4.7

81. R.V. 10.55.7

82. Norman W. Brown, "Creation Myth of the Rigveda." (*JAOS* 62), pp. 85–98.

83. See *The Presense of the Word, op. cit.*, where a most suggestive study is offered on the influence of the 'visual model' of philosophers from Plato, Kant, Locke, to modern days.

84. See *The Presence of the Word, op. cit.*, pp. 111–175. The above notes on the sensorium, with certain personal alterations are based on those pages.

85. R.V. 2.3.9 and 3.29.16 indicate this use of *prajña*. R.V. 10.79.4 equates *pracetās* and *vicetās* in this same sense of heuristic discernment while R.V. 7.4.4 gives both meanings to Agni as the poet–seer possessed of intentionality amongst those deprived of it (*kavir akaviṣu pracetāḥ*). Other instances of the same use or conveying the same idea are found in R.V. 10.87.9; 7.17.4; 6.5.1; 6.13.3; 2.10.3; 6.2; 10.97.4 which is in accord with the above 7.4.4; also 4.1.1; in association with the word *kavi* the word is used in R.V. 3.25.1; 10.110.1; 6.14.2; 8.84.2; 6.14.2; 8.102.18; 7.16.12; 3.29.5.

86. R.V. 3.38.3.

87. Cfr. R.V. 4.47.18, *rūpaṃ rūpaṃ pratirūpa babhūva.*

88. In R.V. 10.53.9 he creates, fashions, the gods.

89. R.V. 1.161 deals with the forms taken by the *Ṛbhus*. It is interesting to note how these forms (as in stanza 5) were derived from *gnā–su*, of sounds, i.e., from sound.

90. As said of *Agni* in 3.5.6.

91. R.V. 1.161.9; 4.33.7; 4.33.2–3; 3.60.2; 4.51.6; 4.33.8; 1.111.1; 1.161.7

92. See *Instant et Cause*, *op. cit.*, First Chapter.

93. See *Epithets in the Rgveda*, *op. cit.*

94. On *Varuṇa* we must have in mind his connection with the *Ādityas*. The main hymns are: 2.28; 5.85; 7.86–89; 8.41.42; and 1.24.25, that is, 10 song–poems. There are 23 other song–poems addressed to *Mitra–Varuṇa*: 11 in book 5; 6 in book 7. Nine more hymns to *Indra–Varuṇa*, 4 in book 7. There is only one song–poem addressed to *Mitra*: 3.59, and there are 6 song–poems to the *Ādityas*. There are no hymns to *Varuṇa* in book 9, yet he is mentioned in 35 hymns of that book.

Uṣas (Dawn) is celebrated in 21 hymns, 14 in the family books. Hymn 4.51 may be taken as a prototype of such hymns. The Dawn maintains the unity where to the naked eye there is only the disunity of night and day. She knows the way (1.124.3 and 5.80.2). Her way is the way of immortality as in 1.113.13. Her way is similar to that of *Soma* (9.106.8) and *Savitṛ* (4.54.2).

The *Aśvins* are celebrated in 54 hymns, half of them in books One and Eight. They are twins. They operate as the 'twilight preceding the Dawn,' or the twilight after the sunset, (5.73.4; 1.181.4; 8.22.14; 10.39.1; 40.4). See, as a model, hymn 7.71.

Sūrya has in all about 12 song–poems. See 7.63 as an example.

Savitṛ has also about 12 hymns. See 1.35. He is the stimulator, the one who keeps all the spheres in continuous flow, 2.38.7; takes all forms, 5.81.2; he bestows 'life succeeding life' in 4.64.2; that is continuity or immortality, as in 4.54.2; 1.110.3. See especially 3.62.10 as *Savitṛ* the stimulator of thought.

On *Pūṣan* see 6.54 and 6.53.

On *Viṣṇu* see 1.154. Also Gonda's *Some Aspects of Early Viṣṇuism*, *op. cit.*

95. See on *Vāyu–Vāta* (the Wind: from *vā*, to blow) 1.134 and 10.168; 186. The Wind, obviously is not a visual image, nor does it have front, back, and directions, which may be as determinable as an object. It surrounds from all over. There are special mentions to gusts of wind and wind in general, as in 4.46.3; 48.4; 2.41.1. It is interesting to notice the relation between wind (touch) and *Soma* (taste): See 1.134.1; 6; 135.1; 4.46.1; etc.

For the *waters* see 7.49. For *Rudra* see 2.33. *Rudra* is immersed in the world of sound (the *Maruts*: thunder, storms, lightning) and touch (*vajra–bāhu*), just like Indra, they are 'bolt–armed' to fight *Vṛtra*'s followers, as in 2.33.13. Rain is connected with them too.

Apām–Napāt and the others may be seen in 2.35. They take the place of *Indra*, *Rudra* and *Agni*, at times.

96. *Agni* is celebrated in 200 song–poems in the Ṛg Veda. In fact, the *Agni* songs stand at the beginning of the 'family books' (from 2 to 7). In fact, all except two books, start with songs to *Agni*.

There is a peculiarity regarding *Agni* which gives us a further clue as to the unity of the sensorium–synthesis investigated here. *Agni* is an earth god. However, through *Agni* the three 'spaces' unite. *Agni* is threefold (1.95.3 and 4.1.7) for so the *devas* made him (10.88.10); has three heads (1.146.1), three stations, three tongs, three bodies, (3.20.2), three dwellings (8.39.8), three kindlings (3.2.9) and above all, he is the source of the three 'spaces' (2.36.4: 'sit down in the three *yonis*,' or 'men have kindled *Agni* in his tripartite seat,' as in 5.11.2.

Soma is celebrated with 120 song–poems. As important as *Indra* and *Agni*, in *Soma* the whole range of the perception through taste, 'touch,' in certain ways, and 'kinaesthesia,' is concentrated.

Sarasvati, the Rivers, mountains, forests, trees, etc. The Ṛgveda has also hymns to the terrestrial waters, in the rivers (10.75), mountains (*parvata*) (meaning at times *Vṛtra* (2.11.7–8) or *Indra*, 3.54.20, and forests (*aranyāni*) as in 10.46.

It is obvious that only people alert to sound can find presence and communion in forests, mountains, rivers, etc. Animism, in fact, is possible among highly oral–aural cultures or people, even though living in a visual culture.

97. See Gonda, *The Vision of the Vedic Poets*, *op. cit.*

98. *Enneads* 4.4.6. It will be interesting to note here, in relation to the sense of touch, the super–abundance of words meaning to pierce, in a sexual manner, or in general perform biological functions. See on this topic: Ivo Fiser, *Indian Erotics of the Oldest Period.* Universita Karlove, Praha, 1966.

99. R.V. 9.3.2; 9.65.12; and 10.99.6

100. What is said of *Vāc* may also be said of Brahman. See: *Notes on Brahman*, *op. cit.*

101. Cfr. 1.164.39; also 10.125.5; 10.71.4

102. See R.V. 10.59.4.

103. R.V. 10.55.2 and 1.113.16.

104. R.V. 10.18.5; 10.60.7; 10.59.8.

105. R.V. 1.35; 5.81.4; 5.82.8.

106. R.V. 1.110.3.

107. A.V. 19.53–54

108. Only once in R.V. 10.42 is the word *kāla* used.

109. R.V. 10.90.

110. R.V. 7.87.

111. R.V. 8.87.

112. R.V. 10.129.

113. See Minoru Hara, "A Note on the Sanskrit Word Nitya," in *JAOS*, 78, 90–96.

114. See Michael Polanyi, *The Tacit Dimension*, Doubleday, New York, 1966. Related bibliography is offered on the subject above discussed.

See also the bibliography offered in *The Presence of the Word*, *op. cit.* Pierre Teilhard de Chardin, *The Phenomenon of Man*, Harper & Brothers, 1959.

Marshall McLuhan, *Understanding Media*: *The Extensions of Man*, The New American Library, 1964.

115. Textual confirmation was offered from R.V. 3.8.2–3; 10.72.1; 10.129.2; etc.

116. R.V. 1.89.9.

117. *āyur viśvayuh*, R.V. 10.17.4.

118. R.V. 1.89.8.

119. R.V. 1.55.8; 1.57.6; 2.16.2; 10.50.1; 6.18.4; 8.15.2; etc.

120. R.V. 1.55.6; 3.36.4; 5.33.6.

121. R.V. 1.127.3–4.

122. See on this topic, Ivo Fiser, *Indian Erotics of the Oldest Period*, *op. cit.*

CHAPTER SIX

1. Miguel de Unamuno, *Tragic Sense of Life*, trans., J. E. C. Flitch (New York: Dover, 1954), p. 139.

2. Montaigne, "Of the Inconstancy of Our Actions," in *Essays, II*, 1, trans. by Charles Cotton, 4 Vols. (London: Reeves & Turner, 1902), Vol. II, p. 142.

3. As may be seen from R.V. 5.40.1; 8.3.17; 24.2; 93.2; 89.3; 10.111.6; 10.133.1; etc.

4. R.V. 8.33.5; 3.34.1 *indraḥ pūrbhid ātirad dāsam arkaiḥ* (Indra, the shatterer of strongholds has gained victory over the *dāsa* by means of mighty words. Note the assimilation of sound into energy); 10.111.10; 9.88.4 applies also to Soma assimilating within Indra's energy taste: "Like Indra a slayer of *Vṛtras* and destroyer of strongholds." Cfr. *Epithets of the Ṛgveda, op. cit.*, pp. 54–56.

5. R.V. 1.85.3; 10.152.3; 8.17.9; 10.49.6; 6.60.3; 5.35.5; etc.

6. *kratu–* stands for intentionality or intentional efficacy. Cfr. L. Renou *Etudes védique et paninéennes*, II (Paris, 1956), p. 58. L. Silburn, *Instant et Cause* (Paris, 1955), p. 24. J. Gonda *Epithets in the Ṛgveda, op. cit.*, p. 37–42.

7. See Chapter Five.

8. See Chapter Three and Five.

9. See R.V. 8.96.20; 4.20.2 (*vajrī maghavā . . . imam yajñam anu no vājasātau* = the *vajra* bearer, the great, I expect to attend the sacrifice in order to acquire *vāja*–power.)

10. R.V. 10.43.6; 6.23.1; 160.4.

11. Cfr. Chapter Five; see also R.V. 1.51.2 where it said of Indra that he fills the whole space.

12. There is no battle (*āji–*) for Indra without Soma. Nor is there Sacrifice for Indra without Soma. See: 1.16.8; 1.81.1; 6.47.6; 7.32.6; 8.2.26; 4.11; 6.40; 33.1; 37.1; 90.1; 92.24; 93.20; 33; 97.4; 9.98.10; 10.152.2 and especially 8.33.14 and 78.7.

13. See note 8 above.

14. R.V. 6.17.6.

15. R.V. 2.12.1–2.
It will not take a great effort of the imagination to realize how, in Indra's power, is regathered (turned in) the dispersed powers of the sensorium. With the note made above 11 and by reading carefully Part I of Chapter Five, it will be easy to realize how Indra's power is the embodiment of the power of (intentionality) the *ṛṣis*, of the gods, who prepare him or his birth, of the Sun, the *Aśvins*, the *Ṛbhus*, the Hawk or Eagle, plants, rivers, *Maruts*, etc.

16. *Vāyu*, the Wind, equals *Mātariśvān* as *Vāta–Vāyu*, the gale or Dawnwind who awakens Agni and fans the flame of life as in 1.112.3.

17. R.V. 1.141.3. Note also how Indra's *vajra*'s function is to bring the enemies to the ground, the original space, or remind them of it.

18. The Lotus, *puṣkara*, stands for the original ground of all existence, or the existence of all the worlds. It is applied in a similar meaning to the Serpent in 7.34.6: "I celebrate with recitations the serpent water–born (*nadivṛtam*)," and since *Ahi* is *abja*, water–born, then Agni is born from the lotus, as coming out of *Vṛtra*. An echo of the same may be seen in SB VII. 3.2.14: "he has crept out of the waters into the lotus–leaf."

19. See, for example, PB XXV. 15.4; PB VII. 5.6; TA Y. 1.1; TB II. 6.13.1 where the identity of the Cave (*Vala*) with *Makha* is suggested, as in R.V. 3.34.10 and SB XIV. 1.1.

20. R.V. 10.51.8

21. In R.V. 10.89.7 *Vṛtra*'s fall is equated to the falling of a tree and in 10.31.7 and 10.81.4 it is asked, "What was the wood, what the tree out of which they carved Heaven and Earth?" Soma and Agni are also called *vanaspati*, lord of the woods.

22. For a more detailed analysis account of these notes and especially for further references in other than the Rg Vedic period on the same ideas and repetitions see:
Ananda K. Coomaraswamy, "Angels and Titans: An Essay in Vedic Ontology," in *JAOS*, 55, 373–419. Also by the same author: "The Darker Side of Dawn," *Smithsonian Miscellaneous Publications*. Vol 94 n. 1.

23. R.V. 1.27.13.

24. R.V. 1.164.30 and 8.39.8.

25. *Ibid.*

26. R.V. 1.164.35.

27. R.V. 1.164.50 and 10.90.16.

28. R.V. 2.3.6 (*tantuṃ tataṃ saṃvayantī samīcī yajñasya peśaḥ sudughe*).

29. R.V. 1.105.9.

30. R.V. 8.32.26; 2.11.18.

31. R.V. 1.164.5.

32. R.V. 2.5.2.

33. R.V. .0.168.4.

34. R.V. 4.3.4 (*ṛtasya bodhi ṛtacit svādhīḥ*).).

35. R.V. 5.60.6 (*Agne vittād haviṣo yadyajāma*).

36. R.V. 1.159.1.

37. R.V. 1.144.7; 3.20.2; etc.

38. R.V. 2.27.7 (*ṛtenādityā mahi vo mahitvam*).

39. R.V. 1.44.14; 89.7; 3.54.10; 6.21.11; 50.2; 52.13; 6.66.10; 10.65.7.

40. R.V. 2.4.3; 3.29.7; 8.19.2; (*agniṃ devā dadhanvire adhvarāya*).

41. R.V. 7.11.4.

42. R.V. 2.1.2.

43. R.V. 8.23.18.

44. *Ibid.*

45. R.V. 2.5.2 and 3.15.4.

46. R.V. 6.16.11.

47. R.V. 2.35.12.

48. R.V. 1.31.2; 10.115.5; etc.

49. R.V. 3.32.12; 6.38.4; 6.40.4; 8.12.20; 13.17; etc.

50. R.V. 3.32.12.

51. R.V. 6.21.2; or in 7.39.7 and 6.19.5 (*somavṛddaḥ*).

52. See Zenaide A. Ragozin, *Vedic India* (Munshi Ram Manohar Lal, Delhi, 1961), 2nd ed., p. 174.

53. R.V. 9.54.9 and 97.11.

54. R.V. 9.72.4.

55. R.V. 9.98.6.

56. R.V. 9.96.10.

57. R.V. 9.67.19.

58. R.V. 9.80.4.

59. R.V. 9.7.2.

60. R.V. 9.73.9.

61. R.V. 9.68.5.

62. R.V. 5.37.4; 8.62.5; 8.82.2; 10.42.8; 160.1.

63. R.V. 9.72.1; 9.97.45; 107.22; 9.103.2; 9.62.5; 8.2.3.

64. R.V. 9.88.2; 86.45; 77.1; 7.47.1.

65. R.V. 9.11.6; 22.3; 81.1; 101.12; 5.51.7; 7.32.4.

66. R.V. 7.40.5; 67.10; 69.8 (*irā*).

67. R.V. 10.94.10 (*ilā*).

68. R.V. 4.2.5 (*ilāvāṃ*); 3.54.20; 59.3; 4.50.8; 10.27.9.

69. R.V. 1.40.4; 3.1.23 (*ilāmagne havamānāya sādha*); 3.22.5; 6.10.7; 7.102.3.

70. R.V. 8.35.14 and 8.10.1.8.

71. *pracetasā adhvarasya yajñasya*, 8.10.4; and in 1.15.11 (*yajñavāhasā*).

72. R.V. 9.61.7; 1.34.3; 47.4.

73. R.V. 3.26.6; 2.36.2; 1.86.2.

74. R.V. 1.43.4; 1.114.4; 4.3.1.

75. R.V. 6.55.1.

76. R.V. 1.89.7; 6.50.2; etc.

77. R.V. 3.20.1 *adhvaraṃ vāvāsānāḥ*.

78. R.V. 10.66.1 *adharasya pracetasaḥ*.

79. See the much quoted 1.164. On the Word and its division see stanza 24 of the same hymn.

80. *divakṣaso agnijihvā ṛtavridha ṛtasya yoniṃ vimṛśanta āsate dyāṃ skabhitvy apa ā cakrur ojasā vajñaṃ ljanitvī tanvī ni māmṛjuḥ.*

81. R.V. 1.76.5.

82. R.V. 3.14.7 and 3.27.12.

83. R.V. 3.15.5.

84. R.V. 3.17.4.

85. R.V. 1.145.2–5.

86. R.V. 4.19 referring to both gods and men as the audience, the objective body.

87. R.V. 1.162.19.

88. R.V. 10.2.3.

89. R.V. 10.124.2.

90. Many texts repeat this same idea. See R.V. 4.10.2; 1.1.4; 10.8.5; 6.9.2–3; 1.45.7. Further schemes of duration may be seen in: Lilian Silburn, *Instant et Cause op. cit.*, pp. 32–48.

91. R.V. 5.1.2.

92. R.V. 2.1.4.

93. R.V. 1.24.1.

94. R.V. 10.5.2.

95. R.V. 1.164.38.

96. Cfr., for example, 10.79.2.

97. Cfr. 5.46.1; 1.164.31; etc.

CHAPTER SEVEN

1. See Chapter Three.

2. See Chapter Three and notes for bibliography.

3. R.V. 10.62.4.

4. R.V. 3.53.7; 10.67.2.

5. R.V. 10.67.2.

6. R.V. 7.42.1.

7. R.V. 10.67.2.

8. R.V. 10.62.1.

9. R.V. 5.11.6.

10. *sahase jātaḥ* (born with a view to conquer through power). Similarly, R.V. 6.38.5 and 10.73.1 (*jamaṣṭhā ugraḥ sahase*).

11. R.V. 1.16.6; 7.98.3; 104.3.

12. R.V. 5.31.3; 10.153.2.

13. R.V. 1.127.9.

14. R.V. 4.50.1.

15. R.V. 6.66.9.

16. R.V. 1.50.13.

17. R.V. 1.11.4; 2.23.3 (*sākam jātah kratunā sākam ojasā vavakṣitha sākam vṛddho vīryaiḥ* = born with power, you Indra, have grown with *ojas*, with manly courage).

18. R.V. 1.130.9 (*sūras cakram pra vṛhaj jātā ojasā*).

19. R.V. 1.47.7 (with the *Aśvins*); 3.51.9 (with the *Maruts*); 10.73.6 (with *Namuci* who is *Vṛtra*); etc.

20. For a detail analysis and abundance of texts on powers and gods see: Gonda, J., *Some Observations on the Relations Between "Gods" and "Powers" in the Veda, A Propos of the Phrase Sūnuḥ Sahasaḥ*, Mouton & Co. 's–Gravenhage, 1957.

21. For other words denoting "power" like *māyā*, see Chapter Three and notes.

22. R.V. 1.27.2; 6.48.5.

23. R.V. 6.18.11; 6.20.1.

24. R.V. 10.10.2.

25. R.V. 9.71.4; 10.115.7; 8.102.7.

26. R.V. 1.164.16; A.V. 2.1.2; etc.

27. R.V. 7.61.4.

28. R.V. 10.61.11.

29. R.V. 1.46.11.

30. R.V. 4.3.14.

31. R.V. 4.3.1.

32. R.V. 2.28.4.

33. R.V. 5.1.7.

34. R.V. 7.39.1.

35. R.V. 3.2.26.

36. R.V. 8.23.9.

37. R.V. 10.5.7.

38. R.V. 10.61.14.

39. R.V. 5.12.2.

40. *Ibid.*

41. *Ibid.*

42. R.V. 6.57.19.

43. R.V. 7.66.3.

44. R.V. 1.124.3.

45. R.V. 1.124.3.

46. *Ibid.*

47. R.V. 4.51.6.

48. R.V. 8.25.3.

49. R.V. 1.75.8.

50. R.V. 7.87.3.

51. R.V. 3.55.13.

52. R.V. 10.61.19.

53. R.V. 2.55.13.

54. R.V. 10.67.2.

55. R.V. 4.3.11.

56. R.V. 2.24.8.

57. 10.62.2.

58. R.V. 10.62.2.

59. R.V. 10.66.8.

60. R.V. 7.43.3.

61. R.V. 10.67.1.

62. R.V. 4.33.9.

63. R.V. 9.97.32.

64. R.V. 9.86.32.

65. R.V. 9.113.2.

66. R.V. 9.66.24.

67. R.V. 9.89.2.

68. R.V. 9.97.4. Two characteristic hymns on *Ṛta*: 5.45 and 7.87.

69. R.V. 1.105.

70. R.V. 9.73.9; 5.12.2.

71. R.V. 4.33.10.

72. R.V. 4.7.7.

73. R.V. 3.54.6.

74. R.V. 4.5.6.

75. R.V. 9.74.4.

76. R.V. 9.68.5.

77. R.V. 4.8.3.

78. R.V. 10.5.3.

79. R.V. 10.131.3.

80. R.V. 10.65.14.

81. R.V. 2.24.7.

82. R.V. 1.160.1.

83. R.V. 1.23.5.

84. For other references to *satya* see the following: 1.1.5; 1.20.4; 1.38.7; 1.52.13; 1.57.1; 1.105.12; 1.179.6; 3.14.1; 3.39.5; 4.17.5; 5.51.2; 5.57.8; 5.79.1; 6.49.6; 6.65.5; 7.49.3; 7.75.7; 7.76.4; 7.83.7; 8.2.36; 7.16.8; 8.40.11; 8.45.27; 9.64.2; 9.73.1; 9.78.5; 9.113.4; 9.113.5; 10.27.1; 10.87.11; 10.87.12.

85. Immanuel Kant, *Critique of Practical Reason*, trans. Thomas K. Abbor, (6th ed., 1909), p. 105. (Underlining mine.)

86. *Ibid.*, p. 119. (Underlining mine.)

87. I find an analogy with my interpretation here in Prof. Ch. Perelman's work on Western Philosophy. See, for example: Ch. Perelman, *Justice* (Random House, 1967). Especially Chapters V and Appendix. See also: "The New Rhetoric: A Theory of Practical Reason," *The Great Ideas Today 1970*, (Encyclopedia Britannica, Inc.).

See also: Ch. Perelman and L. Olbrechts–Tyteca, *The New Rhetoric*, trans. John Wilkinson and Purcell Weaver, (London: University of Notre Dame Press), 1969.

88. Ernest McClain, *Myth of Invariance*: *The Origin of the Gods, Mathematics and Music from the Ṛg Veda to Plato*, (Nicolas Hays, Ltd.: New York), 1976.

See also "Rhythm in Music: A Formal Scaffolding of Time," by Walther Durr in *The Voices of Time*, edited by J. T. Fraser, (George Braziller: New York), 1966.

See also, *Avatāra*: *The Humanization of Philosophy Through the Bhagavad Gītā*, (Nicolas Hays, Ltd.: New York), 1976. Especially Chapter Six on musical criteria and also for my remarks on embodiment.

APPENDIX I

1. This formalization is based on two papers written by Dr. Patrick A. Heelan, in *Philosophy and Physics*. The first paper was read at the Boston Colloquium in the Philosophy of Science. The titles of the papers are:

"Quantum Logic and Classical Logic: Their respective roles."

"Complementarity, Context–Dependence and Quantum Logic."

Both papers are dated January, 1969. However, my own formalization owes very much to the personal assistance of Dr. Heelan who saw in the language–context of the Vedas a concrete example of the thesis formulated in the papers above mentioned, even though my field of application was very distant from the concrete field of Quantum Mechanics on which he is working. Abundant bibliography is provided on this subject in the papers above mentioned and which were published as:

"Quantum and Classical Logic: Their Respective Roles." *Synthese* 21 (1970) 2–33.

2. It is obviously not my intention to 'invent imaginary tribes' a la Wittgenstein, nor try to discover the metaphysics of the 'hopi Indians' through some language analogues a la Worlf. My only intention at this time is a description of the function of a historical language as found in its use in these texts and reflected in the Sanskrit grammar. However, for similarities and differences I suggest the reader might look up:

Language, Thought and Reality: *Selected Writings of Benjamin Lee Worlf*, ed. John B. Carol (Cambridge: Technology Press of Mass. Institute of Technology, 1956).

Max Blank, "Linguistic Relativity: the Views of Benjamin Worlf," in *Models and Metaphors*: *Studies in Language and Reality* (Ithaca, New York: Cornell University Press, 1962). The refutation of Worlf is found in pages 244–257.

APPENDIX III

I

1. This selection of Ṛg Vedic texts is offered here mainly to clarify some of the claims made in this book. Unfortunately, the selection is brief, and it is not chant. However, since practically all of the translations of the Ṛg Veda are partially, or in most cases totally, unintelligible, we hope that these few chants translated here will inspire others to produce at least an intelligible translation of the whole Ṛg Veda.

The following Bibliography is a list of original sources and English translations of the Ṛg Veda which might help the reader of this book to continue, complete, compare or reject what has been here started.

SANSKRIT TEXTS

Ṛgvedasaṃhitā, with Commentary by Sāyaṇa, Ed. by F. Max Müller, 6 Vols. London, 1849–74.

Ṛgarthadīpikā, on *Ṛgvedasaṃhitā*, by Mādhava, Ed. by L. Sarup, 2 Vols. Lahore, 1939.

Ṛg Veda Bhāsya of Sāyana in *Ṛg Veda Saṃhitā*, 5 Vols. N. S. Sontakke, Poona, 1935–51.

REFERENCE BOOKS

Sanskrit-English Dictionary, Ed. by M. Monier–Williams, Oxford, 1899.

Sanskrit-Wörterbuch, Ed. by O Böhtlingk and R. Roth, 7 Vols., St. Petersburg, 1855–75.

Panini's Grammatik, Otto Böhtlingk, George, Olms, Hildesheim, 1964.

Vedic Concordance, by M. Bloomfield, Cambridge, Massachusetts, 1906.

Vedic Index of names and subjects, by A. A. Macdonell and A. B. Deith, I Benares, 1958.

Wörterbuch zum Rig-Veda, by H. Grassman, Otto Harrassowitz, Wiesbaden, 1964, 4th ed.

Vedic Grammar, by A. A. Macdonell, Strassburg, 1910.

TRANSLATIONS

The Hymns of the Ṛgveda, Tr. by R. T. H. Griffith, Motilal Banarsidass, New Delhi, 1973, (revised edition).

Der Rigveda, Tr. by K. F. Geldner, Vol. I, Gottingen, 1923.

Rigveda Saṇhitā, Tr. by H. H. Wilson, Vol. 2, Poona, 1925.

PARTIAL TRANSLATIONS

Bose, Abinash Chandra, *Hymns from the Vedas*, Bombay, London, New York: Asia Publishing House, 1966.

Chethimattam, J. B., and Antonio T. de Nicolás, *A Philosophy in Song–Poems: Selected Poems from the Rigveda*, Dharmaram College, Bangalore 1971.

Griswold, H. D., The *Religion of the Ṛgveda*, Oxford University Press, 1923.

Muir, J., *Original Sanskrit Texts*, London, 5 Vols., 1872–74.

Müller, Max, *The Vedas*, Susil Gupta, Calcutta, 1956.

Oldenberg, H., *Vedic Hymns*, SBE Vol. 46, Oxford, 1897.

Raja, C. K., *Asya Vāmasya Hymn* (R.V. 1.164), Ganesh and Co., Madras, 1956.

Renou, Louis, *Études Védique et Pāṇinéennes*, Publication de l'institute de Civilization Indienne, Paris, 1961–66. Tomes 1–17.

ARTICLES

Apte, V. M., "Is Diti in Ṛgveda a mere reflex of Aditi?" *Bhāratīya Vidya 9* Bombay, (K. M. Munshi D. J. Vol., Part I.), 1949

"The name 'Indra'—an etymological investigation," *Journal of the Bombay University*, 19 (2) Sept., 1950, 13–18.

"Indra as a god of light in the Ṛgveda," *Saugor University Journal*, I. 1952, 105–110.

Atkins, Samuel, D., "R.V. 2.38 A Problem Hymn," *JAOS.* 81:77–86.

"A Vedic Hymn to the Sun-God Sūrya," *JAOS.* 15:419–434.

Bloomfield, M., "The Story of Indra and Namuci," *JAOS.* 15:143.

"The Marriage of Saraṇyū, Tvaṣṭra's Daughter," *JAOS.* 15:172–88.

Brown, W. Norman, "The Sources and Nature of the Puruṣa in the Puruṣasūkta" *JAOS.* 51:108–18.

"The Ṛgvedic equivalent of Hell," *JAOS.* 61:76–80.

"The Creation Myth of the Rgveda," *JAOS.* 62:85–98.

"Agni, Sun, Sacrifice, and Vāc: A Sacerdotal Ode by Dīrghatamas," (R.V. 1.164) JAOS. 88:199–218.
Falk, M., "Sat and Asat," SP (Summary of Papers) *14th All Indian Oriental Conference*, Poona, Darbhanga, 117–20.
Renou, Louis, "Les Connexions entre le Rituel et le Grammaire en Sanskrit," *Journal Asiatique*, CCXXXIII, 1941–42, 156.
"La valeur du silence dans le culte védique," *JAOS*, 69:11–18.
"Ceremonies Védique dans l'Inde contemporaine," *Seance Annuelle des cinq Academies*, Paris, 1949, 1–8.
"Vedique ṛtu," Ach. Or. 18, 431–38. English version in *Indian Culture*, Calcutta (Barua Comm. Vol.) 21–26.
"Etudes Védique," *JA* 240 (on virāj) 133–54.
"On the word ātman," *Vak* 2. 151–57.
"Vedique nirṛti," S. K. Chaterji Comm. Vol. 1955. 11–15.

II

Indian philosophy is traditionally divided into four main periods:[1]

a) 2500 to 600 B.C. *Vedic Period.* There are Four Vedas (Ṛg Veda, Yajur Veda, Sāma Veda, Atharva Veda), each of which includes four other parts: Mantras, Brāhmaṇas, Āraṇyakas and Upaniṣads.

b) 600 to 200 A.C. *Epic Period.* The Rāmāyana, the Mahābhārata, and the Bhagavad Gītā, which is part of the Mahābhārata, date from this period. This latter work is the most comprehensive philosophical synthesis of the earlier and present periods. Buddhism, Jainism, and the six orthodox philosophical schools started to develop in this period. The Cārvāka, materialist philosophy, and the Dharmaśāstras, ethical and social philosophies, also date from this era.

c) *The Sūtra Period* corresponds in time to the Early Christian era. Previous philosophical systems are recorded in 'slogans,' aphorisms and brief statements. Constructive imagination and spontaneous insight gave way, in this period, to reflective, self–conscious thought. Bādarāyana's Vedānta Sūtra (or Brahma Sūtra) is the best known.

d) *The Scholastic Period* is almost contemporaneous with the Sūtra period and stretches to the 17th century A.D. when philosophical speculation declined, not to be revived until our present generation. This period included such well known philosophers as Śaṇkara, Kumārila, Śrīdhara, Mādhava, Vācaspati, Udayana, Bhāskara, Jayanata, Vijñānabhikṣu and Raghunātha.

In this book our primary concern is the *Vedic Period.* Of this period, we are leaving behind the Brāhmaṇas, Āraṇyakas and Upaniṣads to center our complete attention on the Vedas. Yet, of the Four Vedas we will only attend to the Ṛg Veda (for reasons which will be clarified later on). It will, however, be most useful to keep in mind the subsequent development of Indian Philosophy to better appreciate the continuity and mode of philosophizing which is uniquely Indian.

The Veda (in the plural) as we now know them,[2] are four systematically arranged collections (Saṃhitās): 1) verses (*ṛc*) recited at the sacrifice and collected in the Riksaṃhitā or Ṛg Veda; 2) Sacrificial formulae (*yajus*) collected in the Yajuhsaṃhitā or Yajurveda; 3) Melodies (*sāman*) collected in the Sāmasaṃhitā or Sāmaveda; and 4) magical formulae (*atharvan*) collected in the Atharvasaṃhitā or Atharvaveda.

The Ṛg Veda, or Veda of verses, is a collection of 1028 poems (hymns or versified ideas) (*sukta*) (including 11 supplementary ones) divided into ten 'circles' (*maṇḍala*) books. Each poem contains from 1 to 58 verses; the total of verses being 10,552 (including 80 supplementary ones) divided into eight parts (*aṣṭaka*)[3] which are themselves divided into lessons (*adhyāya*), and these in turn into groups of five verses (*varga*). The Maṇḍala are also divided in a mechanical way into 'recitations' (*anuvāka*).

The Yajurveda (*Vāsjasaneyi Saṃhitā*, *Madhyandina* text) is divided into 40 chapters, 1,875 stanzas and prose–units.

The Sāmaveda consists of 1,875 stanzas divided into two main sections (*arcika*).

The Atharvaveda is divided into 20 books (*kaṇḍa*) with 730 hymns, 5,987 stanzas and prose–units.

The Four Vedic Saṃhitā are said by tradition to be compiled by Vyāsa (meaning 'compiler'), while the same tradition attributes to Sakalya the origin or the *padapāṭha*, or recitation by words, which presents the text in isolated words, neglecting the rules of euphone. This recitation was used for mnemotechnic purposes in contrast to the *saṃhitāpāṭha* or 'continuous recitation.' The date of compilation, however, is as foggy as the date of composition.[4]

However obscure and inaccurate the historical dates may be, the fact remains that these documents are the first of the Indian tradition. They also happen to be the first and earliest documents of the Aryan race.[5] Until about a century ago the West did not know that more than twenty thousand stanzas comprising the Veda had been passed by oral recitation for over a period of four thousand years. These same poems are also recited today with the same freshness of inspiration as they were in prehistoric times by the Aryan tribes.

In this book we are primarily concerned with the poems of the Ṛg Veda because the Ṛg Veda is the oldest and germinal source of the other Vedas. The whole of the Sāmaveda except 104 stanzas (5 being repetitions) is found in the Ṛg Veda and sixteen percent of the Atharvaveda verses are also Ṛg Vedic. It would appear, therefore, that although the other three Vedas borrowed from the Ṛg Veda, they had purposes of their own different from the Ṛg Veda. Furthermore, it is around the Yajurveda and not the Ṛg Veda, that ritualistic obsession of Brāhmanism developed and subsequently the counter reactions of Buddhism.[6] The Ṛg Veda, somehow, remained peripheral to the subsequent development of Indian thought, even though, ironically, Indian thought originates here. Historically, the Ṛg Veda has been and is largely still a *text out of context*, a text which can only be retrieved in itself and for itself, by internal comparison and reconstruction, not merely as a linguistic fact, but as a 'comprehensive' linguistic fact. What the Ṛg Veda does not have, no other external source can supply.

The Ṛg Veda Saṃhitā, usually called the Ṛg Veda, is the oldest and most important text of the whole Vedic literature. It was probably composed somewhere between 2,500 and 1,500 B.C., and it consists of older and later elements. On calculation, the bulk of the Ṛg Veda is equivalent to the extant poems of Homer.

It is generally recognized that the majority of the oldest hymns are contained in Books II to VII, ascribed by tradition to different families of singers. A fairly high age is also accorded to Books VIII and IX, while the hymns found in Books I and X are composed of different elements, some of them being regarded as younger additions. That does not mean, of course, that all these hymns are later in origin. In the tenth Book we find many words and grammatical forms which grew obsolete, side by side with new emerging expressions; and we can recognize the later age of these books only as far as their final arrangement in the Saṃhitās is concerned. In fact, although we know the names of the sages to whom the tradition ascribes the composition of the hymns, (some women's names can be found among them), the authorship of the Ṛg Veda as well as of the other Vedic texts presents considerable problems. There is a striking difference between the time of the composition, compilation and final codification of the Ṛg Veda Saṃhitā, and we shall have to be content with the assertion that the bulk of our information comes at least from the second of the second millennium B.C., more or less.

We are far from understanding everything contained in the Vedic Saṃhitās and anyone who tries to translate everything in the hymns gravely misleads his readers by including the belief that they are often unpoetical or senseless. There are many passages whose real meaning is highly doubtful, many hints of myths and occurences are referred to which have not been recorded in later sources. Even in early times, the Indian scholars themselves did not understand everything and were engaged in the interpretation of such obscure passages in special works as the Nighaṇtus, "glossaries," rare and unintelligible words, Anukramaṇīs, "indexes" or legends, myths and other auxiliary material, and finally commentaries, of which we possess the only comprehensive work of Sāyaṇa from the 14th century A.D.

The findings of later Vedic scholars like Delbruch, Grassmann, Oldenberg and Bergaine on the structure and arrangement of the Saṃhitās are well known and also show the arbitrariness of the arrangement. According to them the greater portion of the Ṛg Veda (especially the latter half of the first maṇḍala and maṇḍalas II–VII) follow certain definite principles in arrangement of hymns: Cycles of hymns of the same sage (*Ṛṣi*) or family (*gotra*) are arranged in ascending order according to deity groups; but deity groups are arranged in the descending order of the total number of hymns for each deity; where these numbers are equal, those groups with a longer first hymn are given precedence. Within the same deity group hymns are arranged according to the descending order of the total number of *ṛcs* in a hymn. When the *ṛcs* are equal, the longer meter precedes the shorter. This mechanical sort of arrangement shows that the collection of hymns into the present form ocurred at a time when the original meaning of the ancient poets was either unintelligible or at least somewhat irrelevant to the users of the hymns. The internal criticism of the Ṛg Veda is very much based on the discovery of these rules of recognizing interpolations and reconstructing a more ancient model of the Saṃhitā by breaking hymns which formed an artificial unity into smaller groups, *pragatha* (verse groups), or *tṛca* (groups of three *ṛc*).

FOOTNOTES TO APPENDIX III, SECTION II

1. See J. N. Farquhar, *An Outline of the Religious Literature of India*, (Delhi, Motilal Banarsidas, 1920). See also: J. Muir, *Original Sanskrit Texts on the Origin and History of the People of India, Their Religion and Institutions* 5 Vol. (London: 1868–74); Moriz Winternitz, *Ceschichte der indischen Litteratur*, 3 Vol. (Leipzig: 1905–22), English translations by Mrs. S. Ketkar and H. Koh, 2 Vol. (Calcutta: 1927–33); Surendra Nath Dasgupta, *A History of Indian Philosophy*, 4 Vol. (Cambridge: 1922–49); S. Radhakrishnan, *Indian Philosophy*, 2 Vol. (London: 1923 and 1927); S. Radhakrishnan and Moore, *A Sourcebook in Indian Philosophy*, (Princeton University Press, 1957); Masson–Oursel, *Comparative Philosophy* (London: 1926), Heinrich Zimmer, *Philosophies of India*, ed. Joseph Campbell (Princeton: 1951) Appendix B: Historical Summary, pp. 615–618; Hiriyana, *Outlines of Indian Philosophy* (London: 1932).

2. See Max Müller, *The Vedas* (Calcutta: Susil Gupta Ltd., 1956). The book is a collection of essays which appeared in several publications. It covers essays by Max Müller from 1865 to 1898. See also: Louis Renou, *Vedic India* (Calcutta: Susil Gupta Ltd., 1957); and Arthur Berriedale Keith, *The Religion and Philosophy of the Veda and the Upanishads*, 2 Vol. In the Harvard Oriental Series Vols. 31 and 32 (Cambridge: Harvard University Press, 1925).

3. See Theodor Aufrecht's edition of *Die Hymnen des Rigveda*, 2 Vol. (Wiesbaden: Otto Harrassowitz, 1955). On *aṣṭhaka* (part) see introduction to second Vol.

4. See Sen. Gupta, *Journal of the Asiatic Society* (Bengal: July 1941); also Max Müller, *The Vedas*, *op. cit.*; also R.C. Majumdar, general editor, *The Vedic*

Age (Bombay: Bharatiya Vidya Bhavan, 1951), p. 197; also M. Winternitz, *History of Indian Literature* (Calcutta University, 1959).

5. It would be a grave misunderstanding of the Aryans of the Vedic period if one were to read in them racial overtones of our times. The internal evidence of the Ṛg Veda points to an ideological struggle which applied to both Aryans and Dasyus. As Max Müller says in *The Vedas*, *op. cit.*, p. 13, "If one wants to find the contrary of the Aryan way of thinking (not the color of the skin) one would have to look into the Semitic world. The Aryan ancestry goes back to India, Persia, Greece, Italy, not Mesopotamia, Egypt or Palestine."

There is even greater clarification when one looks within Vedic text for the use of words like *rūpa* (form) *varpas* (concrete form) and *varṇa* (color). The three words have a fluid and inconcrete character in the Ṛg Veda. In general, the three words correspond to an effect (form) produced or being produced and therefore classifiable only according to the aspect or the stage of the manifested external activity. As in the forms of Savitar R.V. 5.81.2; or Viśvarūpa, the Creator of all forms and therefore named as such; or the changes of Soma in the ritual R.V. 2.13.3; or the multiple active manifestations of Indra in R.V. 3.53.8. In this same sense it is said of the wind and its form which remains unseen while perceiving its force R.V. 1.164.44 or its *whispering* R.V. 10.168.4.

Although *varṇa* primarily means color, like the black color of night and the white color of day, in R.V. 1.73.7, still one must be aware of the wider context of activity within which both colors are signified and within which their opposed aspects become reconciled, i.e., the activity within which both day and night are only alternate manifestations, as in R.V. 1.96.5.

"All beauty resides in the color (*varṇa*) of Agni," (R.V. 2.1.12). Yet to translate color in a physical sense, like skin pigmentation, would be a misunderstanding. In R.V. w.5.5 the philosopher-poet affirms that the "cows follow the color of Agni," (*tā asya varṇam . . . sacanta dhenavaḥ*), while Agni is called the *nesṭr*, "the Leader," in the same sense that the butter of the cows and the flames join in an efficient action. Color (*varṇa*) is less a visual quality than a state a state of mind. The "asura color" (*asuryam varṇam*) in R.V. 9.71.2 is that which *rejects* the harming soma to enter within the domain of an activity which is efficacious. *Varṇa*, again, appears as a state of being, a state of mind, rather than a racial quality. It is no doubt this feeble and abstract 'category' which the word '*varṇa*' carries with itself that causes attempts to be made to identify it with 'race' and 'caste.' It has been more clearly the case with relation to the word *dāsa* (servant, slave) and the *ārya varṇa* of R.V. 1.104.2; 2.11.4; 3.34.9. Yet this reduction of meaning to only physical aspect is contradicted by the passages already mentioned and others. The 'Rivers' which carry the *varṇa* of the god Varuna in R.V. 10.124.7 recognize in this god a banner, a sign which makes them belong to his 'race.' *Varṇa* refers to color as a distinctive sign of characterization of a state of being active, as in other aspects *Ketu* is light insofar as it is also a sign of activity. In this sense the poet may call his poem '*śukravarṇa*' (clear–colored) in R.V. 1.143.7 (also R.V. 10.71.2) as a poetic characteristic or the result of a thought-activity which is efficacious. In the same sense it is said of Indra in R.V. 3.34.5. It is also said of the Divine Doors (R.V. 2.3.5) "which open to liberate the class of mortals," (*varṇam punānā yaśasam surīram*) and of the "sacred poets" in R.V. 8.3.3 which are pure (*śuci*) and of a "pure class" (*pāvakavarṇa*).

Cfr. Louis Renou, *Etudes sur le Vocabulaire du Rigveda.* Institut Francais d'indologie. Pondichery, 1958. Bloomfield, *JAOS*, 15, p. 178.

6. See Louis Renou, *Les Ecoles Védique et la Formation du Veda* (Paris: 1947), pp. 209–12, for summary. The historical problem of the genesis of Brāhmanical ritualism is here discussed. See also K. N. Jayatilleke, *Early Buddhist Theory of Knowledge* (London: George Allen & Unwin, Ltd., 1963). The counteractions of Buddhism against Brāhmanical ritualism, pp. 65–68. He offers further bibliography on this subject.

Index